FIRE OF A THOUSAND SUNS

 WEB
PUBLISHING
COMPANY
WESTMINISTER, CO

The George R. "Bob" Caron Story - Tail Gunner of the Enola Gay

FIRE

OF A THOUSAND

SUNS

Foreword by Brig. Gen. Paul W. Tibbets (Ret.)
George R. Caron • Charlotte E. Meares

Published by Web Publishing
P.O. Box 528, Westminster, Colorado, 80030-0528

Illustrated & designed by nellie sudavicius macCallum, Genesis
Holigraphic, Inc., Service Bureau

Printed in the United States of America on recycled paper

Library of Congress Catalog Card Number 95-60313

**Publisher's Cataloging in Publication
(Prepared by Quality Books Inc.)**

Caron, George Robert.
  Fire of a thousand suns : the George Robert Caron story, tail
gunner of the Enola Gay / as told to Charlotte Meares.
    p.cm.
  Includes bibliographical references.
  ISBN 0-9639014-8-6

  1. Hiroshima-shi (Japan)—History—Bombardment, 1945. 2. Caron,
George Robert.   I. Meares, Charlotte. II. Title.

D767.25.H6C37 1995   940.54'25
                                QB195-20029

To My Wife, Kay,
and
In Memory of My Wonderful Parents,
Anne and George

C O N T E N T S

To succeed, to win, to fly and fight another day, you have to have men you can count on.

During the course of my military career, and World War II in particular, I was extremely fortunate. With the 509th Composite Group, I had the very best team of airmen the Army Air Forces could assemble.

Those were unusual times that called for unusual actions in anything but normal circumstances. As the commander of this country's only atomic strike force, I was accorded more latitude and freedom to operate than any commander before or since. I am proud of that record and proud of *our* accomplishments.

The crew of the *Enola Gay* was a unique team unto itself. In the operation of that wonderful aircraft, everyone was a specialist. Each member was hand-picked because they were, in my eyes, *the best of the best.* We had only one man to protect us. Tail gunner George R. "Bob" Caron.

Bob Caron was, in many ways, the typical GI. He worked his way out of the Depression of the 1930s, through school and up his ladder of success. He had an irrepressible desire to succeed, to learn, to know more and to enjoy life.

Simply stated, I knew I could count on George Robert Caron. He never let me down. We, as a crew, benefited from his quick mind, dry wit and his sharp eye. In my view, he knew more about the B-29's central fire-control system than the engineers who designed it. That expertise was invaluable.

This is Bob Caron's story. In the pages that follow, you will meet the man, the boy within and the tail gunner who protected the *Enola Gay.*

Paul W. Tibbets
Brigadier General, USAF, Retired
Pilot, *Enola Gay*
February 1995

ACKNOWLEDGMENTS

There are many people whom I would like to credit for their encouragement and support, and the first would have to be my still-beautiful wife, Kay. For half a lifetime, she has endured my tales and persuaded me to tell them. "You're seventy-five and not getting any younger," she reminds me in her ever-direct manner.

Paul W. Tibbets, then colonel and pilot of the *Enola Gay*, today brigadier general U.S.A.F, retired, generously provided the Foreword.

Because fifty years is a long time to wait to tell one's story, Paul Tibbets and George E. Hicks, historian, writer and director of the Airmen Memorial Museum, Washington, D.C., generously proofed the manuscript to be certain that my remembrance of Air Force events was accurate.

Thomas Ferebee, Theodore Van Kirk and Richard Nelson, fellow crewmen on the *Enola Gay*, kindly provided brief biographical material along with encouragement.

Brig. Gen. James C. Hall, U.S.A.F. (Ret.), graciously gave his enthusiastic endorsement.

Without my publisher and neighbor, Wallace Burke, whom Kay and I met by accident, I might never have gotten this project under way. Like my wife, he believed that my story was worth telling.

Charlotte Meares, my co-author, became an enthusiastic researcher with a gift for writing that pleased Kay and me very much. We had no idea how deeply one delved into facts and history and personal life in order to write about it and how many questions that entailed! I wish to acknowledge her studious efforts with thanks.

Last, but never least, I wish to acknowledge my children, of whom I am extremely proud, my grandchildren and my great-grandchild. While I wish to give you, the reader, the whole story, in the last analysis, I want them to know...and remember.

George R. "Bob" Caron

For their cooperation and encouragement, I wish to thank James Bert, executive director, Strategic Air Command Museum, Bellevue, Nebraska, and Mark Trupp, chief of restoration, who answered questions as I crawled through SAC's B-29. To my pilot brother-in-law, William M. Meares, III, who landed long enough to make certain my manuscript engines were operating as they should, my earthly thanks. nellie sudavicius macCallum, president of Genesis Communications, designed the book inside and out. The Library/Archives Center, Historical Society of Douglas County provided valuable research assistance. Many thanks to our publisher, Wallace Burke, for bringing Bob Caron's story to light, and to Bob Caron for telling it one more time. In August 1945, during one of those many occasions the press interviewed Anne Westrick Caron about her son, she confidently asserted that one day there would be a book about Bob's adventure. As usual, she was right. I feel as though I knew her. Those for whom the only reward for their efforts and contributions is my sincere gratitude and affection include: Linda Johnson, Ph.D., English Department, University of Nebraska, Omaha; my ever-patient husband, Lorran Meares, whose faith in me never waivers, and who dedicated hours to scanning and electronically enhancing the historical photographs for this book; and my family and friends, enthusiastic supporters all.

Charlotte E. Meares

No Dry Run

The sunrise such as the world had never seen began as a seed of reddish-purple light. In one-millionth of an eyeblink, the seed blossomed into a light not of this world, the light of a thousand suns in one.

When the eye-stabbing flash penetrated the goggles intended to shield him, the tail gunner thought he had been blinded. At the signal nearly two minutes earlier, Staff Sergeant George Robert Caron had lowered the dense Polaroids over his eyes and tested them. The bright morning sun had been reduced to an odd, faint purple blob. Nothing more.

Major Tom Ferebee spotted his aiming point, the Aioi Bridge, pressed the trigger of his Norden bomb sight and calmly, but deliberately, announced "bomb away."

At that moment "Little Boy" tumbled from the belly of the *Enola Gay* on its six-mile plummet earthward. Isolated by the blackness of his goggles, Caron counted the seconds after the bomb bay doors burst open.

Freed of its five-ton burden, the B-29 shot upward. Instantly, Colonel Paul Tibbets executed the well-practiced, evasive maneuver calculated to put a safe distance between his crew of twelve and the unknown effects of the blast. No one, not even the physicists responsible for creating the world's first atomic weapon, could predict what its force would do to the specially modified plane. Or to a city of three hundred twenty-three thousand people. For Little Boy, there had been no dry run. Its deployment marked the first time in history a major weapon had gone into battle untested.

The thirty-third President of the United States had inherited a bloody war. The last thing Truman needed was a dud bomb. If the "gimmick" worked, he was sure it would bring Japan to her knees. If not in one devastating and demoralizing blow, then by another and another. He waited anxiously. The scientists who conceived this two-billion dollar baby and the pilot of the plane who had just delivered it also waited.

Its intended victim lay waiting like the outstretched fingers of a six-digit hand. The seven watercourses of the Ota River fanned out gracefully around and between the fingers called Hiroshima, then meandered lazily southwestward until, finally, their estuaries licked the gaping mouths of the Seto Inland Sea.

Japan's admirals and generals recognized Hiroshima's waterways were among her greatest strengths. The city's harbors eased troop deployment, and industry lined the banks of its rivers. In their fitful planning sessions, military strategists had designated Hiroshima as provisional capital and headquarters for the nation's defense—should Tokyo have to be abandoned. Already, they had established headquarters of the Second Imperial Army and military support facilities within the four-square-mile area that surrounded the Aioi Bridge.

This morning had begun no differently than any other. Japan's undernourished young soldiers, eager to die for their emperor, drilled proudly and obediently in the courtyard of Hiroshima Castle. Wrinkled, stooped old men fished from the banks of the muddy Ota. Even one fish would help relieve the pain of hunger in their families' bellies. School children resumed their tasks from the day before, leveling more of Hiroshima's flimsy wooden dwellings, shops and fences to create broad fire breaks that might save her, if and when she came under attack.

On this brilliant morning, August 6, 1945, any one of her citizens whose eyes turned skyward would have seen only the golden glint of an aircraft, scarcely visible at thirty-one thousand feet. Air-raid sirens, which had cried wolf so frequently throughout the past months over a seemingly benign reconnaissance plane or two, had not yet screamed the plane's presence through the stirring streets.

Three times during the night and early hours they had wailed their warning: *B-san. B-san.* The city's weary people felt the effects of another sleepless night. Hiroshima's pulse was rapid, its nerves frazzled. Fathers and mothers wondered when the whining fire bombs that had turned her sister cities into cinders would rain destruction on her. In their restlessness, they had not dreamed their fair city had been reserved for something else, something new, something unimaginable.

At 8:15:17 A.M., Hiroshima time, their wonderings ended.

In his shoulder-wide compartment, tail gunner Caron had been counting. Forty-one...forty-two.... Suddenly, without a sound, the pinprick of energy inside the bomb transmuted into a full-blown explosion.

2

Light from a thousand suns crescendoed to a brightness that seemed to illuminate the universe.

As though billions of years of creation had suddenly and inextricably reversed themselves, the sky ripped open. Within this tumultuous, man-made cataclysm roiled unfathomable temperatures. Just as it had been programmed to do, the bomb released its might eighteen hundred and ninety feet above the city. The explosion released fifty million degrees Celsius, turning matter to energy, mass to ash. Its core reached three hundred thousand degrees. At ground zero, directly below, there was no running away from the fire and fury. Objects were no longer real. Most ceased to exist. Trees, bicycles, tea pots, sleeping mats, houses, people. Vanished. Vaporized. Only occasional eerie shadows on stone, imprinted like photograms by the intense light, hinted the presence of once-living beings.

Coursing eastward after its sharp right-turn dive, the *Enola Gay* raced away from what was.

At the split second of detonation, the forward cabin lit up as though hundreds of flash bulbs had been tripped all at once. Tibbets sensed a galvanic tingle on his tongue, then a metal aftertaste reminiscent of lead.

When the sun exploded, Caron appeared like a negative image—a solarized figure helplessly blinded. He winced from pain, then ripped the goggles off his forehead. His retinas played tricks on him. Everything was awash in brilliant yellow and white. Seconds played themselves out in slow motion. Form and line gradually became more distinct. Color flowed back into bleached-white surroundings.

Eight miles west of the city at the home of a friend, Satoshi Nakamura lingered over his newspaper. He savored another cup of tea. Without warning, the east-facing windows shattered with a force so violent that it threw him to the floor. The reporter for the official government news agency, Domei, picked himself up from the pool of glass and rushed outside. He could not believe his eyes. Over Hiroshima writhed and twisted a growing black cloud. Then it burst into a ball of flame, "like the instant blossoming of a fantastic flower."

Approximately the same distance away, Caron beheld the spectacle, but from a unique perspective. Tibbets knew at that moment his gunner's compartment was *the* place to witness the unfolding drama. The pilot waited for a description of the action below.

"The turret's in the way. I can't see anything yet," Caron reported. Abruptly, that changed. His body registered alarm as apprehension swirled in his belly. His heart pounded like a jack hammer. No human had ever witnessed the form that now threatened to engulf the fleeing plane like some sinister plasma out of a science-fiction movie. The giant, semi-transparent bubble, expanding rapidly like three-dimensional ripples in a pool, was nearly upon them. He tried to scream a warning. It was incoherent. He tried again. Just as his warning reached the crew's ears, the bubble of compressed, super-heated air smashed into the plane. The aircraft bucked, then dropped like an elevator in free-fall from the tenth floor to the first.

"Flak," Tibbets said instinctively, recalling vividly the violent jolt of anti-aircraft fire over Europe. It felt and sounded like the familiar German 88 mm shell.

The hefty Superfortress had been rocked not by flak, but by the shock wave the crew had been warned to expect. Tibbets had remembered almost the instant "flak" escaped his mouth. Four seconds after the first hit, a second giant bubble, the "ricochet" of the first shock wave reflecting off the surface of the earth, again chased them down.

"Here comes another one," Caron loudly and clearly warned. The second collision with the nearly invisible force bounced the plane less violently than the first.

The tail gunner leaned closer to his wraparound windows. A tremendous cloud rose from the ground, billowed past the protruding gun turret and crept into his view. He was awestruck. Still, duty pressed. In a space smaller than an outhouse, he struggled with the unwieldy aerial camera a photo officer had thrust at him just before takeoff. But where to point it? The gun sight was in the way. He called over the intercom to Tibbets and asked for a better angle. A five-degree turn to the left would do. It would give him a clearer shot through his right side hatch.

"Describe what you see," Tibbets prodded again.

Caron pressed his nose to the Plexiglas. Now, he could see the entire live, churning thing. In the hushed waist and forward cabin, everyone listened. His breathy, staccato words spilled out and flooded the intercom.

"A giant column of smoke...a purple-gray turbulent mass...white at the top and fiery red core right down to the base." He remembered Captain William Parsons' term during their preflight briefing—a mushroom, he called the umbrella-like crown that was expected over the cloud's column.

"It's like bubbling molasses down there...the mushroom is spreading out...it's nearly level with us and climbing...very black, but has a purplish tint...the base of the mushroom looks like a heavy undercast that is shot through with red...fires are springing up everywhere...like flames shooting out of a huge bed of coals...smoke is billowing out into the foothills...it's like a peep into Hell."

"Count the fires, Bob." It was the perfectionist in Tibbets that thought he must keep track even of that. But there were too many. After fifteen, Caron stopped counting.

Tibbets turned the B-29 broadside. The crew gasped. Rising boldly before them was the culmination of eleven months' training and the efforts of one hundred thousand workers back home, although the crew would not know that detail until Tibbets revealed it on the flight home. The pilot cautiously skirted the cloud. Like a living tower of hands made by school boys stacking palm over hand, one on top of another until there were no more hands to stack, it grew. Thirty thousand, forty thousand, forcing its curling crown of dust, vapor and heat fifty thousand feet into the blue above Hiroshima.

"My God, what have we done?" The guttural whisper passed through co-pilot Captain Robert Lewis' lips almost without his knowing he had spoken. The utterance was neither a lament nor a hackneyed response. It was not self-condemning. Rather, the expression came from some shadowy, alien part of himself he had not yet come to know. It acknowledged the breadth of collective responsibility. It searched for answers to the incomprehensible. Searched for questions that had been asked only in fiction and poetry. It wondered without judgment at the power to create and the power to destroy in the blink of an eye.

Just as suddenly, came a quite different thought. *This* could be the end of the war!

Caron flashed a reassuring smile at the dark-haired beauty in the photograph as if she were in the tiny tail compartment with him. And, of course, she was. He had slipped Kay's picture into the clear plastic pocket over his oxygen chart and it dangled on a little chain beside him. On the reverse side was a snapshot of his baby daughter, Judy. Especially now, they were the most gorgeous sight in the world. And if the ominous black cloud that loomed above the *Enola Gay* convinced the Japanese to surrender, he would soon be with them.

With little elbow room to finagle the cumbersome K-20 camera, the gunner aimed again at that towering, still climbing thing. He squeezed the shutter trigger. Over the roar of the engines he heard the loud *kerthunk* as the vacuum assembly's piston sucked the thin film firmly against the pressure plate. He shifted position as best as he could and squeezed the trigger again and again. Photography, second to airplanes, had been his passion, but he could not have guessed that the documentary images from this last-minute assignment would make front pages around the world. Right now, there were too many other things to think about. What he was seeing seemed so "unreal."

As he fired off frames, his mind drifted with the cloud. He imagined scientists' excitement when their experiments revealed that an infinitesimally small particle called an atom could be "split," and from that unnatural act enormous quantities of energy would be released.

Since childhood he had taken things apart and put them back together. He had to know how and why things worked as they did. For hours on end at Wendover's base library, he would contentedly lose himself in physics books. It was in that remote, sandy, northwest corner of Utah, brushing Nevada, during those long months of training for this day, that he had been introduced to a famous Berkeley physicist and his atom-smasher. Now all that sleight of hand had come together in the form of a cloud.

Tibbets was only peripherally thinking about atoms. With the dangerous evasive maneuver successfully behind him, he gave himself over to the still rising column and collided with a rhetorical question: Had such unbridled force set in motion a new dawn? Mercifully, the immediate task of gathering more mission data sufficed for an answer. He shared his prescience with no one. Instead, as though telepathic, he voiced the words in Lewis' mind: "I think we've won the war."

Almost as an afterthought, he remembered the wire recorder on board. He asked each crewman to express his thoughts about the event they had just witnessed. "For posterity," he said, adding, "Watch your language."

One by one, they did. Shumard, Stiborik, Nelson, Beser, Lewis, Parsons, Jeppson, Caron, Ferebee, Van Kirk, Tibbets, Duzenbury. Where were the words to explain what they had just seen? Or how they felt? Well-worn phrases spilled into the microphone connected to their intercom. "Amazing." "Stupendous." "Spectacular." Each of them added a commentary about the enormity of it all, its inevitability for ending the war...*surely, it would end the war.*

The crew could never be absolutely certain of their exact words that morning. They would never hear them again. Neither would any high-ranking government official. Once the wire recorder was placed in the hands of an information officer on Tinian, the small island in the Pacific they had left just six hours earlier, it would mysteriously disappear.

Bombardier Ferebee and weaponeer specialist Navy Captain Parsons were in no mood to be bogged down in reverie. Parsons needed to prepare a detailed strike report. He wiped his broad forehead. The President was waiting. So were top brass on Tinian. Tibbets already had prepared the short message they wanted to hear:

> CLEAR CUT, SUCCESSFUL IN ALL RESPECTS.
> VISIBLE EFFECTS GREATER THAN TRINITY.
> HIROSHIMA. CONDITIONS NORMAL IN AIRPLANE
> FOLLOWING DELIVERY. PROCEEDING TO REGULAR BASE.

Private First Class Richard Nelson radioed the pilot's brief strike report. Then he transmitted Parsons' more-detailed, coded message to Guam for the eyes of Major General Thomas Farrell, chief deputy to General Leslie Groves, bomb project commander.

Little remained to be done. The radioactive cloud continued to drift menacingly toward them. Tibbets swung the *Enola Gay* southward toward Tinian onto the flight path the Allies had named the "Hirohito Highway," after the Emperor himself.

"Junior," as Caron nicknamed the nineteen-year-old Nelson, monitored the radio on the long return flight. Every few minutes Captain Lewis pestered him. "Any reports yet of Japan's surrender?" It was too soon for such a breakthrough. Furthermore, stunned Japanese officials were issuing no statements.

The crew also fell silent. Tibbets lifted the oppressive stillness.

"Hey, Bob. How was the ride back there?" Once, on a practice run, the Colonel had nosed a B-29 into the same dive-turn maneuver with robust assertiveness. The "g" forces plastered the tail gunner against the compartment's frame and made him feel like "the last man on a giant 'crack the whip.'"

"Better than the quarter ride on the Coney Island Cyclone, Colonel."

"Just pay me the twenty-five cents when we land."

"Sorry, Colonel. You'll have to wait till payday."

Harry S. Truman crowded the microphones clustered in front of him. In the few months since he had assumed office, his Missouri drawl had become familiar to radioland listeners. Now, the President was seconds away from the most earth-shaking, electrifying message any political leader had ever delivered.

> The world will note that the first atomic bomb was dropped on Hiroshima, a military base. We won the race of discovery against the Germans. We have used it in order to shorten the agony of war...to save the lives of thousands and thousands of young Americans. We shall continue to use it until we completely destroy Japan's power to make war.

"The first atomic bomb was dropped...." It was an assemblage of words that had never before been spoken. Now, all at once, Truman was revealing to a startled nation that the United States had developed a secret, revolutionary new weapon and, although it had not been ready to use on Hitler, its deployment against Japan could end the war and save countless thousands of young lives.

That was what mothers at home had been praying for.

4:30 P.M., Wednesday, 8 August 1945

Dear Bob,
So, the Carons are on the "front page." And lil Annie is still on her feet to tell about it. There's so much been happening since 11 o'clock last night (here's another reporter). First, Bob, I am so darn proud of you that the lump in my throat is like a watermelon, and Dad, too. He had to stay home today, too much was happening. I hope you won't mind anything we might have said; it has no bearing on your secret mission, because we really didn't know. I just had my usual hunches, or hunch, ever since I heard the news on Monday about the bomb, I was writing to you at the time. Then last night Gabriel Heater said "The B-29 that dropped the atomic bomb was piloted by Col. Tibbets of Florida." Then I knew, so I stayed up till the 11 o'clock news came on. That's when your name was announced, that's when the phone started ringing and it hasn't stopped since. Most of the pictures I had are being used, they are all over the front pages. Do you mind, Bob? After all, you are a world-wide famous person along with your gang. I only hope Kay is O.K. and I think I will try and call her tonight. Don't imagine she heard it last night. They all asked me for pictures of Judy. I said I didn't have any yet. No doubt Kay has new ones and they will ask her there for any. Dad was asleep, I had to wake him and it goes without saying I was not the calmest person in the world, because I didn't know if you all were safe. Until

a woman reporter from Newsday *told me you were. Lynbrook says they are all proud of you, they started calling us to tell us so last night. Dad is buying all the papers to send to you, also Kay. Some of the "copied" news items in the city are balled up, guess you can see that on reading them. Am making stew, so have to make the dumplings now. So long, God Bless you and keep you safe.*

Love,
Mother

Occam's Razor

ain made it feel colder than forty-six degrees, and gloomier. Winter could set in any time. This morning's October 31, 1919, *New York Times'* headline glared back at George Jay Caron and sent a chill up his spine.

GOVERNMENT LIKELY TO ASK COURTS TO HALT COAL STRIKE;
REGULARS GOING TO WEST VIRGINIA, ROADS TO SEIZE FUEL;
WILSON APPROVES FIRM MEASURES TO HALT EMERGENCY

He passed up his usual *Journal American*, tucked the rolled *Times* inside his overcoat, flipped a nickel into the newsstand tin cup and turned a heel back to the apartment before the coin stopped ringing.

George rustled halfway through the paper before he finished his first cup of coffee. Before long, coffee would be about as strong a brew as he could get. Two days ago the Prohibition Enforcement Act passed over President Wilson's veto. It labeled any beverage "intoxicating" that contained half of one percent alcohol or more. *That wasn't enough to make the fuzz on your ears stand up, much less put a buzz in them. What was this country coming to? Those Anti-Saloon Temperance Leaguers were interfering with a man's right to the pursuit of happiness through the amber glow of fine Irish whiskey. At least the Eighteenth Amendment wouldn't go into effect until January 16. That meant a sturdy French-Irishman could still pour a little cheer for the holidays.*

George turned the pages and was attracted to an article on airplanes. As was his habit, he read to his wife.

TO BOMB AFGHAN RAIDERS
BRITISH TO USE AIRPLANES UNLESS TRIBESMEN CEASE ATTACKS
Airplane bombs are to be used against the tribes of Waziris and Mahsuds in Afghanistan unless the tribesmen discontinue the continual attacks on British posts and convoys and the raids into British territory, which they have indulged in during and since the recent troubles with Afghanistan.

Representatives of these tribes have been summoned to British headquarters to hear the British ultimatum. In case they do not comply with the terms, they will be given time to remove their women and children and will then be subjected to an intense aerial bombardment.

He took a long breath as though storing up for the next installment, then continued.

AERONAUTICAL SHORTSIGHTEDNESS
Just before he reached the age of retirement the other day, Rear Admiral Fullam made a plea for a capable aviation service for the army and navy. It was his opinion that in the future no fleet would be able to attack or defend itself effectively from the sea alone; that, in fact, it would be doomed if weak in the aviation arm; and it was his conviction that no enemy would ever be able to land on our coasts if squadrons of airplanes were available to bomb the transports and landing parties.

That was news of interest to George. But not to Anne Westrick Caron. She preferred to dish out a little of her rare teasing.

" 'Flatbush Bargain...' " she fired her salvo. "This sounds like just the place to raise a family. She read him the classified advertisement word for word: 'Superb residence, seventeen rooms, three baths, billiard room, seven master rooms, *servants' quarters*, hot water heat, electricity and gas, vacuum system (raising her eyebrows), three-car garage with living rooms; *restricted*.' " She looked at him and waited, as if expecting him to be clairvoyant. He knew what she wanted, but pretended not to.

"Well?" she coaxed. "Guess how much." When he responded to her game with a shrug, she grew impatient and continued reading.

" '... Forty-two thousand dollars. Worth sixty thousand. Evans and Evans Attorneys at Law. 5 Beecham Street.' "

"You should have married an attorney instead of a carpenter," he whisked at her.

Anne wondered aloud who bought houses like that. Certainly no one she knew. Their few friends who could afford not to rent purchased nice little houses for a respectable three thousand or four thousand dollars.

George wished he could build her dream house. Since prosperity hadn't knocked at their door—and probably wouldn't any time soon—he wasn't going to let their discussion take a dead-end turn and spoil his good mood. Heaven knows, everything else that morning had conspired to. The weather. Headlines about strikes. Depriving a man his shot of eighty-proof.

Still, over all the doom and gloom, he felt playful. Good-naturedly, he resumed reading to her about one of his favorite topics.

"America is sorely behind England in construction of airplanes," he editorialized to his wife, who by now was thinking more about the strange sensations in her swollen belly than the machinations of governments.

"It says here, 'In July fourteen planes had been built in the United States. Great Britain built two thousand....' " He let the words fall off, realizing his audience had just left the auditorium.

On Halloween 1919 a very small George Robert Caron drew his first breath of the world's largest city. When his mother and father brought him home to their cramped, drab apartment, they laughed that she had received a trick rather than a treat. There was no need to say aloud what this yawning infant, rocking in his father's arms, meant to them. The world was turned upside down. But this night, in the warmth of their Flatbush bedroom, the churning political climate in Russia, even King Ferdinand of Romania's successful block of Communism in Hungary, faded as swiftly as the tail of a comet.

Socially, economically, politically, 1919 had been a bizarre year. Ice cream sales froze all records and topped one hundred fifty million gallons. Actress Lillian Gish was sultry in the silent film *Broken Blossoms*. Wall Street's boom in "war baby" stocks sent prices soaring. Bethlehem Steel was up fourteen hundred percent. General Motors stock rose by nine hundred forty percent.

The Carons and millions of other New Yorkers didn't have to be told that their cost of living, too, had soared—by seventy-nine percent in the last five years. Still, middle-class Americans were better off than their eastern European counterparts, who were dying of starvation. Even without crop failure, the shortage of manpower fated their agricultural prosperity. At a time when the Viennese should have been celebrating Christmas, they were, instead, tightening their belts. Bread rations had been reduced to four ounces per week.

In the months and years following George Robert's birth, his parents read with growing concern about anti-Semitism fomenting abroad. Yet the news was not all bad. The worldwide press discovered the personable, bohemian genius Albert Einstein. The "new figure...whose investigations signify a complete revision of our concepts of nature," received the Nobel Prize when Bobby was three. Einstein had been concerning himself with more than science. He had been observing with trepidation the rising influence of an unpredictable man named Adolph Hitler. When the name appeared in headlines for his daring November 8, 1923, Beer Hall Putsch, uneasiness coursed through the Berlin scientist. Others also kept a watchful eye on the insurrectionist who within a decade vaulted himself from inciter to Chancellor of Germany.

Five days after Hitler's appointment, President Franklin Delano Roosevelt admitted to the American people in his first inaugural address that challenges lay ahead: "In the field of world policy, I would dedicate this nation to the policy of the good neighbor." He would soon discover not every world leader felt a moral obligation to live by the Golden Rule.

Anne tucked the straggler curl that persisted in falling over her forehead back under one of the tortoise-shell combs. The pair had been a birthday present from George. Smoothing her apron with her palm, she traced the contours of her full hips. A twinge of regret swept over her, then evaporated. Fried potatoes browned nicely in the skillet. They were, no doubt, partly responsible for her "rounding out," as George called it. On their wedding day, she barely tipped the scale at ninety-eight pounds. Although her husband was no giant—he stood only five feet eight inches—next to him, she had been the lissome dragonfly.

From the moment he saw Anne that day on Long Island, George had been attracted to her liquid blue eyes, gentle complexion and feminine curves. It had pleased him to learn they shared an Irish heritage. George's French-Canadian father brought a robust exuberance to family life and insisted on the proper pronunciation of Caron.

Meal preparation mechanical, Anne focused on their son. Unless he shot up suddenly, and soon, he would probably remain shorter than his father.

Though she couldn't know it, Bobby was thinking of height, too. But the altitude he was contemplating had nothing to do with how tall he might grow. Elbow cemented to the table, chin resting on curled fist, he had infinite minutes ago soared past participles, clanging pots and pans and over-bright lights to a loftier place.

Feeling settled was a strange and wonderful sensation. They had moved six times in the last eleven years. It wasn't that making new friends was all that tough. It just meant he had to work a little harder to fit in. Most of his friends stood four to six inches taller and looked like the football tackles many would become. Bobby—*Why does Mother insist on calling me that?*—didn't have the physique for such combative sports. Not that it mattered much. He was quite satisfied to tone his muscles and his mind on the smooth paved side streets off Nostrand Avenue, where it paid to be a featherweight and skates sped him into raucous games of swift-dodging, fast-thinking "hockey." Already he could lob a handball in school courts or empty alleys better than most anyone. Though he consciously worked at it, he hardly needed to improve his dexterity. He only wished he could see things more clearly.

Growing up in Brooklyn had been no hardship. A mighty oak that would have been a sapling on that first Independence Day turned the empty lot on Avenue "U" into a fort, a jungle, a hideaway. For Bob, every day in the freedom of this wilderness in the midst of concrete and steel felt like his personal Independence Day. Ever since he could climb, he picked his way, sometimes barefooted, to the top of the great tree along its broad, sweeping boughs. Even without looking down, he could feel when someone was watching. If that someone was a girl, he lengthened his reach and dared narrow, creaking limbs. He and his friends double-knotted a heavy rope to a sturdy branch and, from twenty feet off the ground, swung out into the vastness of space and back again. They were Tarzans. Daring pilots. Underwater adventurers. Magically, the tree conformed to the shapes and fantasies of their dreams. Sometimes, when their energy was spent, Bob and his best friend, Herb Fink, settled lazily into boy-size niches, covered their faces with their Brooklyn Dodgers' baseball caps, and in this private world shared secrets that could never be revealed in quite the same way anywhere else on earth.

By nine o'clock every summer morning, a team's-worth of boys had assembled in the empty field to play baseball. Bob was a nimble short-stop. In a single, swift motion, he could scoop the ball from his mitt and have it airborne. When a batter hit a high ball that disappeared against the clouds, Bob's fantasies would trail skyward after it.

For special occasions, even during lean times, Anne packed a picnic basket, rolled up beach towels and loaded her two children (Bob had acquired a sister, Doris) onto the train for Coney Island. On any sweltering day masses of humanity dotted the warm, coarse sand like bright confetti.

"You're brown as a berry," his mother repeated again and again. Dripping on her sandy towel, her son absorbed her warmth and beamed jubilantly. In the surf, like on the playing field, he lost track of time and space. Everyone, especially Doris, might as well be on another planet. It was enough to flow with the current far beyond the clamor, determine the precise moment to launch out over a wave, ride its rolling force at hurtling speed, then feel it break across his shoulders as it dropped him in the shallows.

He couldn't stay out of the water long enough to dry in the sun. On the train home, his damp woolen bathing suit itched under his clothes and grew damper and itchier with sweat. His mother let him have the window seat. As the city whizzed by, he stared straight ahead, focusing on an imaginary point, letting himself slip far, far away, until he could feel the flutter of the long white silk scarf tied around his neck. Taste the wind on his lips and feel the chin strap of his leather pilot's helmet through gloved fingers.

Bob knew better than to give Father a reason to pull the razor strap off the wall. No lame excuses for chores left undone. No denial of responsibility for a poor grade. George always made it clear where the buck stopped. "That's how it is, son." Yet the distance between how things were and how Bob wished them to be was fairly insignificant. There were always branches to climb, tall tales to tell, secrets to share with Herb, home runs to hit and brag about over Friday night's fish supper. And there were enough chances to prove to neighborhood bullies that he had the right stuff.

"That's a fine boy you have there, Mrs. Caron," his teachers had said more than once. And Mrs. Caron would look across the breakfast table from Mr. Caron and tell him so.

One burly driver of a city Checker cab would have told her differently. Responding to a whistle and hailing arm at Avenue "S" and 27th Street, the driver pulled alongside the curb to pick up his party. In an instant, the young prankster and his buddy lunged past the streetlights and into an alley. The infuriated cabby, having sat out the quiet night with hardly enough fares to pay for his supper, aimed the yellow and black taxi straight at the fleeing boys. Screeching his brakes and rolling out from behind the wheel, the cabby waved his chubby fist and fired obscenities at the butts and heels that had just barely managed to clear the fence in front of him.

Praise didn't flow like a river at the Caron house, but it did trickle enough that there was little doubt in Bob's mind that he and his little sister were loved and respected. He felt it in his father's steady hand as they built model airplanes together at the kitchen table, mustering scraps from dust bins and trash heaps. He smelled it in the steam of a simmering stock pot filled with little more than a scrawny pig's knuckle, a fistful of beans and a handful of herbs grown in pots on the windowsill.

Admiration went three ways. Bob felt it, too, between George and Anne. Sometimes it embarrassed him. Mostly, though, it warmed him. He watched surreptitiously as little tiffs melted into expressions of quiet resolve and finally flowed into reconciliation. It always happened so subtly that he could not be sure where and when the battle began or ended. That the would-be adversaries emerged victors and allies never ceased to amaze him and was a lesson he would never forget. He observed as Father signed their pact with a sheepish grin, sealed it a robust embrace and delivered it with a wet kiss. Then Father would traipse out the door, his vibrato whistle echoing down the hall, down the stairs, growing fainter and fainter, until, finally, it was lost in the cacophony of 27th Street.

Silence in Brooklyn was an elusive treasure. Sirens screamed. Car horns honked. Trolleys clanged. Feet shuffled and clunked up and down flights of creaky stairs. Doors slammed. Wives shrieked at husbands. Husbands bellowed at wives. Toilets flushed. Pipes rattled. Children laughed.

Doris slept through the din in the tiniest of the apartment's two bedrooms. George and Anne took the other, with precious little space to spare. The lumpy couch in the living room would toughen Bob's mettle—an exercise in mind over matter that let sleep come anywhere in years to come, even on a rough hardstand in the shade of a B-29 wing.

Every other day the iceman wielded his frigid load up the three flights. Every morning Bob toted the splashing dishpan of meltwater to the window and tossed it into the street.

When George had steady work, life for his mother and younger sister was easier. But jobs came and too often went. And with them came and went apartments ever closer to promising futures that, one by one, drifted farther and farther from the American Dream. Like hundreds of thousands of laborers, George Jay Caron had become a pawn to a Jekyll-and-Hyde economy.

When house construction waned, George hired out to several display shops that built exhibits for store windows and convention halls. Before long, his supervisor recognized his skills and made him a foreman. It was during one of those brief interludes between apartments that the family enjoyed the comforts of a home. The Caron men created a basement workshop where at day's end they built model planes. Sometimes George carved them out of wood. Occasionally on Saturdays, he took Bob with him on the subway to his shop in the industrial area, where they worked until mid-day then rode the subway home and relaxed building more model planes.

On game Sundays, Bob and one of his baseball buddies walked, or rode the trolley, the four miles to Ebbets Field. For a quarter, they had seats in a section of the farthest bleachers and spent the afternoon in the company of heroes like first baseman Dolph Camilli.

In the fall and spring, Bob could easily cover the three-quarter mile distance to school in a breathless dash and slide into his homeroom seat before the second bell had rung. In the afternoon, Nostrand was an avenue to adventure. Not far from home, a water works long vanished had been transformed into a baseball diamond—with ample outfield for solid home runs. For a few hours, boys of all shapes, sizes and colors mingled in freedom. They discovered a neglected neighborhood golf course was better suited to running and catching than driving and putting.

After school and on Saturdays, a narrow storefront sandwiched between wide-front businesses attracted boys five to ninety-five. They swarmed excitedly outside the window, buzzing and vying for positions against the glass.

"Look at that one," a tow-head shouted. All eyes fixed on the Handley Page V/1500 model airplane dangling at the end of fishing line suspended from the ceiling. A nearby placard informed that the bomber after which the model had been created had flown for the first time in 1918. The card said the Handley's one hundred twenty-six foot wingspan held four three hundred seventy-five horse power Rolls Royce Eagle VIIIs and was unique because of its heavy bomb-load capacity and tail gun position.

Perched on a pedestal nearby, a Soviet TB-1 twin-engine, cantilever low-wing monoplane aimed its miniature nose toward the entrance.

"What'd ja get?" interrogated Bob and fellow oglers as schoolmates emerged from the store.

Kits were great, for those who could afford them. Bob couldn't. Although he wouldn't fully appreciate the depth of his relationship to his father until he was older, Bob cherished the hours he and "the great kite maker" pored over model airplane plans. Tacked to a big sheet of plywood that rested flat on the kitchen table, the construction prints were edged with tiny, precise notations about modifications and errors. Shoulder to shoulder, the two patiently worked their way through wing and fuselage sections to motor assemblies. When things got too serious, they poked and teased each other. Occasionally, a project fell victim to sabotage (peanut butter on more than one critical measurement would do it).

Securing the plans themselves involved espionage and intrigue. Intrepid Aunt Grace (her name may have influenced her success) had risked her job at the printing company to steal model airplane plans run on its presses. To Bob, she was a master spy, a hero. For him she stealthily confiscated plans for the SPAD, British SE-5, Nieuport Bébé and Fokker D-8 right out from under her supervisor's nose. Aunt Grace always transferred the contraband from her big brown purse to the hands of the waiting aeronautical engineers at the prearranged location—the Carons' living room. The payoff was Anne's responsibility—an Aunt-Grace-size serving of peach cobbler crowned with sweet cream.

Necessity, the mother of invention, meant substituting flour and water for "dope," the good glue normally used to adhere tissue paper to the fuselage and wings. Anne's perfume atomizer with the purple silk bulb, donated as her contribution to the effort, misted the tissue paper lightly so that it shrank smoothly and tautly against precisely cut and sanded balsa frames.

"We could get rich selling these," wide-eyed Herb said one day, elevating a model admiringly. Bob had little confidence in his friend's construction ability. But Herb did have a way of talking kids out of nickels and dimes. Their short-lived business venture didn't go bust—Herb sold three—but supply soon exceeded demand, and the partners learned once they added in a small profit, neighborhood boys couldn't pay the price.

"Besides," Herb whined, "I can make more money *fishin'*." Bob knew a resignation when he heard one. Fishing in Brooklyn meant baiting a line with a saliva-softened wad of chewing gum and steadily lowering it between the grates in the sidewalk. When it was centered just right over the catch, its caster would let it plunge ten to twelve feet straight down to snare a coppery penny or silvery dime. Quarters nearly always got away. They quivered momentarily at the end of their line and, finally, amid "Aw's" and "shucks," freed themselves of the tacky lures and fell back into the depths.

The pulse of Brooklyn throbbed in these arteries. Under Nostrand Avenue the IRT zipped through tiled tunnels green with fluorescent light. Turnstiles clanked and groaned with the endless ebb and flow of commuters. A few blocks away, Flatbush Avenue crossed the mighty Nostrand and marked the end of the line.

The bird's-eye view of Nostrand disclosed a rich and colorful assortment of sights, smells and sounds. When he was on the roof of his apartment building, Brooklyn belonged to Bob. New York belonged to Bob. The skies, too. The roof was his runway, his cockpit, his ticket to space. One bright afternoon it was nearly his ticket to disaster.

That day, he cradled the model plane with the rubber-band motor in his arm and raced up the stairs. He couldn't wait to fly the new plane, barely completed the night before. When it was in position for takeoff from the tarpaper runway, he gave the propeller a final turn. Its flight pattern, he calculated, would include several smooth, semi-circular turns before it descended and landed on the sand strip of the vacant lot next door.

Seconds after the plane cleared the half wall, Bob knew it wasn't going to happen quite that way. A thermal lifted the plane and carried it in a wide sweep over Nostrand Avenue. He watched helplessly as it assumed a force of its own, gliding over buses, taxies and pedestrians, finally spiraling in an ungodly death dive toward an oncoming trolley.

"Stop! Stop!" The trolley's conductor shouted futilely, determined to avoid a crash with the flying object, or worse, with cars that were by now intent on it, not him. He waved his arms then clanged the bell wildly. But the die had been cast. On impact with the front of the trolley, the aircraft burst into splinters of balsa and fluttering fingers of foil. Although his trolley window hadn't been shattered and a traffic accident had been narrowly averted, the conductor shook his fist and let fly a string of expletives at the unseen pilot.

The Battle of Nostrand Avenue had been lost. But Bob wasn't prepared to lose the war. His creation had been dashed. Not his dreams. It was time to go back to the drawing board. More lessons in aerodynamics were still to come.

For Bob's idol, aviator Charles Lindbergh, 1932 was a painful year. His twenty-month-old son had been kidnapped and murdered, although a ransom of fifty thousand dollars had been paid. Police arrested Bruno Hauptmann and, after a sensational trial, he was sentenced to the electric chair. For Hungarian Leo Szilard, 1932 was the year he discovered the works of English author and social thinker Herbert George Wells. It wasn't Wells' famous 1898 *The War of the Worlds* that sent shivers up the physicist's spine, but his 1914 novel, *The World Set Free.* What unnerved Szilard most was the author's prophesy that man would harness atomic energy and use the new technology in a global war to destroy entire cities. In Wells' fantasy, England, France and America formed an alliance against Germany. The Hungarian shuddered.

To the physicists who were exploring atomic energy potential, science, as always, was neutral. Whether a discovery was used for good or ill wasn't their responsibility. Ethics was not the domain of test tubes and centrifuges, spectrographs and cyclotrons.

Whirling around in the mind of American physicist Ernest O. Lawrence as early as April 1929 was a device for creating massive quantities of atomic energy. In Lawrence's design, nuclear particles were accelerated within a circular magnetic field.

Several months before, the technique had begun to spin through the curly, dark-haired head of Leo Szilard. Short, often pompous, the Jewish-descent physicist, who had added his inventive genius to Albert Einstein's in Berlin, had already pondered the feasibility of a mechanism that released more energy than was required to produce it.

Szilard's calculations created embryonically the concept of "critical mass." Based on his formulations, an explosion was possible "if the thickness [of the material] is larger than the critical value." When the configurations for his atom-splitting device were complete in January 1929, he applied for a patent.

But a design wasn't *the* device. The scientist preferred inspiration to perspiration and lavished long contemplative hours wrinkling up neck-high in his think-tank tub. Lawrence, on the other hand, was an energetic implementer as well as an innovator. A year after conceiving his accelerator, he fleshed out a small working model and nicknamed it "cyclotron." Within two more years, he wrote in the *Physics Review* that to create the circular magnetic field in his full-scale version would require an eighty-ton magnet.

Although he had aspired to be a pilot rather than a physicist, George Robert Caron would stumble on this and other fascinating cyclotron information in a dusty military base library in the middle of nowhere, far from the intellectual congregation called Berkeley. But that would not happen for eleven more years.

By March 1934, Szilard was, as usual, in hot water up to his neck. Neurons fired rapidly across the synapses in his brain. Immersed in his ball and claw-foot, white cast-iron London laboratory, he conducted mental chain-reaction experiments. Which element, he mused, as he frequently replenished the hot water turned cold, could emit two or more neutrons for each neutron captured?

"It suddenly occurred to me that if we could find an element which is split by neutrons and which would emit two neutrons when it absorbs one neutron, such an element, if assembled in sufficiently large mass, could sustain a nuclear chain reaction."

Along with its famous baths, Rome produced scientist Enrico Fermi, who coaxed fruit from Szilard's barren vines. Cultivation, so unpalatable to the Hungarian, turned the fertile earth at Fermi's laboratory. While it had the potential for bountiful harvests, theirs was an uneasy alliance battered by torrents of ego.

Like Lawrence, Fermi didn't let the grass grow under his feet. He engaged in prolific experimentation. A shy man of Occam's razor passion, he worked for hours and days alone, struggling to reduce a principle to its simplest form. In 1934, he had accomplished the "alchemist's dream," creating a new, radioactive element by bombarding uranium particles with fast neutrons. Although he would not know the significance of his experiment until later, he had succeeded in splitting the atom.

Unlike Fermi, the dashing, charismatic Lawrence was at his best among his students, colleagues, even reporters, stimulating everyone around him. He grafted the branches of his ideas onto the young tree of nuclear knowledge and watched as in 1939 the new growth sprouted a Nobel Prize. The publicity and prize money would help him achieve his goal: inaugurating at the University of California at Berkeley one of the nation's foremost physics research centers. In Harvard physicist J. Robert Oppenheimer he would find not another master grounds keeper like himself, but the perfect complement, an idea architect whose mind was a diverse garden of theories.

The garden had sprung from a tiny seed some twenty-five centuries earlier. Greek philosopher Democritus, contemplating the nature of matter, speculated that everything could be divided into minute particles that could not be divided into anything smaller. He called these invisibles *atomos*, simply, "non divisible."

For more than two millennia, what the atom was and wasn't stumped scientific thinkers. Was the seemingly indivisible divisible? Indeed, was the atom a real—or merely "convenient"—explanation for the behavior of chemical reactions? By the end of the nineteenth century, Western science concluded that the atom, for all its coherence, was divisible after all.

At Manchester University during World War I, New Zealand physicist Ernest Rutherford had been the first to discover the atomic nucleus. Later, at Cambridge, his assistant James Chadwick would find a third component of matter, the neutron. Although the neutron was as massive as the proton and contributed to an element's atomic weight, Chadwick discovered that since it carried no electrical charge of its own, it could be useful in exploring the nucleus itself. The perfect apparatus for producing neutrons, with a few modifications, was Lawrence's cyclotron. About the time World War II began, German physicist Otto Hahn and his team demonstrated that splitting atoms could initiate and sustain a chain reaction of successive splittings. Researchers in Europe and America made similar findings.

Throughout the politically unstable years that followed, many scientists were forced to seek safe havens. They found them on the campuses of major American universities. With open arms, California Institute of Technology in Pasadena welcomed aeronautical physics pioneer Theodor von Kármán when he fled Aachen, Germany. Later, Von Kármán was to head the prestigious Guggenheim Aeronautical Laboratory funded by aviation philanthropist Daniel Guggenheim.

The European brain drain had begun. Startling numbers of non-Aryan academics, stripped of their positions in 1933 by the first of Hitler's anti-Jewish laws, sought sanctuary in neighboring countries, then emigrated to the United States. Over the next eight years, as many as one hundred refugee physicists settled in New York, Illinois, California, Massachusetts and New Jersey, lured by academic Meccas that promised intellectual freedom and financial security.

Princeton University dangled a five-million dollar research endowment carrot before the eloquent father of relativity who, ironically, as a child had been slow to speak. Its Institute for Advanced Study was less interested in Einstein's capacity to expound theories than to beget them. In March 1933, after his life had been threatened, his Berlin house searched, the mentally and physically muscular émigré with twinkling eyes and raucous laugh renounced his German citizenship. For Einstein, parting had not been such sweet sorrow. He despised what Germany had become.

Flights of Fancy

T
he land to which great thanksgiving anthems were sung melted into its richness myriad souls for whom the imagined was preferable to the known. From its strange newness stirred the winds of promise. They blew across ocean seas and whispered to tired shores, "opportunity and a land of plenty awaits." Beleaguered souls dared to dream. Toting in suitcases and satchels the icons of their cultures, the exodus trickled imperceptibly into the river of immigrants that flowed through Ellis Island. They were seasonings for the soup that was already simmering. To the opposite coast, where the imprint of the orient—literally, rising in the sky—had been firmly set, came the Japanese. Handfuls of them previously had known only a place between the mountains and sea, a place called Hiroshima.

Each Japanese dawn, the heavens greeted the earth in a warm embrace. In the ritual long ago, the great Sun Goddess Amaterasu became full with the energy of life. To her was born a son, and to him a son, Ninigi. The Sun Goddess instructed her Imperial Grandson, "Go and rule over the Luxuriant Land of Reed Plains below, that our descendants may inherit it. May our Imperial lineage continue unbroken and prosperous, co-eternal with Heaven and Earth." Carrying the three symbols of divine authority, a sword for justice, jewels for mercy and the mirror into which his grandmother looked and saw truth reflected, the young god descended to a snowy peak. Ninigi peopled the land of volcanoes, lush mountains, plentiful streams and rushing rivers. Finally, in 660 B.C., Jimmu, the great-grandson of Ninigi, was crowned the first Emperor of Japan.

In the span of two and a half millennia, a unique culture deeply influenced by China and Confucianism evolved and flourished. During the twelfth-century, the Samurai warrior class emerged. Fierce warlords, called shoguns, ruled. For seven hundred years, Japan remained insular, little-changed. Then, in 1853, United States Commodore Matthew C. Perry shattered Japanese isolationism and flung open its gates to the West.

Fourteen years later, another legendary grandfather, Koin Kido, and his band overthrew the shogunate and restored Japan's long-exiled Emperor Meiji to the royal throne established by Amaterasu. It was not so unusual then, that the destinies of the Emperor Meiji's grandson and the grandson of the Koin Kido should become entwined. The future Emperor Hirohito and Kiochi Kido ran and sparred in the courtyard and learned the art of being warriors.

When Hirohito ascended to the throne in 1926, he recognized the dedication and loyalty of his long-time playmate and conferred upon Marquis Kiochi Kido the title Lord Keeper of the Privy Seal. Officially, the Marquis stamped the Emperor's signature seals on Imperial decrees and documents. Unofficially, he was the Emperor's eyes, ears and voice. As self-proclaimed gatekeeper and chief adviser, Kido had become a most influential man. And he intended to use his influence to empower the Emperor. Koin Kido and his band had been guided by the conviction that to offer one's life for a divine being was not a price, but an honor. And thousands willingly impaled themselves on the sword in the Emperor's name. They did not doubt Hirohito's divine lineage

The great disbeliever was Hirohito, himself. Outwardly expressing these or any other feelings, *ninjo*, was not the prerogative of the Emperor. *Ninjo* could be exalted through art, poetry and, of course, lovemaking. Hirohito believed himself no different from any other man. Wealthier, better educated, but just as mortal. That was a dangerous self-indulgence cautioned Kido. People needed a divine figure to give purpose to living and dying. The Emperor had Japan at his feet. Everyone understood that it belonged to him. Wealth brought certain freedoms. It built a laboratory where he spent untiring hours huddled over butterflies, insects and fungi that he had personally collected. It opened the domain of the undersea world to his insatiable quest for discovery. But the Emperor's divine status was also his prison. While his own countrymen were not permitted to gaze directly at their ruler, the rest of the world was not so obligated, and could view him as a marine biologist of significant achievement. Outside of his homeland, he could smile and wave and wear his earthliness without shame and indulge his mortal self in a day of golf or a hearty bacon and egg breakfast.

While upon him was bestowed everything, he would have preferred to own nothing. Luxury, unlike life, was an inconsequential largess. Riches were to be found not only in simplicity, but also in serenity.

The warrior he pretended to be as a child was not in the man. So much did he treasure tranquillity that Hirohito declared his reign *Showa*, Enlightened Peace.

Yet the path to enlightenment was strewn with obstacles. One of them was limited natural resources. Political and military leaders embraced the concept of Japan in the center of a great circle of influence, possessions that would not only enrich her, but would also enhance her world status.

The Japanese military had begun to flex its muscles during the First Sino-Japanese War of 1895, when it gained Taiwan. As Britain's ally in 1902, Japan fine-tuned its navy in the Anglo tradition. It had learned well and crushed the majority of the Russian fleet at Port Arthur and Chemulpo in 1905, adding territory in China ceded by Russia and bringing the nation to international prominence. Within half a decade it annexed Korea. During World War I, the emerging nation lost no time occupying German enclaves on the coast of China, along with the Marshall, Mariana and Caroline islands in the Pacific. In 1931, Japan established a puppet state in Manchuria, and six years later invaded North China. Chiang Kai-shek, struggling to nationalize and unify China, mobilized his military in an effort to check incursions by both the warlords and the Communists. Boldly, Japan allied with its former enemy, Germany, in a triune pact with Italy and opened hostilities against the United States.

The Imperial military did not expect interference from the Emperor. It was politically free of his divine intervention to prevent war and morally free to use his divine name to conduct it. In a few swift strokes, the Japanese military claimed a wealth of territory in the Philippines, Hong Kong, Singapore, Malaya, Guam, Wake Island, Burma and the Dutch East Indies.

W hile Japan took what it didn't have, George Robert Caron invented ways to turn whatever was on hand into something he wanted. His five-barrel gun, three rubber bands to a barrel, was so effective it was banned from Flatbush Avenue. Then came the scooter, fabricated from one dismantled Chicago ball-bearing roller skate and a two-by-four. Bob converted the cardboard Majestic Cleaners tucked inside its laundered shirts into zip guns; the wheels and axles of his sister's baby buggy into the undercarriage of a wagon.

Fortunes were made and lost on the same day. The Crash of 1929 turned futures into worthless pieces of paper. By the time Wall Street's fever signaled illness, the disease had progressed too far. The nation plunged deeper and deeper into the dark abyss of joblessness. Eventually one-third of the labor force, sixteen million workers, would face unemployment.

Franklin Delano Roosevelt, who had fought crippling poliomyelitis in 1921, as governor of New York was again on the battlefield, this time negotiating his state's economic quagmires. On April 7, 1932, during an emotional radio broadcast, he told troubled Americans that he would do everything he could for "the forgotten man at the bottom of the economic pyramid."

Voters believed him and sent Herbert Hoover packing. Recapturing the American Dream had all the drama of recapturing the pennant with Red Barber giving the play-by-play.

During Roosevelt's first one hundred days, his "everything" curriculum started with the three "R's"—reform, recovery and relief. He ramrodded radical fiscal and social reforms through Congress to stimulate the economy and reorganize industry and agriculture. Guided by the pluck of Raymond Moley and other Brain Trust advisers, the President continued the initiative begun by Hoover and pulled even more rabbits out of the bureaucratic hat. But some of the magic of the New Deal would be overshadowed. For example, the National Recovery Administration, established by the National Recovery Act of 1933, was declared unconstitutional two years later. Funds for programs such as Hoover's Reconstruction Finance Corporation, which helped pay for war plants and disaster damages, were being rapidly depleted.

The United States was still reeling from the eleven-and-a-half-billion-dollar war credit line it had extended to European countries. As the ripples of the Depression swept onto European shores, only Hungary and Finland had not defaulted on loan payments. Federal coffers earmarked to finance New Deal proposals would not be refilled by debtor nations.

The success of some programs, such as the Work Projects Administration of 1935, was not an illusion. As workers constructed one hundred sixteen thousand buildings, seventy-eight thousand bridges and six hundred fifty-one miles of roads, their paychecks bought goods and services. But more than brick, steel and wood was being used to rebuild the nation. The Federal Arts and Federal Theatre projects set the stage for actors, directors, writers and scene designers to expand or launch their careers. Experimental theater brightened the Depression sky with rising stars, among them Orson Welles' highly touted Mercury Theater. The Federal Writers' Project recognized the contributions of talented literary artists.

Yet, for American journeymen, factory workers, small businessmen and skilled laborers of all kinds, economic rebirth was protracted and painful. George Jay Caron didn't expect relief overnight.

From his third-floor window, Bob contemplated the soda fountain across the street. A fountain-candy store and accompanying curb-side newsstand sprouted every third block in Brooklyn's less affluent neighborhoods. Fifteen-year-old Bob paid special attention to this one not because it tempted with hot fudge sundaes or fifty kinds of penny candy. Bob wasn't looking to spend money, but to make it.

"Sure can use you," said its owner, who complained his lazy son had dropped the ball. "Tell you what. I'll give you a buck and a half a week to deliver the *Daily News, Daily Mirror, Times* and *Herald Tribune* every morning, Sundays, too. Be here when the bundles arrive at 5 A.M."

The paper-route money covered a few expenses and, for most of the week, Bob's school lunches. The remaining day, Bob packed a cheese sandwich and bought a carton of milk.

There was little extra of anything. Still, families, friends and neighbors shared what they had. Herb Fink was making do with even less than Bob. When Herb's father died, his mother tried to compensate for the lost income by renting out their downstairs rooms. More than the space, they needed groceries and shoes for a growing boy.

Mrs. Fink fascinated Bob. Her slim face was always radiant. She laughed a great deal, and like his own mother, never complained. He would watch her long, veined hands slice a loaf of bread so thin that the pieces arched rather than fell flat. As gently as if she were handling brocade, she would lay down a pink, round sliver of bologna and top it with the second thin slice of bread. Having cut the sandwich on the diagonal, she would put half in front of each boy.

Wives and mothers stretched dollars and took on added work. Three days a week, Anne Caron boarded the trolley and headed across town, where she spent the day scrubbing, ironing and preparing a meal for a gravely ill woman. On the trolley heading home, she would cup her hands in her lap and shut her eyes, mentally distancing herself from standers crowded in the aisle. Their wrists secured in ceiling straps, they, nevertheless, teetered with every lurch and start. Instinctively, she tucked her sore feet under her seat and pressed herself nearly through it. Within minutes, their over-closeness, the loud bell and harsh lights no longer invaded her seclusion. She drifted into a private, peaceful world without struggle. Her elbow relaxed its grip on the tightly rolled newspaper she faithfully brought home to Bobby.

"Take *all* the papers," her feeble employer had urged, knowing that the paper collector would pay Bob a nickel for every hundred pounds he bundled.

It took about forty nickels to buy his first pair of Chicago ball-bearing roller skates. The steely, high-pitched sound of their wheels grated rhythmically on the concrete as one foot, then the other, raked along the dimpled sidewalks that latticed for miles.

One afternoon, Bob's mathematics' teacher broadened his horizons when she had welcomely digressed from problem-solving to tell her class a story about wooden-wheel skates at the roller rink. Wooden wheels? What could be better than his skates? As she paused between sentences, Bob seized the moment. "Oh, *those* things," he gestured with a flip of the wrist. "They're just cheapskates." When the teacher and the class recovered from their laughter, he leaned back in his chair, stretched his legs into the aisle and sprouted a satisfied grin. Who wanted to skate round and round the inside of a building anyway?

Unlike the busy cobblestone main thoroughfares, the residential side streets were smooth macadam, a quiet roller hockey haven. By saving old rubber heels that the boys used for pucks, the Czechoslovakian shoemaker vicariously joined in their games. For fifty cents, a boy could buy a real hockey stick. As the sun dipped behind the mountains of bricks and brownstone, boys with skinned knees skated home past young couples pushing baby carriages and late commuters wearily emerging from the underground.

From the subway to Brooklyn Technical High School, the freshman walked briskly fifteen minutes down DeKalb Avenue to Fort

Greene Place. Tech rose like a seven-story ship in a harbor of sampans. Tenements flanked its west side. A large park opened on the north. On the south side, the gymnasium with its indoor track and high ceiling heated up on sunny days and was a cool place to work out when it was gray. A two-story aeronautical shop took up most of the area to the east of the gym.

Acclaimed as one of the best tech schools in the country, Brooklyn always had a waiting list of students who wanted to get in. Each spring, eighth-graders across the city took Tech's standard admission test. Bob was glad to have made the grade. In addition to carrying a full load of academic subjects, he would study engineering and physics. The intricacies of how things worked had piqued his interest since childhood. Calculations were a game, not an assignment.

On an unseasonably warm fall day, he rummaged through trash cans for ginger ale bottles to redeem for their five-cent deposit when something distracted him. Carefully, he separated the book from damp bags and bottles. *A Treatise on Civil Engineering* was stamped in gold on its brown linen spine. On its title page, "D. H. Mahan, LL.D., late professor of Civil Engineering at West Point, 1877." Bob sat down on the curb and gently turned its fragile pages. The first plate was a fine lithograph of the East River Bridge. By the time he had gotten to Chapter IX, "Natural Features of Rivers," page 494, collecting bottles no longer seemed of great importance.

The big park across from Tech had been one of his class surveying projects. Drafting, learning about molecular structure in chemistry, calculating stresses on materials, physics: it all seemed more play than work and a good foundation for becoming a pilot.

A "bombshell," Herb called her, poking Bob in the side. The blond was pretty, yes, but sexy? No. Bob hadn't noticed Edna Sanders at other YMCA dances, but he noticed her now. Surprised by his boldness, he asked her to be his date the following Saturday. She didn't have to think twice.

The track team, which ran together off the field as well as on, congregated at the "Y" for Saturday evening coed splash parties. After letting off steam in the pool, boys and girls paired on the dance floor, laughing as they jitter-bugged. Wallflowers, knots twisting nervously in their stomachs, froze unspeaking in their chairs.

Sometimes a classmate or team member invited the group to a party at his house. When booze flowed freely one night, Bob was surprised to see his friend's parents filling the glasses. Mellowed from having emptied several of his own, Bob marveled at Edna jitter-bugging. Fleetingly, he wished he could dance like that. Then someone else attracted his attention. His focus blurred and cleared again on a cute redhead.

"I'm Irish, too. French-Irish," he told her. The redhead laughed at his presumptuous introduction. Although Edna had been dancing with someone else, she saw no equity in Bob's flirtatiousness and insisted that he take her home. She pouted throughout the elevator-train ride there. When he moved in for the usual goodnight kiss, she turned away.

The night was still young, and train fare jingled in his pocket. He was pleased the redhead hadn't left the party. She stood near the window, saying something that made his friend laugh. Bob liked her entertaining, refreshingly exuberant personality. Since Edna had given him the cold shoulder, he could guiltlessly ask her for a date to Coney Island.

A few weeks later, Edna let Bob's invitation to a movie bridge the rift between them. Although they agreed occasionally to date others, their friendship became a strong bond that lasted throughout high school. Bob's track teammates applauded his taste in girls and approved of his patching things up with Edna. Jealousy and envy had no place among them. Whether they ran cross-country in the fall, or competed in meets on the National Guard Armory's two hundred twenty-yard track in the winter, they were a brotherhood.

Edna, Bob's parents and Doris were in the bleachers for his first major competition, the one-mile relay. The fastest runner on the second team, he had been positioned as anchorman. His muscles tensed as the first runner took off, then lost ground. The third runner was half a lap behind the rest. Sweat beaded on Bob's face. When the baton finally hit his hand, the anchorman figured he didn't have a chance. Although he couldn't see Edna and his family in the wall of faces, or hear her cheers over the roar, he felt her pulling for him. Energy burned in his thighs; he thrust his chest forward and lengthened his stride. Before many seconds had passed, he closed the gap between him and distant runners. Willing his entire body into the push, he found himself in their midst. Coach cupped his hands around his mouth and shouted, "C'mon shorty. You're gonna make it."

Bob heard nothing but his blood pulsing through his veins.

"You did good, " coach said at the finish line. "You almost had it."

The razor strap came down off the wall for the last time late one Friday night when the cock-sure, would-be aviator was fifteen. Bob was already waiting at the sidewalk when Herb Fink arrived. The two were more than ready to release a week's worth of rampant hormones and pent-up energy with as much physical contact as touch football allowed. As usual, the guys were meeting at the big, well-lighted lot next to the gas station five blocks away. There was plenty of time, Bob assured Herb, to run into the corner drug store for a penny cigarette.

Under the street lamp, they lit up, let the curl of smoke riffle through their noses and waited for the light to change. When it did, they were too preoccupied to notice the man in the dark topcoat and fedora who approached them from the opposite side. When he stopped and stared, the boys laughed and puffed and kept on walking.

"I wonder what *that* old geezer wants," Herb said.

"Who knows," Bob shrugged him off. Speaking was more for effect than communication. He was only interested in making his cigarette vibrate on his lower lip as he talked the way Bogey did.

For a few hours, football put the inconsequential encounter behind him. Whether or not the need for physical catharsis had been sated on the field, it was about to be challenged in the living room.

Before the door closed that other world behind him, George Caron ordered, "Get the strap, son."

Bob stared at his father blankly.

"I'm that 'old geezer' who caught you smoking."

By late June 1935, electric fans were already oscillating sticky tenement air, pulling faint breezes past curtains that hardly fluttered. Without warning, George's carpentry work evaporated like morning mist. There was no money for rent.

"You just tell Anne and the kids they're staying with us till you get squared away," Uncle Bill boomed as usual, his husky arm flung over George's shoulder. Aunt Kitty and Uncle Bill weren't family but might as well have been. The brownstone tenement they owned in old Brooklyn provided them with a comfortable living and enough left over to build a boarding house on a substantial wedge of land in northern New Jersey on Lake Parsippany.

Doris and her mother shared a pleasant downstairs bedroom. Bob settled into one of the eaves in the attic, where a little four-paned window looked east over the lake. He shoved the cardboard box with his neatly folded clothes against the wall and stretched out on the folding cot. Pillowing his head with upturned palms, he stared at the rafters. Lake Parsippany for the whole summer. A grin crept over his face and he closed his eyes.

"Chicken."

"Ain't either."

"Then let's see you do it."

Thinking that maybe the guys were right, Bob stood with his toes more off than on the fifteen-foot diving platform. His breakfast threatened to be his lunch.

"Jump." The injunction rose more loudly from within than from below. He gulped air, stepped into nothingness, grabbed his knees and let gravity take it from there. His brain registered terror, then, inexplicably, wild pleasure. The one hundred twenty-five pound cannonball boomed into the depths without grace, but without panic.

On his fifth jump, he waited, poised at the end of the board, until their eyes were on him. Imitating the show-offs he had admired all morning, he sprang from the board like he'd been shot from a bow, remembered to tuck his head between his outstretched arms and knifed his way through the surface of the water, the cheers and clapping gurgling in his ears.

On one of those memorable days, he discovered Edith Scheno. Rather, she discovered him and introduced herself. Orphaned at a young age, Edith was already an accomplished singer whose future seemed assured. She was confident, happy, vivacious.

Bob discovered only a few evenings later that her cheeks flushed when he kissed her. As they canoed the placid lake, her mellifluous laugh danced across the water and was absorbed in the pines that ringed the shore. She eagerly shared experiences new to him: roasting potatoes in buried coals until their skins were black and their centers tender and moist; fresh-water bait fishing. At midnight, when they gathered with friends for a bonfire on the beach, she curled up in the sand in front of him, pushing her round shoulders between his knees. Without reservation, she looped her arms around his legs as naturally as if they were her own. Tangled, laughing, they remained for hours, one fire going out, another igniting.

For the first time, he wanted to reveal to someone other than Herb his hopes, his dreams. It was all so poetic, the temptation to bare his soul to this woman-child, this Siren. He wanted to take her through the journey of his sixteen years, sit beside her as she saw him through the pages of his family's photograph album. He wanted to watch her eyes light up in recognition as she discovered the little print of him perched ecstatically on the cockpit of the magical biplane ("I was only three. But airplanes were already my *first* love." He would emphasize "first."). He wanted to be with her.

Amid the fires that burned that summer, the flame of entrepreneurism, not quenched from the business experience with Herb, flickered again. This time, ready supply and inexhaustible demand fanned it to life. The appetite of Lake Parsippany's dinner guests for sweet corn on the cob seemed virtually insatiable. The restaurateur couldn't keep up with it. If he circumvented local produce stands and bought "bootlegged" corn, he could increase his profits. For every field-fresh ear Parsippany's young businessmen could stealthily load into gunny sacks by moonlight, the restaurant owner would shuck out one cent.

Bob was as eager as the other boys to make a buck, but he had no stomach for stealing. Although he was fast and efficient, his gut tightened with every ear he pulled from the stalk. All he could think of was the farmer who tilled, planted and fertilized the field, struggling—like his own father—to make a living for his family. He would never forget his experience with stealing years earlier. The marvelous emerald green and gold fountain pen with its own leatherette hinged case was as vivid now as it was that terrifying day that he pocketed it. As quick as a flash, he had the elegant writing instrument in his hand. It had happened so spontaneously he was stunned. He felt sure someone would notice how guilty he looked as he slipped past the imprisoning doors to the freedom of the street.

At home, the coveted pen became an albatross. What could he do with it? The next day, classes dragged on mercilessly until the final bell. It took greater effort than usual to push open the heavy glass department-store doors. Breathing rapidly, he mingled with shoppers until clerks were occupied. With trembling hand, he removed the fountain pen from his pocket and eased it back onto the display case.

Uncle Bill's shutting down the boarding house on Labor Day signaled the end of a another passage. Bob and Edith said their good-byes without promises. A few tears traced a path down her cheeks before her independent spirit took hold. Pulling Bob's arm around her shoulder, she led him along the shore.

"This one is to remember me by." After her long kiss, she ran toward the road, turning once to smile and wave.

Families all around the lake were packing for home. Home for the three Carons was a yet-unseen furnished suite of rooms above a fish store that George had found a few days before. The small carpentry contracts he had secured would cover the rent and little more.

The new apartment was narrow and dark. Its few windows in the front and rear barely lifted the tiny rooms out of gloom and despair. With the exception of the kitchen, rooms in the center of the apartment were lifeless. Anne's kitchen faced the "airy way" passage between buildings and the window of the kitchen opposite hers an arm's length away. Bob shared a cubicle-sized bedroom with his sister. He had learned from his parents not to complain. Instead, his model airplanes, skates, books, cap and baseball mitt mingled with Doris' few dolls, dollhouse and puzzles.

Occasionally, the family scraped together enough change to spend the evening at a local cinema. Box offices lured moviegoers with free dinnerware, and Anne clutched the treasured plate, cup or saucer along with her soggy handkerchief.

On Fridays she fought fire with fire. The smells of her own frying fish temporarily overpowered the nauseating medley of halibut, herring, anchovies, squid, octopus, eel and heaven knows what else that seeped through the floorboards and up from the alley, where the scraps turned to fertilizer.

The President urged patience. "If we can boondoggle ourselves out of this Depression," he said in his January 18, 1936, speech to the New Jersey State Emergency Council in Newark, "that word is going to be enshrined in the hearts of the American people for years to come."

Anne's patience and perseverance were rewarded with a tidy, more spacious apartment in a three-story brown brick building just five blocks away. On a side street, the new home was just out of range of the incessant clanging of trolley bells and thunderous, earth-shaking rumble of the subway. Yet the station access was convenient, and Bob daily rode the subway to Tech.

Their building, the end of the apartments in that section, offered a clear view of businesses queued liked dominoes along busy Nostrand Avenue. At noon, the corner luncheonette and drugstore buzzed with activity and increased patronage for businesses on both sides. The tailor was one of those who benefited from the drugstore traffic.

Catty-corner from the drugstore, St. Jerome's Church thrust its gray spires against the steel sky. Its bells peeled sad-glorious and had no competition during the early Sunday morning hush. On yellowing walls hung Stations of the Cross, dulled by long city days and nights, yet potent and enduring in their solemnity.

After evening Mass the priests and nuns left their deific duties in the hallowed halls and sidled up to the soda-fountain for that extra ice-cream dip the new soda jerk scooped into their dishes.

Bob's generosity with someone else's profits had put the young man in a league with the President—as measured by the standards of New York's Democratic Governor. Repeatedly during his 1936 campaign speeches, Alfred E. Smith attacked Roosevelt's spendthrift New Deal programs, branding them philanthropy and complaining that "nobody shoots at Santa Claus." Perhaps the governor was right, thought Bob. Even the nuns and priests hadn't rejected the free scoop of ice cream.

As long as his youngest employee kept customers happy, the luncheonette's owner would leave Santa Claus alone. When business was slow, the owner insisted Bob focus on homework at a small table at the end of the counter.

His second year at the luncheonette, Bob's wage doubled to ten cents an hour. When the contents of the mayonnaise jar he had dumped periodically onto his bed amounted to five dollars, he bought a used bicycle, or more appropriately, an *abused* bicycle. A handy-man's special. He replaced one missing pedal with a carriage bolt. Everywhere he went, he carried spare bolts, nuts and a little wrench in his hip pocket. Rust and all, the two wheels expanded his horizons and increased his earning power.

The druggist sent the eager-to-please youth pedaling one Sunday morning to another pharmacy a mile away to replenish stock for which he had misjudged demand.

"Just six?" asked Darby, who had become accustomed to his friend's lack of purchasing foresightedness.

"That's it for today," Bob assured him. He stacked the boxes on his handle bars and steadied them with his palm for the dangerous ride back. As Sunday morning traffic increased, he careened onto the sidewalk, whizzed past his apartment house to the drugstore and braked abruptly as four middle-aged ladies freshly virtuous from Mass stepped out in front of him.

"Bobby...," his mother gasped. She had hardly recovered her breath when the women recognized the six bright blue boxes jumbled at their feet. Facing all directions, large letters that unmistakably spelled KOTEX glared back at their disbelieving eyes.

With his own transportation, Bob could take on additional clients and less auspicious assignments, if not riskier. For the tailor, Bob sharpened his balancing and maneuvering skills until he could steer with his knees, lunge off curbs and bank around corners, all the while looking like a human clothes rack, a crisp wool gabardine suit hanging primly from each outstretched arm.

Once Saturday afternoon deliveries had been completed, the bicycle became an earth-bound airship. Its big tires effortlessly gobbled the cobblestones to the runways of his heroes.

Floyd Bennett Field, the municipal airport for New York, was more exciting than the model plane store. Framed by the bay, its landing strips were touchdowns for famous pilots. Oftentimes, the ruddy flyers would cast egos to the wind and, for five dollars, take other dreamers aloft.

Fifteen minutes with high flyers Al Williams, Roscoe Turner or Jimmy Doolittle would have been worth every penny. But in reality it had taken him nearly a year to save that much for the transportation that brought him here. Bob would stay grounded. His time would come. He felt no remorse over opportunity missed, no self-pity. He simply made the best of what he had, just as he always did. Propped on the seat of his bike, or stretched out on the cool grass, he contentedly searched the sky for a black speck and listened for the inevitable, distant buzz of engines. Sometimes he was lucky enough to catch the sweeping, daredevil stunts of acrobatic pilots.

One Saturday he had pedaled the ten miles to see the Lockheed Vega, *Winnie Mae*, in which Wiley Post had made his solo flight around the world.

Bob slipped cautiously into the side door of the hangar and stared at one of the sweetest sights he had ever seen. The *Winnie Mae* was beautiful. The mechanic on a tall ladder was inspecting one of her Parker hydraulic fittings, turning it in his grease-black fingers. It's a "goner," he pronounced to his audience of one, then tossed the fitting onto the floor.

Bob stooped to retrieve the *Winnie Mae* souvenir, then looked up at the mechanic. "Sure, kid, take it." The round, grimy face smiled understanding.

Clouds like curdled milk hung low over the city the afternoon Bob glimpsed Generalissimo Italo Balbo. The suave Italian had braved a world tour in his twin-hulled Savoia Marchetti. Airborne in Italy, crossing Africa, the Pacific, South America, flying north into Central America, Balbo finally landed with other seaplanes in the bay. The dreamer on the rusty bike committed the image of the Marchetti to memory.

"That's one dollar." The shopkeeper recounted the fistful of change plunked on the counter and rang up the sale. Bob burst out of the store with the Univex camera under his arm.

Determined to teach himself about apertures, focal lengths and depth of field, he read books and articles. Within a week he purchased the necessary chemicals—developer, stop bath and fixer—to process film in the bathroom, much to Doris' dismay. From now on, he was going to create his own pin-ups. The beautiful bodies on his bedroom walls would belong to trophy racers, a Ford Trimotor and, in the years to come, the first models of the new B-17. George and Anne not only approved of his obsession with anything that could fly, they encouraged it. George had introduced his son to planes at age three.

Living midway between the ground floor and the roof, Bob hovered in his Brooklyn world. Toy people and taxies animated the streaked streets below. Gray and brown stone walls converged overhead. Sky wasn't a place where fields and fence rows vanished in the pale blue mist, or where a vast purple dome crowned a shimmering prairie. Psychologically and spiritually, out was up.

When finally on December 5, 1933, the Eighteenth Amendment was repealed to whoops and hollers, President Roosevelt sent a plea to Americans. "I ask especially that no state shall, by law or otherwise, authorize the return of the saloon, either in its old form or in some modern guise."

New York raised its glass and passed the whiskey. Bars, pubs, saloons, beer halls and lounges returned and flourished, without need of "modern guise." Anne's kitchen faced the rear of one such drinking establishment. On occasions when the Carons had guests for dinner, George dispatched Bob to the pub's back door with a quarter in one hand and his tin-plated lunch pail, nicknamed "Growler," in the other. They called the beer run "rushing the Growler."

At Anne's kitchen window, a pulley reeled shirts and pants out into the city air and reeled them back again. The other end of the Carons' line was securely fastened to a pole near the rear door of the bar. The arrangement looked suspiciously like a private delivery service.

One evening, dinner guests and their stunning twenty-year-old daughter were amazed by the seemingly endless flow of cold brew. Not one to miss an opportunity to tease an attractive female, Bob scuttled her off to the kitchen for a look at his "automatic" beverage dispenser—Anne's clothesline.

He groped for words. "Just a simple...hydraulic system engineered to dispense refreshments at a moment's notice." He opened the window, anchored the Growler on the line, reeled it out a few sample feet and reeled it back. "Simple," he said, again, leading her down the garden path as far as she would go.

"Not at all," she said, impressed. "It's quite...clever."

The Great Depression had brought that out in Americans— being clever, cultivating the fine art of making do. Almost everyone was making silk purses out of sows' ears.

Bob was always hunting sows' ears. He never knew quite where they might turn up—garbage cans ripe with last night's supper scraps, junk lumber piles teeming with wildlife. Or what they might turn up—bottles and pieces of scrap metal to redeem, lightweight wood for kites and model airplanes, string, envelopes with stamps to add to his collection, readable copies of *Popular Mechanics,* the *Saturday Evening Post,* or *Liberty.* The real objects of the searches, the *pieces des resistance,* were their illustrations, photographs and articles on airplanes. In fact, anything to do with aeronautics would be blotted off, cleaned up and taken home. Sometimes, the urgency of an article demanded it be read on the spot.

Rummaging yielded strange usable discards. Once he had unfolded slightly soggy plans for a crystal radio set. The family's first radio, a Zenith console with dials on top, sat proudly next to Father's chair. While the console was meant for a gathering to enjoy a half-hour of Fibber McGee and Molly, a crystal radio was a solitary experience. Its operator wore earphones and strained to the crackle.

Bob bought a crystal, salvaged a little wood, touched the tightly coiled copper catwhisker tickler to one point on the crystal and was shocked to be in the right place at precisely the right moment to hear a beautiful and familiar voice. When the song was over, the New Jersey station announcer informed listeners that the melodic voice on the record they had just heard belonged to Miss Edith Scheno. Bob was mesmerized. The first station he picked up mysteriously reconnected him to his summer romance. For the rest of the night, he drifted dreamily on the airwaves.

The power of radio as a public relations tool wasn't lost on the President. Over the airwaves he conducted casual fire-side chats, one-sided conversations with Americans from all social and economic backgrounds. In their living rooms and automobiles, they listened intently for signs of prosperity.

They didn't hear them, however, in his second inaugural address, January 20, 1937. Instead, he told them what they already knew: "I see one-third of a nation ill-housed, ill-clad, ill-nourished." The living, breathing statistics to whom he had pitched his campaign promises brought him back to play a second season and counted on him to strike out the opposition.

In June, Pittsburgh sold pitcher Waite Hoyt, at thirty-seven a "fading veteran," to Brooklyn. Much to the astonishment of everyone, including Hoyt, he pitched so well that, at the end of the season, he ranked fourteenth among all major league pitchers. Out of twenty-two seasons in baseball, he had played in seven World Series.

Sports weren't the only places to find unexpected heroes that year. Spencer Tracy won an Academy Award for his character portrayal in *Captains Courageous*. Delaware author John Philips Marquand, whose gently satirical novels took readers into the lives of rich New Englanders, won a Pulitzer Prize for *The Late George Apley*.

In October, Roosevelt's Chicago speech sent the truism, "War is a contagion" ringing in people's ears. It had become self-evident: the spreading cancer claimed the innocent along with the wicked.

Coincidentally, stage and screen became absorbed in the same thematic concerns: the virtue of youth and lost innocence. Brooklyn composer Aaron Copeland brought *Billy the Kid* to life in ballet. Spencer Tracy gave a powerful performance in *Boys' Town*. Cary Grant was contemplating the problems of *Bringing Up Baby*. Charles Boyer, Basil Rathbone and Claudette Colbert rehearsed for the hot radio program "Hollywood Hotel."

During his April 14, 1938, fireside chat, Roosevelt returned to his campaign issue, putting people to work: "Not only our future economic soundness but the very soundness of our democratic institutions depends on the determination of our government to give employment to idle men."

The administration inaugurated programs to create employment and urged Congress to ramrod through the Fair Labor Standards Act to guarantee a twenty-five-cent per hour minimum wage and a maximum work week of forty-four hours, enforced by the Division of Wage and Labor.

The American Federation of Labor expelled militant labor leader John L. Lewis for spearheading within the AFL a minority movement that advocated workers be organized according to basic industries. In 1938 the AFL disbanded the Committee for Industrial Organization, and Lewis changed its name to the Congress of Industrial Organizations, reordering its work force, which emerged as a powerful voting block. A unique symbiosis was to occur between government and industry that would revolutionize both warfare and domestic life. Among the revolutionary technologies of 1938 was a strong, yet light, synthetic thermoplastic material called Nylon.

A new term, "recession," appeared in the political lexicon to soften the hard edge of depression, just as Hooverites coined "depression" to alleviate the terror evoked by the noun "panic." Dr. Roosevelt diagnosed the chronically ailing economy as suffering from recession, which sounded as though it could more easily go into spontaneous remission than could depression. To boost the economy back to health and balance the 1939 budget without a larger dose of taxes, he prescribed "a little finesse."

Fishing in the warm Caribbean with his friend and spokesman Robert H. Jackson, the President cast his line into the blue. "The country is not running into a major depression," he told Jackson convincingly. Despite his wishful thinking, however, the *New York Times* business index for the fourth quarter showed a greater decline than during the thirteen months that followed the 1929 crash. For certain, the nation needed an infusion, a tonic to soothe its raw nerves.

For southern Californians, that infusion came as two parts hydrogen and one part oxygen. Billions of gallons of it were about to be pushed, pulled and cajoled more than three-hundred miles through deserts and mountains. Harnessing the Colorado River employed thirty-three thousand engineers, electricians, welders, machinists, drill runners, steel workers, crane operators and muckers. The world's longest aqueduct was scheduled to be completed before George Robert Caron's twentieth birthday.

At the same time a small army was taming the force of a mighty river, the bantam engineering student was channeling his talents constructing Tech's disappearing stage. The only person with welding skills who could squeeze into the narrow crevices and under the low beams, he spent hours in solitude completing the project. He would have been surprised to learn that the physical and psychological ability to wrangle into tight places would someday come in handy.

His Brooklyn Tech classmates were scheduled to graduate in January, but Bob wouldn't be among them. More than his vision had failed. History had somehow fallen between the cracks. As New York's academic year ended in January instead of June, attending a make-up term put him in line for June graduation. It wasn't so much that Bob was more interested in the present and future than in the past. The crux of the problem was simple. He was merely selective about whose past and which historical events would lay claim to his energy.

Aviation history and the biographies of famous flyers were more to his liking. He had read voraciously about Edward Vernon Rickenbacker, the Columbus, Ohio, air ace who had downed twenty-six enemy aircraft during World War I. While Bob was cramming for his senior year exams, Rickenbacker would become president of Eastern Airlines. On May 21, 1927, when twenty-five-year-old Charles Augustus Lindbergh astounded the world with his New York to Paris flight in the *Spirit of St. Louis*, Bob was not yet eight. The aviator's wife, Anne Spencer Morrow Lindbergh, had just completed *Listen! the Wind*, a chronicle of the famous duo's flights. Howard Hughes of Houston, who had set several aviation records, was busy forming the nucleus of the Hughes Aircraft Corporation.

Stretching graduation into the spring term had its benefits. Track season was coming up, and it gave Bob time to take an extra course in advanced algebra. For pin money he swept the lunchroom and piled chairs on tables. His structural design teacher invited him to join the floor-manager squad, answering telephones and running the office between history and algebra classes. The academic and extra-curricular activities filled his days and evenings.

Before sleep finally claimed him, he escaped briefly into the pages of the *Saturday Evening Post*. He imagined himself Alan, the ruggedly handsome hero in "The Dark River," whose friendship with the sensuous Naia ripened into steamy Tahitian love. As the school term ended, so did the sixth of the nine-part series, which by now had conveniently joined the couple in holy matrimony before ship-wrecking them on a reef. There, on the pearly beaches of the uninhabited island Tetmatangi, the mated lovebirds discovered newfound pleasures in the crystalline days and warm, tropical nights that stretched before them as limitless as the pulsing Pacific.

In the auditorium as big as a movie theater, Edna Sanders had eyes for only one young man in cap and gown. As her steady of four years received his diploma, she stood and clapped with devoted enthusiasm, playing back the awkward, wonderful and painful years that took them both through adolescence.

The rite of passage was marked by a diploma and blue annual. Anne Westrick Caron found her son's photograph on page eleven at the end of the second column. She looked thoughtfully at the image, as if seeing him for the first time. What day, what month, what year had the boy become a man? When did the childlike features sharpen into a sculpted mouth, straight brows over sparkling hazel eyes? Someone had attempted to contain the sum total of the individual born to her eighteen years earlier in a few cryptic lines beside his photograph.

GEORGE R. CARON, 552 EAST 29TH STREET, BROOKLYN, NEW YORK. STRUCTURAL COURSE; TRACK; MODIFIED T; CROSS COUNTRY; SENIOR SERVICE SQUAD; FLOOR MANAGER'S SQUAD; SURVEYING SQUAD, CAPTAIN; MODEL CLUB; SENIOR JEWELRY COMMITTEE; MATH AND ART CERTIFICATES—GOAL: CURTIS-WRIGHT AERONAUTICAL INSTITUTE.

High Flyer!

Transforming Dreams Into Reality

"I've got just the car for Bob," a friend of a friend said to George Caron. "Let you have it for two hundred dollars." Only fifty of the maroon roadsters had been made, and George could see this one was in mint condition. Its sporty lines were ahead of their time and would be revived later in the MG. With side curtains and rumble seat, the garnet jewel was a showstopper.

George's salary had been increasing gradually, enabling the family to rent a pleasant house on 29th Street. For the first time, there was a little cash left over after paying the bills. The graduation present would help make up for all the gifts over the years that he couldn't afford. Bob had been saving for a junker. But the roadster was something really special. He pulled out his wallet.

George Jay had seen the handwriting on the wall. Despite predictions to the contrary, no housing boom hoisted contractors, carpenters, plumbers and electricians out of the financial basement. Earlier in the year analysts blamed the sluggishness not on a flagging demand for homes, but on the building industry itself. Growth, they claimed, had been stunted by its failure to follow the lead of the automobile industry, which provided a consolidated production and marketing package. Sprouting from columnists' editorial flower boxes were their newest seedlings labeled "Housing Guild." The Guild was intended to facilitate the same tidy needs' consolidation for home buyers that had served car buyers.

To combat the vagaries of the construction industry, George had opened his own display and exhibit business on Murray Street, Manhattan. It was a risky time for entrepreneurism. But from observation he had learned that big businesses and corporations were taking exposure and their public image seriously. Great portions of their budgets were being spent on marketing, especially on trade show exhibits and displays. That's where George would find his piece of the pie. On target, he soon had a half dozen union men working for him, plus a non-union son, although the work he could assign to Bob was limited.

George bid on a project for an up-and-coming company called International Business Machines. Its founder, perfectionist T. J. Watson, insisted that his displays reflect the quality and integrity of the products. When George's shop consistently turned out that kind of quality, under bid and on time, IBM became his regular client. The shop produced displays for its Madison Avenue and 57th Street world headquarters. To supplement the IBM contract, the shop produced special-event and holiday windows that changed every few weeks. Anne was proud that people came from all over the city to see them.

Captivated by the storefront exhibitions, passersby would linger, entranced, discovering something missed before in the magical montages—interplays of the displays inside and the reflected world outside. The accidental metaphor that mirrored the American Dream had not been missed by the 1938 Nobel laureate in physics. As Jewish ostracism had spread to Italy, thirty-seven-year-old Enrico Fermi escaped to New York with his devoted wife and confidante, Laura, and their two children. For Fermi, son of Italian peasants, the windows to this new world held a special meaning, a new beginning.

Beginning anew and improving one's station in life was an idea unthinkable in Japan. Tradition "fixed" every individual in his place according to class, family position, age, sex and occupation. That was *on*. It was set by one's ancestors, parents and, especially, the Emperor. Life's journey was not a pursuit of personal fulfillment, but a repayment of the Emperor's goodness, *chu*, and of one's obligations to parents, *ko*. Those who shrank from their obligations lost face and were shamed. Even a soldier who had been captured by the enemy reneged on his debt to the Emperor.

Like a wildfire, the West's depression jumped geographical and ideological boundaries. The responsibility of *chu* and *ko* were becoming increasingly heavy. By the time Bob Caron had settled in as an assistant in his father's union shop, Japan had already occupied all China's richest and most populous provinces and much of its coastline.

Will Durrant related the tragedy of Japan to *Post* readers in his poignant, June 1938 article, "No Hymns of Hatred."

> Japan has improved a great deal of what she has borrowed [from China]; and in the minor arts and the graces of life she has surpassed the teacher and

mother whom she now attempts to destroy or enslave. Her militarism was taught her by the West. When she was peacefully agricultural, isolated and self-contained, we insisted, in 1853, that she open her ports to our trade; now those chickens have come home to roost. China finds events revenging themselves upon her through the rape of one after another of her provinces by the very people to which she has given her subtle and delicate culture. We are willing that our children should die for America, if that must be, but we are not content that they should die in a war that might have been avoided by historical perspective, mutual understanding and good will.

Concurrently, Edgar Snow attempted to help Americans understand the complexities of the Japanese expansionism policies in China. In "The Sun Also Sets," he wrote: "Already the Japanese conquerors have destroyed or captured about three-fourths of China's modern industry, reduced China's foreign trade by one-half, penetrated more than four hundred thousand square miles of her territory...extended to nine provinces, including the national capital. Yet it is a paradox that the longer the slaughter lasts, the more doubtful the final issue becomes. ...It can no longer be doubted that Japan aspires to rule all Asia, put the white races into retreat, and finally dominate the world."

Soils in nearly every direction felt the imprint of Japanese Imperial Army and Third Reich boots. As Germany overshadowed Austria, the League of Nations watched with tied hands. When Hitler swallowed the Rhineland, Hungarian physicist Leo Szilard climbed out of the intellectual security of his bathtub laboratory and, like colleague Enrico Fermi, fled to New York. Once Szilard had championed the free exchange of ideas among scientists. Now, he feared the information he didn't want Hitler to obtain might already be at his fingertips. "There is every reason to feel paranoid," he dramatically vindicated his anxiety to colleagues. "Right this minute Hitler is probably assembling an atomic bomb."

The Brain Trust continued to generate formulas for recovery. Through the pages of the *Saturday Evening Post* and other leading magazines, Raymond Moley promised Americans that their "sensible installment buying" would stoke economic fires and "keep factories busy and more people employed." He pledged that "It provides the things that transform dreams into reality for our people." As consumers made purchases, the government bought time.

Since employment at his father's union shop was temporary and it was now evident Bob would need to postpone his education at Curtis-Wright Aeronautical Institute in New York, he stoked a few fires of his own. Every few days he dropped in at Tech's placement office.

Just after the new year, Tech sent him for an interview at 23rd Street near 7th Avenue in midtown Manhattan. Universal Fixtures, manufacturer of modular steel shelving and steel lockers, hired him immediately for his drafting and construction experience. His new boss, Ann Brady, offered him twelve dollars and fifty cents a week, no fringe. After a few months, Brady said, he could expect a two dollar and fifty-cent raise.

Universal had just landed a big contract with Hostess Cupcake to install lockers in the locker rooms at the New York World's Fair grounds in Queens County, not far from LaGuardia Field. Bob generated cost estimates, customized floor plans with the modular units and coordinated material delivery.

While the cupcake company's glamorous hostesses rehearsed their routines, Bob worked in their empty locker room. One afternoon, they returned unexpectedly early. As though he were the invisible man, they slithered out from their skimpy costumes, showered, changed into street clothes, used the stalls and bantered about boyfriends. Their presence put him in the most unusual and delicious predicament. Universal paid him to do a job. He stayed and did it. Brady was wrong. There definitely were fringes.

Twice a week, as a change of pace from sack sandwiches and the automat, Bob lunched at a little Italian restaurant across the street where "Papa" cooked his spaghetti in the window and his raven-haired daughter waited tables. Which attracted him most was a toss-up—the beauty or the feast. For twenty-five cents, Papa heaped Bob's plate high, then agonized as the novice cut the spaghetti into bite-sized pieces.

Papa waddled over to Bob. His fat aproned belly dotted with sauce protruded over Bob's table.

"Hey kid," he asked, his sweaty face glistening like olive oil, "why you cut-a my pasta? That'sa no way ta eat it. You suppose-ta roll it on-a your fork."

"Sorry, Papa. But I'm Irish. That's the way *we* eat it."

"Oh," Papa sighed. He shook his head and retreated to the security of his window.

Near the window of their second-floor sitting room in a Seventieth Street brownstone, upper Manhattan, physicist Fride Meitner sipped tea with her husband, Leo Frischauer. She was becoming exceedingly concerned for her sister Lise. After thirty-two years in Germany, Lise had never become a citizen. Fride feared she was in imminent danger.

Like the majority of scientists in 1938 whose positions and safety were jeopardized by Hitler's anti-Semitic laws, Lise Meitner, former director of the Kaiser Wilhelm Institute, planned her escape. At 60, looking ever more Parisian than Austrian, she fled over the Dutch border to the safety of Stockholm. There she became affiliated with the Swedish Academy of Sciences and retained her communications with physicists to unravel the mysteries of the atom. Working with her ingenious mathematical calculations from his post in Britain, her nephew, Otto Frisch, succeeded in proving that an atom could be split.

In a few short years, Frisch would also emigrate to the United States, thousands of miles from his aunt Fride, stringing out equations—based on his Aunt Lise's original notations—on chalky blackboards at a remote laboratory not far from Santa Fe, New Mexico.

The Northeast was experiencing a typical winter in 1939 when Otto Frisch made a startling discovery. He and his brilliant colleague Rudolph Peierls were determined to identify at what point critical mass could be achieved and how much fissionable material was necessary to sustain a chain reaction. Frisch could hardly believe his eyes. He retraced the steps of his previous calculation. There appeared to be no errors. The figures remained the same. He shoved his scratch paper at the quizzical Peierls. Both men had anticipated that the volume of uranium 235 necessary for an appreciable chain reaction must be staggering. Perhaps tons. These new figures suggested otherwise. A reaction would not take thousands of pounds of the heavy uranium isotope, but as little as one or two pounds! And so little, undoubtedly, could be compressed smaller than a baseball.

But what force would a chain reaction from so little uranium yield? Again, Frisch put pencil to paper. In an inconceivable four-millionth of a second, he explained, staring penetratingly at Peierls, before the chain reaction stopped, the explosive force could be greater than that at the center of the earth, with temperatures rivaling those in the interior of the sun. They both recognized the import of Frisch's findings, should they be correct: an atomic bomb might after all be possible.

There remained, of course, the not-insignificant problem of separating a few pounds of rare isotope U^{235} from the more accessible plutonium U^{238}. Frisch and Peierls were certain that a massive production facility could extract appreciable amounts in a "modest time," perhaps in a matter of weeks.

The two men speculated that if they had come to these conclusions, quite likely Hitler's scientists had also. Perhaps they had been too hasty to label their bath-fancier colleague's paranoia irrational. It was possible that an atomic bomb was being conceived at that very moment in both camps. For which camp it was an offensive and which a defensive weapon would be a matter of perception and the geography of birth.

Full of anticipation, the physicists forwarded their calculations to Australian Mark Oliphant, who agreed that the only defense against a "superbomb" would be the deterrent effect of mutual possession. It was the germ that in the years to come would grow into nuclear proliferation. There was urgency, Oliphant echoed their fears, as Germany had access to the world's only heavy-water factory, used in the process of obtaining fissionable material and to reserves of uranium ore in Belgium and the Belgian Congo. All it lacked was its own atom-splitter. By overrunning France, Hitler closed his fist around the country's cyclotron .

Cyclotrons were not limited to California and France. Japan's leading physicist, Yoshio Nishina, had built a cyclotron at his Tokyo laboratory, the Riken. With the aid of a Berkeley-trained assistant, Nishina began work on a sixty-inch version of his original, using a massive two hundred fifty-ton magnet. Ironically, the plans for Nishina's new device had been donated by the Berkeley guru of cyclotrons himself, the dapper Ernest Lawrence.

Leo Szilard was fast reversing himself on the efficacy of free exchange of scientific information. After his own March 2, 1939, experiment with Canadian physicist Walter Zinn, confirming uranium fission made a bomb possible, Szilard exacted a pledge of secrecy from his international colleagues. He was relieved that they were willing to clamp shut their notebooks and voluntarily withhold papers from publication.

In Czechoslovakia, spring 1939 was not a time of rebirth and renewal. Hitler had successfully frozen the little country into another winter of despair. Her uranium mines were his for the taking.

By July, Szilard, who always preferred the free, unfettered feeling of hotel rooms to the confines and responsibility of a home, was as settled in New York as the vagabond could be. Luckily for him, fellow Hungarian physicist Eugene Wigner had not required much coaxing to chauffeur his short, petulant ally to Peconic, Long Island. The sixty-year-old man vacationing at his friend's cottage on Old Grove Road, whose help they were enlisting, was Albert Einstein.

Indeed, the disheveled pacifist agreed. There was reason to be alarmed at Hitler's access to the richest uranium deposits in the Belgian Congo. Perhaps a letter to the State Department would alert it to the severity of the crisis. But to whom should it be sent? Better to take it to the top. The President must be made aware that a superbomb was possible and that Hitler surely was focusing his scientific minds in that direction.

Szilard had hoped Charles Lindbergh would personally deliver just that message from Einstein to the President, but the Colonel never responded to the Hungarian's numerous requests. When the aviator publicly issued his position supporting neutrality, Szilard deferred to Wigner's original suggestion, and the messenger by default became the chief economist for the National Recovery Administration, Dr. Alexander Sachs. The vice president of the Lehman Corporation and Roosevelt's old friend agreed to hand deliver the letter at the President's earliest convenience.

"Sir," began Einstein's August 2, 1939, letter, "some recent work by E. Fermi and L. Szilard...leads me to expect that the element of uranium may be turned into a new and important source of energy in the immediate future. Certain aspects of the situation seem to call for watchful and, if necessary, quick action on the part of the Administration. I believe it is my duty to bring to your attention the following facts and recommendations. It is conceivable...that extremely powerful bombs of a new type may thus be constructed."

While Sachs waited for an audience with the President, Hitler's tanks tracked across the Polish border. Two days later, on September 3, Britain and France declared war on the Third Reich. Within the week, Roosevelt responded to Hitler's aggression and called a national emergency. The President's generous Lend-Lease policy would demonstrate his support for Britain.

In the meantime, Einstein's timely letter hadn't budged from Sachs' hands. Not until October 11 did Roosevelt have time for his trusted economist. Their warm reunion in the President's second-floor study was brief and promised a breakfast encore. Not until then would Sachs finally stop dancing around the nuclear issue. The President immediately grasped the import of the new information. "What you are after, my friend" the President replied, "is to see to it the Nazis don't blow us up first."

On Sachs' urging, Roosevelt formed the Uranium Committee, a group charged with exploring the delicate, yet latently potent issue. Within a few days its three committeemen met with Szilard, Wigner and their cohort Edward Teller. Reluctantly, and certain that the idea of a bomb right out of science fiction was presidential folly, the Uranium Committee agreed to dole out two thousand dollars—petty cash, indeed—for Szilard to begin a nuclear project that would ultimately burgeon to two billion dollars.

The paltry sum could hardly be conceived of as research and development funding. Scientific exploration and Committee investigation quickly mired. The President, himself, was up to his chin in European quicksand.

Szilard ghost wrote two more letters to Roosevelt for Einstein to endorse. "Interest in uranium has intensified in Germany," he wrote in the March 7, 1940, follow-up. When the second letter drew no response, he chased it seven weeks later with another urgent appeal to form an organization capable of researching nuclear energy's "practical applications." While no such organization would get off the ground for another two years, Szilard had inadvertently launched the Manhattan Project.

"Heads," I Win

B ob took the stairs leading to Tech's main hall two at a time. In the ground-floor employment office, Frank LaVista thrust his workman's hand in his former student's, then pulled up a chair.

"W. L. Maxson is looking for a junior draftsman," he opened without preface. "I told them I'd send them over the best in the city." LaVista, a major in the reserves, slapped Bob on the back, "You've got an 8 A.M. interview with their chief engineer, McLaren."

Universal Fixtures had treated him well. He had no complaints. The money was nothing to write home about, but it beat being unemployed. Plus, it had its perks. Working on the World's Fair grounds for three months, he had almost unlimited passes to exhibits and performances. Still, Bob longed to plunge into an engineering position that financially released him from the need to continue working part-time at his father's shop.

Maxson's was one of the older buildings on West 34th Street in Manhattan. The L-shaped brick complex covered the entire city block and rose fifteen floors, although there was no thirteenth. Pete McLaren—"Just call me Mac. Everyone else does"—met him at the receptionist's desk. His plump fingers closed around Bob's hand and he pumped it enthusiastically. His face was pleasant, almost handsome. He stood nearly Bob's height and limped slightly because one leg was shorter than the other.

Immediately, even before he knew what he might be hired to do, Bob wanted the job.

"Twenty-five dollars a week sound OK to you?"

The soon-to-be draftsman tried to hide his surprise. Ten dollars a week more than he was making now!

"When can you start?"

"I'd like to give Universal a week's notice."

P roject engineer Jack Vaughn took an instant shine to Bob. The feeling was mutual. Every inch of Vaughn's five-foot-ten frame was lean muscle. His thick, wavy hair was prematurely gray, and he parted it fashionably on one side. He would have turned any woman's head, but Bob thought he was a particularly handsome man's man.

"Jack's a helluva nice guy," Bob's new co-workers confided. "He'll kid around with you. But you can't pull anything over on him."

Bob had no intention of pulling anything over on his new boss. He found Vaughn approachable. No question was a stupid question. "Always glad you asked," he'd say.

For the first few weeks his orientation consisted of maintaining the blueprint machine, filing prints and running errands for Maxson himself, a chain smoker who was always running out of Pall Malls.

Several times a day Vaughn leaned over Bob's drafting table and inspected his mechanical drawings. "Looks good, Bob. You're getting there. Good job."

Before long, Vaughn assigned Bob to work on the ballistics gunfire control for the Seacoast Computer. The sixteen-inch guns, which could fire twenty-five-hundred-pound projectiles at a maximum range of twenty-five miles, were strategically placed in barbettes at coastal artillery fortifications to protect American harbors up and down the East and West coasts. Six feet by six feet by three feet wide, the computer was designed to aim at enemy ships from long distances. A half-dozen men were needed to run it. Plotting information on its curved charts required cranking a mechanical device by hand. As its pointer tracked across its charts, ballistics information, such as azimuth and elevation for the correct aim on the target, was simultaneously relayed to the gun controls. The gun's complicated firing mechanisms were calculated for temperature of the explosive, temperature of the air, rotation of the earth and latitude of the gun sight.

When that data had been gathered, Bob plotted the many firing tables into graphs. The graphs were then arranged sequentially so that the information could be transferred electronically onto a foot-wide roll of paper. By moving the ink stylus left or right, he located the data point and punched it with the stylus. Using ships' curves, he smoothed the dots into a fluid line. The resulting master charts were transferred accurately to non-shrinking cloth impervious to humidity.

Occasionally Bob went into the production area to corroborate measurements. Vaughn used those opportunities to explain assembly and machining processes. Bob would skip lunch to watch a machinist demonstrate the lathe. Sometimes he would run a drill press under the supervision of its regular operator. Knowing how the machines made the parts he designed seemed the best way to design better parts.

Neither Bob nor his high-school sweetheart, Edna Sanders, was quite sure who was breaking up with whom. Saying good-bye seemed easier when they both agreed it was for the best. Like in the movies, she said.

Bob had little time for anything other than work and studies. He had enrolled in Brooklyn Polytechnical Institute and Monday through Thursday nights attended mechanical engineering, physics and composition classes. His college adviser said he could earn his degree in *only* eight years.

George helped Bob build a drafting table for his room. When he stumbled in after a long day at Maxson's and classes, Bob shut himself up in his room, and his parents didn't see him again until morning.

Most of the time, he felt that he learned more at work than he was learning in the classroom. The senior engineers stretched his solid Tech background, challenged him to solve problems and consulted him with theirs. When he demonstrated that he knew the laws of electricity, Vaughn gave him assignments to make up electrical schematics.

Over time, his boss became his friend. It never seemed to impede their working relationship. Vaughn brought his wife and daughters to visit Bob and his parents at their new Lynbrook house. His own door was always open to his junior draftsman. When he purchased an expensive exotic fish aquarium, he asked Bob to bring the 35 mm German Dollina camera he had just bought on credit. Vaughn expected Bob would snap a few amateurish photographs. He hadn't expected his young employee to set up a tripod, take a light reading and arrange lights for the shot.

"Where'd you learn to do that?" he asked, surprised.

"Books."

"Forewarned is forearmed," repeated the bearer of the Einstein/Szilard letter to the President less than three weeks before Bob's twentieth birthday. Roosevelt imagined that Hitler would stop at nothing to add an atomic weapon to his war arsenal. But what could the President do about it? He had his hands full. The nation was still recovering from the Depression, plus it had been burdened with the weight of devastating floods and droughts.

Through the words of John Steinbeck's sensitive novel *The Grapes of Wrath*, Americans were touched by the hardships of Dust Bowl farmers, who left behind their buried land to toil in Southwest fields as migrant laborers. For his compassionate and insightful portrayal of their plight, the California author was awarded the 1939 Pulitzer Prize.

Roosevelt tried to convince himself and the nation that the worst was over. For some people that was true. For others, the worst was yet to come. George Caron had been among those who came close to hitting bottom. He had been lucky when he gambled his future on the display shop. Working six and seven days a week, he made it turn a profit. For the first time in their lives, the Carons could afford to buy a house in Lynbrook on a quiet street lined with portly maples and oaks. The decade-old three-bedroom, two-story, white stucco house was trimmed with brown shingles on the second floor. A street-side dormer provided good light in the attic. George immediately screened the full-length porch that stretched across the front of the house. From the porch to the sidewalk, a well-manicured green begged for bare feet.

As he signed the bank loan, reality hit. After nearly twenty years, he was finally able to make Anne's dream come true.

Bob wanted most of all to fly. Poor vision shattered that dream, and he was forced to be pragmatic about his future. Attending college in the evenings after work had seemed like a wise decision. But tuition was expensive. When he learned that Brooklyn Tech offered an aeronautical engineering certificate program free to alumni and Major LaVista was teaching it, Bob dropped out of college and enrolled in the four-night-a-week program.

Although he had already put in a full day at Maxson's, the evening hours flew by. Bob studied the theory of flight, disassembled and reassembled the high-wing observation plane LaVista had coerced the Army Air Corps into donating and designed replacement fittings.

On a new course, he reassessed old priorities. The maroon sports car with its button-down curtains that offered little protection against New York's elements had to go.

Bob turned the key in the ignition of the two-year-old Ford. The sharp black convertible with a white top and rumble seat vibrated to life and inched into traffic. Wind whistled softly where its roll-up windows sealed against the top, but the icy blasts stayed outside.

One cold afternoon in February 1940, chief engineer McLaren called Bob and Gordon Anderson, another Tech draftsman, into his office.

"I hate to do this," he said, looking down at his feet. "I've got to let one of you go. With the Seacoast project over, I don't have enough work for both of you. You're both first-rate, and I don't want to favor one of you over the other."

He wanted off the hook. Picking winners and losers was up to Bob and Gordon.

"Call it," Gordon said, waiting to flip the nickel in his palm.

"Heads."

"Tails."

Bob collected his week's severance pay and his wits. He had no idea what he was going to do next.

"Funny you should call today," LaVista said. "The chief inspector at Republic Aviation wants a Tech boy."

Bob knew where it was—out on Long Island in Farmingdale, not ten miles from where he lived. He had been commuting to Maxson on the Long Island Railroad that slid under the East River and ended up at Penn Station. A job at Republic would be closer to home.

"Ask for Bill Ebert."

"What's he looking for?"

"Guess you'll find out when you get there."

Bob misjudged the morning traffic. A steady stream of eastbound commuters flowed along the Southern State Parkway at the thirty-five mile per hour speed limit. Pushing the accelerator to the floor, he zipped past them, and the light brown sedan. The patrolman in the unmarked police car pulled out after him, placed the flashing red light on his dash and let his siren rip.

Job interview or no job interview, he wasn't sympathetic. Bob made it to Republic barely on time with a ticket in his pocket and a twenty-dollar fine.

"Why not put in a full day, just to get to know the place?" the chief inspector suggested. Bill Ebert's new employee bought a sandwich and milk from the lunch cart and joined the men who were breaking at the back of the building in the warmth of the sun. They didn't seem to mind that he eavesdropped on their easy banter. A gregarious fellow related to his captive audience that on his way to work a cocky kid driving a fancy convertible got nabbed for speeding on the four-lane. "Served the dummy right," he added.

Bob cleared his throat. "I'd like to introduce myself. I'm that dummy."

Republic Aviation, founded by Russian aeronautical engineer Igor Sikorsky, had grown from a one-man shop to a major contractor for fighter planes. The P-43s were rolling off the assembly line when the Swedish air force called for fighters, Sweden's version of the P-35. She would see only a few of those planes, however, as the United States Army Air Corps appropriated them for the war overseas. To the dismay of the Corps, they proved no match for Nazi Messerschmitt Me109s.

At Republic Bob inspected switches, brackets, forgings, relays and the magnaflux of electrical components. He dipped a magnetized part in oil in which iron filings has been suspended and looked for patterns of filings in areas of fractures or defects. Sometimes he checked parts at the assembly line. Then at lunch-time, he climbed into the cockpit of a nearly completed plane and fantasized he was its pilot.

During his random accuracy checks, Bill Ebert would stop at an inspector's station and tighten the man's ratchet micrometers so hard on a part that they needed a time-consuming recalibration on the Jo-Bars.

After observing Ebert's ritual for a few days, Bob placed a special order to Massachusetts for Starrett mics. His co-workers teased him for having to be different, until Ebert tried to put his newest inspector through his usual harassment.

"What the hell is this?" he snarled, thumbing the Starrett mic down as far as it would go.

"Its a thimble-friction mic," explained Bob. "It can't be over-tightened and thrown out of calibration."

Ebert grumbled, tossed the mic in Bob's toolbox and stomped off.

In May 1940, Hitler tightened the screws on Denmark and pushed his panzers through Holland and Belgium. It was a fulfillment of Szilard's worst fears. The uranium reserves of the Belgian Congo were at the fingertips of a madman. Szilard and Einstein would have to grandstand again for administrative attention.

Roosevelt was doing something, but, in the eyes of the scientific community, it appeared to be pitifully little. The day Paris fell, he at long last authorized the Office of Scientific Research and Development to explore more fully the potential of nuclear energy.

Adding to the President's already full plate, Republican Wendell Lewis Wilkie unexpectedly announced that he intended to challenge the incumbent's bid for re-election. Although he had supported the President's foreign policy and judiciously refrained from dragging New Deal reforms onto the partisan platform, he believed voters wouldn't return Roosevelt to the White House for an unprecedented third term.

But the media and Wilkie underestimated the power of the fireside chatter. Roosevelt knew what hit home. On October 30, 1940, with a Boston crowd riveted to his promises, he seized their minds and plucked at their heart strings: "And while I am talking to you mothers and fathers, I give you one more assurance. I have said this before, but I shall say it again and again: Your boys are not going to be sent into any foreign wars."

Americans wanted to focus on America. Kenosha, Wisconsin, director and actor Orson Welles created an enduring cinematic masterpiece in *Citizen Kane*. Female moviegoers swooned over Cary Grant in his latest film, *The Philadelphia Story*.

Love was triumphing over war in film and fact. At the June 1941 wedding reception for one of Maxson's engineers, Bob ran into Jack Vaughn.

"How's Republic treating you?"

"Fine, Jack, but I'd rather be on the drawing board."

"Why don't you give them a week's notice. I'd like to have you back."

Bob mingled with the guests and was pleased that so many of the Maxson engineers had sought him out. As the evening wound down, Jack made him an offer he couldn't refuse. "Would you come back for a five-dollar-a-week raise?"

Bob had heard right. Tough Bill Ebert was sorry to see his enterprising young inspector go.

Although Maxson's had wrangled a new contract for the Seacoast Computer, Vaughn had other plans for Bob. He was needed to design a gun turret that could be lowered into a mounting ring in the fuselage of the Navy's Brewster attack plane.

Four-abreast, Maxson engineers hunched over drawing boards across the expanse of one floor and drafted under incandescent lamps with cup-shaped metal reflectors clamped to each table. With the passing hours, natural light from waist-high, horizontal swing-out windows traced shadows across the floor.

To the north of the Maxson building, a large meat-packing plant ground out putrid smells that wafted in on faint breezes and permeated clothing and nostrils, hanging nauseatingly in the cavernous spaces. When they could stand the stench no longer, employees closed off their exchange of air with the outside world and suffocated in the fetid air.

A small overflow addition had been built on the roof to accommodate additional project engineers, including those designing an offensive remote-controlled plane. Vaughn saw to it that when they needed extra manpower, Bob went on loan. "Good experience," he called it.

And it was. The main assembly required detailed, intricate drawings. All measurements had to be calculated based on the aircraft's center of gravity, or CG. Most planes were nearly symmetrical side to side, and small lateral weight shifts had little effect on their flight characteristics. The fore and aft CG was much more critical. Control could be compromised, even lost, if the CG moved outside of a narrow range just ahead of the center of lift forces produced by the wings. As everything from fuel tanks to bomb racks had to be located with the CG in mind, Bob worked with the engineers to assure that his installations would not dangerously shift the aircraft's center of gravity.

Armed with his newfound knowledge and imagination, Bob designed the control pedestal and the elevation mechanism for turrets with four .50-caliber machine guns. These guns, used extensively by the Allies throughout Europe, were intended to be mounted either on the ground or on half-tracks.

One Saturday, everyone except Bob and the chief engineer had clocked out. Earlier in the day, the company photographer had called in sick, and Mac wanted a photograph of one fully assembled turret before it was to be shipped.

"Higher," Mac urged. "I want you to shoot down into the cockpit and show the mount."

Bob climbed onto the workbench and stretched to shoot down onto the turret. His shoe hit an oil patch that someone had neglected to blot and his own CG shifted. His left hand held the camera up as he went down. But as he landed, the long, narrow spout of the stainless steel oil can skewered his flailing right arm, angling deep into his wrist.

Slowly, he worked the daggerlike nozzle out of his forearm and pressed a white handkerchief against the gaping red hole. Mac paled. Feeling worse than Bob, he accompanied his injured employee to the company doctor in the next building. "You'll live," he teased as he cauterized the wound, adding that Bob was lucky the impaling had missed a main artery.

Dotty Gaborc had agreed to the blind date only because her brother, Arthur, talked her into it. Bob had agreed to it only because Arthur, one of Maxson's junior designers, had shown him Dotty's picture. Professionally, the Queens model for a swanky Fifth Avenue department store went by the name Lorraine Leeds.

When the two laid eyes on each other at her door, they burst out laughing. Bob, in his most dashing suit and tie, cradled his injured arm in a sling. The breath-taking model, radiant in red, had one of her shapely ankles hidden under a cast and hobbled to the door on crutches.

Arthur had been right. Dotty was incredible. But while Art could fix up a buddy with his sister, the thought of lining up his own date terrified him. Asking anything more of Ann Lizak, the cute little waitress with the Hungarian accent, than "two over easy," raised his blood pressure.

"Tell her you'd like to take her to dinner and a movie," Bob coached. With his continual prodding, Art stumbled over the words. His first date with the petite waitress turned out to be a dead end. Uncle Gaborc, who worked at the city morgue, had an emergency autopsy to perform, and Art thought it might be more exciting than chicken-fried steak at the diner. For Ann, who deftly sliced up cherry pie, carving a cadaver was not on her menu. She dashed out of the lab before she left something behind. Dumbfounded, Art stayed, fascinated with the Friday-night dissection.

Gordon Anderson liked his bodies warm and moving and sitting on the back of his motorcycle with both arms wrapped tightly around his waist. He was pleased to discover his old Tech chum Bob was back at Maxson's. Whenever possible, they took their lunches to the roof. From their fourteen-story vantage point, they watched the *Queen Mary* and *Normandie* dock along the Hudson River a few blocks away. Shipbuilders were busy refitting the *Normandie* for its new role as a troop transport. On February 10, 1941, Maxson employees lined the roof, stunned to see the mighty ship sprawled on her port side in her ice-filled berth, a fireboat still spraying her steaming hull. The preceding night, she had listed precariously at forty-five degrees with the incoming tide until, finally, she rolled and fires erupted.

The small summer cabin on Long Island was nestled near the bay. For George and Anne, the American Dream had not only become a reality, it was emerging in dazzling Technicolor. Whenever they could, the family converged on their quiet retreat. From the comfort of neatly painted white Adirondack chairs, family and guests slipped under the spell of the waning down-East light, mesmerized by the moonlit, placid water.

Bob said good-bye to the classy black rumble-seat Ford and traded it for a 1940 Chevy convertible that provided his friends the comfort and warmth of a real back seat. Double dating in the Ford had taught him that pretty girls dressed for an evening on the town shivered at the thought of riding in a rumble seat.

The jingle had been convincing. "You'll be ahead with a Chevrolet." The auto maker was keenly aware that it was selling not the virtues of a machine, but the fantasies of a nation that longed to leave hardship behind. Untold hardships were yet to come.

To meet wartime demands, Chevrolet's factories also forged ahead with armored cars, 90 mm guns and shells, components for Pratt and Whitney engines bound for cargo planes, fighters and bombers.

Across the country, manufacturers revved up production, added assembly lines, increased their shifts to feed the gaping maw of war. While Germany tore into Britain, the Bell System ripped a sixteen-hundred-mile furrow for defense from Omaha to Sacramento. In one slick operation, it dug a trench, laid transcontinental telephone lines and buried cable. Those lines would soon be buzzing with long-distance defense calls, teletype, telephoto and radio transmissions to the tune of four hundred twenty million dollars. Companies that now served two masters—the government and consumers—knew the public-relations value of not keeping its defense efforts hidden under a bushel basket.

On Monday evenings, radioland listeners tuned into NBC Red Network's "The Telephone Hour." Voices of stage and screen personalities floated on the airwaves and seeped into living rooms, where they sang, wept, laughed and botched lines of dubious scripts or unleashed white-knuckle thrillers on eager audiences. Gene Lockhart, Simone Simon and Edward Arnold showed moviegoers how to deal with *All That Money Can Buy.* Gary Cooper and Barbara Stanwyck ignited the screen with *Ball of Fire.* Alfred Hitchcock aroused *Suspicion,* directing Cary Grant and Joan Fontaine in the blockbuster.

Thousands of promising young British pilots sent to America for training brought in their duffels a little blue book called *Notes for Your Guidance.* The valuable and often comical treatise on cultural differences tactfully informed, "During this war, and probably thereafter, our fate is closely bound up with that of the United States." Travelers to America should not be misled by the similarity of the two languages, or mistakenly presume that the two people and countries are practically the same. Such is not the case, the little book assured. For example, as anyone who had read American history knew, the Deep South was like another country altogether. Its language, customs, even food, were a world apart from both Old and New England, with which Britons had a better chance of identifying.

In addition to the exchange of military expertise, countries were pooling their intellectual resources. Throughout the United States and across the Atlantic, physicists were competing and cooperating, yet, at the same time, agreeing to keep their findings under wrap. Physicists working on splitting atoms were still preoccupied, splitting hairs over the relative merits of "fast" and "slow" fission, and U^{235} versus U^{238}.

When the Japanese army swaggered into northern Indo-China, it was confident that the United States would do little more than raise an eyebrow. Certainly, its penetration did not violate American interests enough to stir military resistance. Its army hadn't calculated on a multi-nation concerted effort to shuttle American B-29s over the Himalayan

"Hump" for access to Japan, much less clandestine operations to produce a bomb with the force to annihilate it.

To the small but powerful Japan, its own atomic bomb could mean fulfillment of its global fantasy. In April 1941, the Imperial Army Air Force issued an order. Develop a nuclear weapon. The swords of the Rising Sun must gleam in victory.

On September 6, Japan's military leaders met secretly in the presence of the Emperor to chart Japan's course among the treacherous seas of Western democracies. These sessions served little purpose beyond discharging protocol. This day, as others, the militarists had not come for the Emperor's advice or wisdom. Not unexpectedly, he preempted their treatises on the virtues of war to read aloud another of his grandfather's poems:

> The seas surround all quarters of the globe
> And my heart cries out to the nations of the world.
> Why then do the winds and waves of strife
> Disrupt the peace between us?

When he had finished, he laid the paper on the lacquered table as gently as though it were a sacred scroll. The poem kept Emperor Meiji's spirit of peace in his heart, he told the rigid faces before him. "It has been my wish to perpetuate this spirit."

Kiochi Kido shared the Emperor's desire. But he was well aware that such dissident sentiments could bring about his early death. The fearsome Kempei-Tai watched Kido as it watched anyone at cross purposes with the government. Would the Kempei-Tai one day secret him away to be tortured according to techniques described in its official manual? Kido knew the Emperor's heart. He, too, wanted to liberate rather than enslave, welcome a new dawn of prosperity rather than the sunset of Japan's potential.

Kido believed that too many of her politicians placed blind faith in the Greater East Asia Co-Prosperity Sphere to fulfill her destiny. Clearly, when Japan fanned its domestic rule over the spheres of others, like an unwanted suitor it had been rebuffed. "Shortsighted nations," government officials had grumbled. "Wasn't political, social and economic power achieved through coalescence worth the loss of individual sovereignty?" But the peoples who had been "coalesced" saw domination, not the realization of a grand and glorious dream.

In their own spheres of influence, many of Japan's elder statesmen were as powerful as the figurehead Emperor was powerless. In fact, the crown jewel of Japan could do little more than rubber stamp the policies of his government. It would take initiators who wielded more influence than Hirohito to get peace negotiations moving.

"Defense production is rolling," Bassick Caster Company proudly announced, showing off in patriotic ads its assembly line-scale versions of the home casters its customers knew.

Offense, in the form of heavy German tanks, was also rolling—straight into the Soviet countryside. The alarm sounded again from scientific circles. Now that Hitler had grasped virtually all corners of Europe, he seemed indefatigable. Einstein's letter suggesting a weapon of unprecedented power quietly but persistently tugged at the President's imagination. In early October, he tapped his presidential emergency fund and sidetracked monies to support research and development. For the time being, the fledgling project would be known simply as "S-1."

Admiral Joseph Richardson, commander of the Pacific fleet, broached William D. Leahy, then chief of naval operations, bluntly in 1939. Pearl Harbor was vulnerable to a sneak attack. The fleet must be relocated. When Leahy demurred, Richardson spoke to the President. Pooh-poohing the commander's anxiety—he was acting like an old woman—Roosevelt was adamant, the fleet would stay right where it was.

Two years later, on Sunday morning, December 7, Richardson's concerns were horribly and agonizingly vindicated. Without prior declaration of war against America, Japan launched "the day that would live in infamy." Three hundred sixty carrier-based Japanese planes sank the U. S. S. *Arizona*, pride of the American fleet, along with the *Oklahoma*, *California*, *Nevada* and *West Virginia*, damaged three other battleships, three cruisers and three destroyers. Two hundred planes were destroyed on the ground. When the smoke cleared, nearly twenty-four hundred Americans had died.

By the time Bob arrived at his parent's cabin on Long Island, it was cold and misting. He had driven out leisurely with the Chevy convertible to pick up his favorite rocking chair. The car radio blared popular music while he snapped the boot neatly over the folded roof. His fingers had already become numb when the program was interrupted by a special bulletin. "God," he whispered to the trees. "Now we're in it for real."

At an Imperial Conference, Emperor Hirohito renounced the plan to attack Pearl Harbor laid out by his Samurai tradition military strategists. Hirohito read them another poem:

> When I regard all the world
> As my own brothers
> Why is it that its tranquillity
> Should be so thoroughly disturbed?

But what did a deity know about the strategies of war? Two weeks after its attack on Pearl Harbor, the Imperial Army again did as it pleased. And this time, what pleased it was to capture Guam and Wake.

Congress' formal declaration of war on Japan only heightened awareness of the gradual changes that had been taking place in Americans' everyday lives as strife escalated in Europe. Consumers had noticed the conspicuous absence of some goods and shortages of others. Prestone informed consumers in double-page advertisements that its antifreeze stocks would be shipped where they were needed most, to defend tank and aircraft engines on front lines.

The government's clarion call to pitch in for the war effort went out to a variety of production corners. "Defense now, homes later," B. F. Goodrich announced in its full-page ads, explaining that government had "prioritized" the manufacture of its Koroseal™ products. The miracle waterproof fabric of shower curtains and table cloths was ideally suited for cable insulation on airplanes and warships. Like many companies "drafted" for national defense, Goodrich doubled, tripled and quadrupled its production levels, yet struggled to meet escalating wartime demands.

Information advertising became a valuable public relations' tool for industries, many of which were as indispensable to the war effort as they claimed. Goodyear's expensive color advertisements urged consumer patience. The company assured new-tire buyers confronted with dealerships unable to keep popular sizes in stock that there was "not so much a rubber 'shortage' as a demand 'longage.' " At length, it explained rubber was one of many vital wartime commodities stockpiled by the government. Goodyear employees worked around the clock to produce new defense products such as barrage balloons, bomber wings and tails, self-sealing rubber-lined fuel tanks, gas masks and rubber tank track treads.

> So it is that from Goodyear factories meant for building things to enlarge life and make it better, now must flow in a swelling tide the things our country needs if we are to hold what we have. This is no choice of ours.... But when the decision lies between helping our government prepare for impregnable defense of such things (all that America holds dear), or running the risk of having them swept away, there is no option. Compared to holding it, what else matters?

Street-corner sandwich shops to multi-million-dollar corporations rallied under a united banner to preserve all that America held dear. In an unusual public-relations twist, the electric power company credited itself for "putting the gun in Johnny's hand," while U. S. Rubber assured consumers that children were still free to sleep and wake and play not only by the "flame that burns from the torch of Liberty, but by the undimmed brightness of the lights in ten million streets."

During the summer of 1941, the nation faced a multi-million ton shortage of iron and steel scrap. In Middletown, Ohio, Armco Iron and Steel Sheeting mobilized a community-wide drive to get junk out of attics, basements and barns and into rail cars headed for meltdown. Children wheeled in battered toys. Mothers donated frying pans. Barbers trucked in their old barber chairs. Armco then replanted the successful campaign in Ashland, Kentucky, and Butler, Pennsylvania. Later that fall, the government imitated Armco's drive and launched its own nationwide campaign for scrap, yielding a half-million additional tons destined to be trucks, tanks, guns, ammunition and a host of other defense matériel.

The Office of Production Management also scrapped for domestic and foreign suppliers of seven metals essential to national defense. Manganese was one of the most vital strategic metals needed. Every ton of steel produced required twelve and one-half pounds of it. The soft alloy tin, used in bearings, was needed for plane props. Tungsten not only provided the filaments for incandescent lamps, but also hardened special steels. Antimony, used in storage batteries, turned steel brittle for use as shrapnel. Nickel and chrome were vital to the electroplating process. Stainless steel manufacture also required chrome. Mercury, used extensively in gauges, was also important in the operation of detonators.

Americans would be directly affected by the acute need for copper and nickel. By 1942, the scarcity of the metals for defense use would spawn the Emergency Coinage Act, authorizing the United States Mint to issue "steelies," zinc-coated steel pennies and nickels made of silver.

Throughout the remainder of 1941, the nation found little to cheer it. It recalled vividly the face of despair from Dorothea Lange's 1936 photograph of a migrant mother. The Hoboken, New Jersey, photographer had startled the nation with her powerful Depression portraits and riveted sensibilities to the plight of rural America with a concern that transcended objectivity. In their 1941 book *Let Us Now Praise Famous Men*, Walker Evans' sensitive documentary photographs and James Agee's evocative narrative would not let the suffering of Southern tenant farmers be forgotten. The poignant images of Margaret Bourke-White illustrated articles in *Time*, *Life* and *Fortune* with shocking realism that haunted even after the page had been turned.

Still, defeat was not in Americans' vocabulary. When Bob's Brooklyn Dodgers lost the 1941 World Series to the New York Yankees, he figured that even if he couldn't affect the outcome of the Series, he could do his part to affect the outcome of the economy. He made a cautious, modest investment in the symbol of rural America, a cheap corn-cob pipe and a can of Prince Albert tobacco. While it had been an unconventional purchase for an urbanite, Bob thought the ritual act might also soothe the soul. It did. Before long, he hazarded a four-dollar investment in a briar Kaywoodie.

Roosevelt risked nothing and cemented Churchill's lasting friendship when on January 30, 1942, in response to his sixtieth birthday greetings, he cabled: "It is fun to be in the same decade with you." His message would have made a good song title. But the Filipino and American troops on Bataan were not singing. They were dying. On April 9, Bataan fell to the Japanese. Thirty-six thousand Americans were captured and forced into a brutal death march to their prison camp. Thousands never made it.

During Bob's high school years, history had been a vague allusion to an even vaguer past. The ebb and flow of nations and power seemed irrelevant, even burdensome. Now, its consequence to the present was a world at war. Hundreds of thousands of young men—some voluntarily, others out of duty—left the security of home to serve in far-away places. The battles they fought assumed greater than newsreel significance. Word for word, on the train to and from Maxson's, Bob read newspaper reports of spring and summer struggles for Pacific-island strongholds.

He was especially interested in the daring April 18 raid on Tokyo, Yokohama and other Japanese cities by sixteen B-25 bombers from the carrier *Hornet* commanded by forty-five-year-old Major "Jimmy" Doolittle.

At work with his friends, at home during dinner, Bob discussed the significance of the major battles making headline news. On May 4-8, during the Battle of Coral Sea, the United States carrier *Lexington* was sunk, taking fifteen Japanese warships down with her. For three days in early June, in the Battle of Midway Island, the Japanese Navy suffered demoralizing defeat. When the carnage was over, four of her first-line aircraft carriers, three cruisers and three destroyers were gone, two hundred seventy-five Japanese planes had been shot down, and four thousand eight hundred Japanese were killed or drowned. Three hundred seven American troops lost their lives. On August 7, Marines landed on Guadalcanal and Tulagi in the Solomon islands for what would become a six-month battle for occupation.

August sizzled with activity at home and abroad. A little-known scientist named Klaus Fuchs, who had been naturalized a British citizen, would weave himself into the web of American atomic bomb development and spin long, connecting threads of secret information directly to Moscow. Cartoonist Billy DeBeck introduced readers to the phrase "heebie-jeebies." Upton Sinclair won a Pulitzer Prize for *Dragon's Teeth*, the third of his eleven novels, featuring hero Lanny Budd. Aaron Copeland's ballet *Rodeo* opened in New York. Irving Berlin reminded Americans that they had something to sing about with his "I've got plenty to be thankful for."

On the homefront, people were thankful for relief from steamy days, for letters from battlefronts, for overtime that made payments on bungalows and convertibles, for Roosevelt's insistence that the game must go on "for the sake or morale" and baseball fans everywhere.

Bob had been grateful for all those things and more. Yet, as he routed out the last of the ground turret's bugs, he had trouble concentrating. The problem wasn't the oppressive summer heat. Something else tugged at him. Because he worked in an essential industry, designing guns to kill the enemy, the draft board issued him another deferment. But a deferment wasn't what Bob wanted.

The day after Labor Day 1942, Bob called his boss and said he was sick. As he climbed the stairs to the Army Air Forces' Headquarters on Whitehall Street in Lower Manhattan, he thought he never felt better. He was charged, as though all the electrical impulses in his body tingled with energy.

Fired by the urgency that they had frustratingly tried to arouse in the President, physicists at Columbia, Berkeley, Princeton and Harvard probed for answers to the many and varied atomic questions.

The Japanese Navy pressed its own sense of urgency for an ultimate weapon on Dr. Joshio Nishina. On July 18, 1942, it had commissioned him to spearhead a research committee to study the potential of a nuclear bomb. Given present knowledge and raw materials, reported the committee, it would take up to ten years to produce such a bomb. By December 7, exactly one year after the invasion of Pearl Harbor, the Navy pressured the committee to revise its forecast to a maximum production schedule of two years.

In Washington, the heat was on the War Department. Charged with responsibility to build a nuclear weapon, Secretary of War Henry Stimson overnight became Roosevelt's adviser on atomic energy. Although oversight was Stimson's responsibility, what he needed was a butt-kicker who could produce a bomb at any cost.

Behold the Turtle

"Haste, with or without waste." That was General Leslie Groves' motto. Every morning he entered his office, Room 5121 of the War Department, 21st Street and Virginia Avenue, and faced the drawing of a turtle with its head stretched forward. A single line beneath it read: "Behold the turtle! He makes progress only when his neck is out."

Pound for pound, Groves was every bit the S.O.B. Stimson was looking for to infuse a bomb project gone nowhere. On September 17, 1942, the Secretary of War presented the forty-eight-year-old, whose gall was matched only by his girth, an opportunity to stick his neck out even farther than he had when he took on construction of the Pentagon. Groves had every confidence Stimson had picked the right man. The West Point engineering cadet and football player hadn't earned the nickname "Greasy" for nothing.

Like a two-hundred-fifty-pound missile, Groves crushed opposition. In less than twenty-four hours, he had blasted away his first project bottleneck—finding uranium.

Incredibly, two thousand steel drums of the valuable stuff, weighing twelve hundred fifty tons, had been stored since 1939 in a nondescript warehouse on Staten Island. At the New York office of a Belgian firm, its elderly managing director disclosed how it got there. Belgium secretly shipped the uranium to the United States to keep it out of Axis hands. No one knew quite what to do with the two-million dollar's worth, until now. Greasy bought it for one dollar sixty cents per pound.

It was a beginning, and the general was ready to twist a few arms for the rest. At Du Pont headquarters in Wilmington, Delaware, he latched onto its president, trapped him into commitment with motherhood and apple-pie questions, then challenged him to put company money where his mouth was. As far as Groves was concerned, corporate conscience was measurable in dollars, and loyalty to country was spelled B-U-I-L-D B-I-G.

What Groves had in mind staggered even the imagination of the Du Pont senior executive.

In less time than most people take selecting a house, Groves gave the go-ahead for a five hundred forty-four million dollar electromagnetic uranium separation plant in Oak Ridge, Tennessee. Code-named "Y-12," it was to be operated by Tennessee Eastman, a subsidiary of Eastman Kodak, which would eventually hire eighty-five thousand employees. Kellex Corporation, a subsidiary of M. W. Kellogg Company, soon had on its drawing board a gaseous diffusion plant for separating U^{235}, which would become the largest, most complex factory in the world. Another plant was scheduled to be constructed in Hanford, Washington.

Whenever Groves cracked his whip, tigers jumped through flaming hoops. Answering only to Stimson and the President, he bypassed bureaucratic red tape with bulldozer efficiency. When he discovered that silver was required for the electromagnetic plating method of separating uranium, he thought first and last of the United States Treasury.

Single-handedly, the generously built chocolate addict masterminded a vast, secret empire—megalithic production facilities employing more than a hundred thousand skilled laborers and technicians—all told, thirty-seven installations in nineteen states and Canada.

The scheme of the thing was so grand that it was difficult to fathom even for seasoned New York *Times* science reporter William L. Laurence, consigned to report on the Manhattan Project.

> If a Rip Van Winkle had gone to sleep at the turn of the century and awakened to behold modern airplanes, radio, television, and radar, he could not have been more surprised than I was when I first visited the mammoth plants in which U235 is being transmuted into plutonium.

The gigantic electromagnet used in the process occupied many tens of thousands of cubic feet. Its proportions staggered Laurence. "Nothing approaching a magnet of this size was even considered before the war," he wrote. And he had seen only one of many such magnets.

Earlier in the year, the University of Chicago attracted chain-reaction research, pulling it away, by mutual consent, from Columbia. Directed by Aurthur H. Compton, chairman of the university's physics department and a Nobel Prize winner, the work continued under the cover of the "Metallurgical Laboratory," cryptically Metlab.

When Groves bestowed his considerable personage on Metlab, Szilard wondered how anyone could work with such an egotist. Groves, no doubt, felt the same about the dreamy scientist with the Messianic complex. As Groves circled the scientific bull pen, he was alert for the flare of nostrils and pawing hooves that signaled an attack. In his case, brawn had not ruled out brain. He had, after all, graduated fourth in his class at West Point. For all their credentials, the "eggheads" didn't threaten him. In fact, he found the charismatic Ernest O. Lawrence was more than approachable, he was likable.

Lawrence's latest efforts had resulted in the Calutron, which separated the rarer isotope of uranium from the element. The Calutron accelerated atoms through a vacuum tube. As atoms were forced past a powerful magnetic field, they curved into circular paths. The lighter U^{235} atoms separated from other atoms and were isolated in a receiving container.

Fascinated, the general accepted the tall, boyishly charming scientist's invitation to inspect his Berkeley lab.

Beneath the huge cyclotron magnet suspended from the domed ceiling of Lawrence's secular cathedral on Radiation Hill, even the colossus Groves paled. For a rare moment, the grand-scheming general stood speechless.

"How pure does U^{235} have to be for use in an atomic bomb?" he asked, regaining his purposefulness.

"I think Oppenheimer should answer that question," said Lawrence without demur.

As easily as a cook draws hungry campers to his table, Oppie had lured seven theoretical physicists to Berkeley for an intense summer devoted to the mysteries of critical mass and chain reactions. While the campus greened and bloomed and all but the most dedicated students shunned the echoing corridors, Oppie sequestered his physicists in two rooms towered in LeConte Hall. Steel mesh covered their windows. Save Edward Teller, they seemed all of one mind. Teller had a wild hare. He wanted to produce a "super" hydrogen bomb that would make the uranium bomb seem like little more than a firecracker. Teller could hatch whatever eggs he wanted on his own time, but in Oppie's nest, the miniature brain trust was sitting on U^{235}.

Groves recalled the name Oppenheimer, all right. He had read the physicist's dossier. Jewish. Brilliant. Pink. In fact, during a predictable period of passion, he had embraced Marxism and gone so far as to roll beneath the sheets of a Communist organization. Groves knew about his privileged background and fated, tempestuous, communist lover. Although Oppenheimer the scientist stood naked before him, the dossier didn't tell Groves about the flesh and blood man. The dossier did not disclose that the man's emotions took him on roller coaster rides. Or that he never forgot what he learned, but failed to learn much others had forgotten. Or that he was obsessed with detail, craved recognition and abhorred inactivity. Groves filled in these blanks. The willowy man answered his questions forthrightly and succinctly. He knew it at once. And it made up his mind. To hell with the FBI's reservations. Oppenheimer was his man.

In Oppie, Groves had found the "who" of his newly named Manhattan Project. He, himself, had solved the "what"—uranium to meet short-term and long-term demands. All that remained were the "when" and the "where." The "how" would be up to Oppie. Any man who could teach himself Sanskrit for fun should have no difficulty in working out that equation. He had not planned, however, for his new director to select a site. Nevertheless, shortly before Thanksgiving, Oppie drove the general to a remote mesa in the enchanting New Mexico mountains and announced, "This is it."

It was the Los Alamos Ranch School northeast of Santa Fe, where in the summer of 1922 a pallid Oppenheimer had been sent by his father to toughen body and soul. The spindly boy found himself amid Territorial-style timber and adobe buildings and rustic Fuller Lodge. Hot springs secreted in a wilderness of junipers, towering ponderosas and piñon spiraled puffs of healing steam into the cool evening air. The magic had been worked. Once these mountains had been Oppie's salvation. Perhaps they might be so again.

The haughtily handsome general and the fragile, mercurial scientist were strange bedfellows. Groves had seen Oppie's mesmerizing effect on others. He was confident that other scientists would soon follow this pied piper into the wilderness in pursuit of the "technically sweet" problem.

Ironically, on the same day Secretary of War Stimson had charged General Groves with the task of overseeing development of the atomic bomb, George Robert Caron, with wide-eyed idealism, began his military career at Camp Upton, Long Island.

The young man whose lifelong dream to be a pilot had been dashed by circumstances beyond his control spent his first day in the service of his country filling out forms—in duplicate, triplicate. His precise signature flowed over so many documents that he felt as though he had signed his life away in one great and final Declaration of Dependence. By afternoon, George Robert Caron had become Serial Number 12143134. The first "1" indicated he had enlisted.

On the ferry to Governor's Island, Bob wondered what part he would play in the ongoing drama. He didn't doubt that he had done the right thing. *Surely, war isn't about killing an enemy, but about securing a peace. No nation has a right to annihilate another, but an obligation to preserve the principles it lives by.* He released a long, exasperated sigh. *What the hell do I know about what war is and isn't? All I know is that one day I'd never be able to face my kids if I stayed home.*

Camp Upton, the old Revolutionary War fort, served as an army post and reception center. Young men came and went through the turnstile of namelessness. Induction procedures were uncharted territory in the waters of experience. They initiated a long list of changes within and without the man.

Bob brought with him to his physical rumors about white-coated strangers who poked and prodded endless streams of bare-butted young men.

"Do you like girls?" asked a psychiatrist, once the physical was over?

"I sure do, Captain. Do you want to see the pictures in my wallet?"

Examiners declared Bob's body and mind fit for service, with one exception. At Maxson's he had begun wearing glasses to correct vision in his weak left eye. Determined to remedy that problem as methodically as he resolved others—with research and perseverance—he had purchased a self-help book to improve vision. For nearly a year before enlistment, he faithfully followed its recommended exercises, focusing on near objects, then refocusing far. The disciplined effort strengthened the muscles and improved vision without returning it to normal.

The morning after his physical, George, Anne and Doris drove the new inductee to Penn Station in midtown Manhattan. Like the other recruits, he carried only one small suitcase. He would send it home in a few days with his few civilian clothes. As a group, they boarded the Long Island Railroad for dispatch to Camp Upton. Bob took a seat by the right window nearest the platform, where his parents and sister watched and waited. A chorus of wolf whistles arose from the seats behind him. He turned and realized the GIs were expressing their appreciation of the pretty girl in the light blue suit who stood between his parents. Doris smiled brightly and waved back at them.

Everything quartermaster issued was stiff, scratchy, or both. The still-tagged, crinkly tan uniforms. The fatigues that could stand upright on their own. The unyielding lace-up shoes. Even the two thick wool blankets.

Just as stiff were the batteries of IQ and mechanical aptitude tests meted out in liberal doses. A lieutenant assured Private Caron that his high scores, coupled with his experience designing gun turrets, would guarantee him armament school. Bob assumed he would receive orders any time for such an assignment.

As Bob hurried up and waited, a surly sergeant began to toughen his new batch of recruits. After several consecutive, fifteen-hour shifts of KP, the tenderfoots were intimate with every square inch of leather in their unbending new shoes.

Within the week, blister-foot Caron received orders for Bowman Field at Louisville, Kentucky, for one-week basic training, and from there, attachment to a troop carrier at Florence, South Carolina.

The peat-damp air of the South Carolina woods buzzed with insatiable mosquitoes and gnatty no-seeums. To soldiers finishing a long day of drilling and running obstacle courses, the folding cots in their canvas tents looked as inviting as hammocks on a South Sea isle. Although his days as an athlete were further behind him than Caron cared to remember, the workouts increased his energy; he felt invigorated. The part of him that craved precision found enjoyment in the choreography of close-order drill.

"You're not in the right place," his Captain replied, when Caron asked him what someone with his experience in armament was doing in the troop carrier squadron.

"Unfortunately, that's the way the army works," the Captain added, although his implied sympathy was no consolation.

The nurses' training facility at the nearby hospital was true consolation. Passes in their pockets, Bob and a barracks' mate would conveniently drop by the hospital just as the shift changed. Soldiers' uniforms would usually guarantee a date. Sometimes they would wile away an hour, engaging a pretty off-duty nurse in conversation over coffee in the commissary.

When orders came through, transferring him to troop-carrier headquarters in Indianapolis for reassignment, Caron had his duffels packed in a hour. He traveled alone, and when he arrived, he was assigned a tent behind the flight line. A small pot-bellied stove helped offset the cold, when the men in the tent could scrounge up enough firewood. There was never a need for reveille. Every morning pilots fired up the new Curtis C-46 Commandos.

A pass to town temporarily dislodged the "how am I serving my country stuck in Mid-America?" feeling. For the GIs, passes meant girls. A cheery blond, whom he had dated several times, invited Bob to join her at a Halloween party. But first, he wanted to stop at a telephone booth.

"Call us collect so we can wish you happy birthday," his mother had written earlier in the week. Caron sat in the little cubicle and answered their eager questions, while the blond in his lap ran painted fingernails through his hair, nibbled on his earlobe, and the windows steamed up.

Too Many Cooks

E ven for the middle of November, San Antonio felt like the Bahamas compared to Indianapolis. Still, Kelly Field in the southwestern portion of the city was another meat-processing plant, a replacement center where GIs waited to be reassigned.

Caron volunteered to take more tests in the hope he could get an assignment that made use of his skills. In the meantime, at Duncan Field he dismantled old B-18s for spare parts. It was the first hands-on contact with airplanes he'd experienced since Maxson's.

Many exotic planes came and went through the old Army Air Corps base. A few of them were early 1930s Douglas twin-engine bombers, forerunners of the DC-3. They were not very sophisticated by 1942 standards and gradually had been phased out. Caron and his crew dismantled their instrument panels and other control equipment for spare parts.

Boeing had developed—in addition to the B-17—one of the biggest airplanes in the world, the four-engine B-15. It had been designed with bomb bays in the fuselage as well as two more between the fuselage and the inboard engines. When he heard that the experimental B-15 had been flown into Kelly Field, adjacent to Duncan, the would-be flyer rounded up a jeep to go see it. The ground crew was working on its engines and gave him permission to go through the one-of-a-kind plane.

On days off, Caron explored fastidious San Antonio. Only one hundred fifty miles from Mexico's border, it exuded a unique cultural aura and beauty that flowed from antiquity to the present. Pink adobe missions, gardens brilliant with hollyhocks and gladiolus and seasoned buildings with storied pasts spiced the pleasant streets. San Antonio's repose stemmed from a very different deeply historical context than Caron's own ethnically diverse Brooklyn. It felt as though the spirits of Santa Anna, Davy Crockett and Jim Bowie lingered at the Alamo. Certainly, the impressionable private would remember it.

When Caron's captain discovered he had an engineer in his company, he ordered the precisionist to letter and paint squadron signs. Caron didn't mind, but he would need to get supplies: a few brushes, oil paint, turpentine and wood.

The captain authorized another squad member to go along, handed his new sign-painter a small roll of cash along with keys to his tomato-red Oldsmobile convertible, then wondered about the wisdom of sending two young men to town with his flashy car.

A San Antonio artist's supply store had everything they needed. But just in case they had missed something important, for inspiration Caron and his helper cruised up and down its main streets. They waved at the friendly natives who waved spiritedly back at the uniformed men in the dazzling, blaze-bright convertible.

"It took you long enough," the captain barked when the corporal had finally returned his car keys. "What were you doing? Chasing girls?"

Wasn't that what being a bachelor was all about?

San Antonio was a hot town in more ways than one. Mexican civilian mess hall cooks concocted fiery, south-of-the-border dishes with scovil ratings high enough to sear the spines off a cactus. It wasn't the stuff a Flatbush boy had grown up on. Caron passed up the opportunities to cauterize his innards and sat quietly alone at the base exchange, savoring a sandwich and a cold glass of milk.

One day on KP, a Mexican cook was teaching Caron the fine points of making chili for an army. First, he had to light the oversize gas stove. He kneeled on the floor to light it from the bottom as the cook had shown him. Suddenly, the accumulated gas ignited explosively, shooting flame at the right side of his face. His forehead, cheek and hair burned. His eyebrows and eyelashes disappeared. The dispensary treated his burns, and the barber trimmed his stinking, melted hair. It had been a painful lesson, but it curtailed KP.

On the morning of December 2, 1942, Caron drilled with his squad at Duncan Field. In frigid Chicago, Metlab scientists constructed their first nuclear reactor near the corner of 57th and Ellis Avenue, on the indoor squash court beneath the stands of the university's old Stagg Field football stadium. Brick by graphite brick, they built a three hundred fifty-seven-ton pile, embedded with pure uranium.

At 10:37 A.M., Chicago time, Fermi, Szilard, Compton, Wigner and about forty other senior physicists took a deep breath and allowed the energy from splitting atoms to split others within the confines of the graphite pile. Chicagoans were unaware that the architects of the chain reaction fervidly hoped it wouldn't "run wild" and blow the windy city into Lake Michigan. In the afternoon, Fermi and Szilard stopped the reaction. Chicago remained intact.

That day, a State Department release revealed a moral imperative for their work. *In memoriam* for the two million Jews who had perished in concentration camps and the millions more whose lives were in imminent danger, the government declared December 2 a special day for Jewish mourning. The world grieved.

Drilling, preparing for inspections and painting signs wouldn't win the war. Caron's frustrations grew. He welcomed the invitation to a New Year's Eve party with a friend at her family's home. The afternoon of the party, the orderly room first sergeant told Caron he would be spending the evening taking mechanical aptitude and armament tests, instead. As his friends rang in the new year, Caron penciled in answers. When the tests were over, so was the revelry. But he had bought his ticket to armament school at Lowry Field in Denver.

The rickety railroad cars looked and felt more like cattle haulers than transportation for people. The train groaned and jostled, and its couplings wrenched and tugged at each other as if they were going to release their clasp. The string of cars finally clanked and screeched to a halt in Dalhart, Texas, for a layover. Bone-jarred passengers filed into the all-night cafe that served greasy burgers and limp fries. Passengers reboarded with a still-pained look. Caron tried to stretch out on the hard cane seat. Throughout the night, he shifted and squirmed as the train rattled and droned past patchwork farms and tiny towns that slept through its shrill, spine-chilling crossing whistle.

At daybreak, the antique lumbered into Trinidad, Colorado, for a brief stop. The foothills that rose abruptly from the plain energized Caron, and he forgot the soreness in his tailbone. Beyond the first range, gossamer wisps of moisture stroked the snowcapped peaks and seemed reluctant to drift away. The train resumed its lurching northward trek and, as the vistas intensified, so did Caron's enthusiasm for this magical place.

He found himself preferring the crisp, invigorating air of the platform, photographing mountains, rivers and streams, to the warmth of the car. Long after nightfall, the train pulled into Denver.

Lowry Field's student barracks were sterile, but after the train ride, their antiseptic smell and appearance were not unwelcome. Besides, he would sleep indoors, not in a tent. Somewhere between dark and dawn, he died and went to heaven. After breakfast, his senses returned, and he was alert and ready to report to Power Turret School, where classes and hands-on experience were scheduled like factory shifts: day, swing and graveyard. Caron began with swing shift. Classes for six days, one day off. In between there were close-order drill and barracks' inspections.

Colorado winter was something new altogether. It amazed him how he felt warmer at zero degrees in Denver than at thirty-two in New York. It seemed as though no matter where in the city he went, the ruffles of mountains that lay to the west were always visible, always beckoning.

The consolidated mess hall resembled a gymnasium. The men marched in, received their trays and stood behind their seats until everyone assigned to the table was present. At arm's-length intervals along the tables were salt, pepper, ketchup and other condiments, including bottles of Tabasco sauce.

"What's this stuff?" Caron asked, holding up the little bottle.

The GI across from him recognized a sheltered schnook when he saw one.

"It's like ketchup."

The patsy sprinkled the surrogate ketchup liberally on his food. With the first mouthful his face reddened, but the Tabasco wasn't wholly responsible. He had left himself wide open for the boyish prank. He figured he deserved it. The price he'd pay was going hungry. Or so he thought.

When he tried to dump his supper at the service line, a second lieutenant stopped him and pointed to a sign. **Take all you want, but eat all you take.** He motioned Bob back to a table to clean up his tray.

P ower turret instruction also started hot and heavy. Six days a week classes drilled maintenance on various turrets for different planes. The Sperry upper turret on the B-17, the ball turret and the consolidated turret of the B-24 nose and tail, the short-lived Bendix retractable turret. All training focused on assembling, maintaining, but never firing the .50

caliber guns. As quickly as instructors planted malfunctions, Caron located and corrected them.

Shortly before the two-month-long classes ended, students were given an opportunity to test for a new class on an electronic remote-controlled power turret for a highly secret airplane. Only twenty eight would be accepted. In a hangar with several hundred other test-takers, Caron sat in the one-arm folding chair and concentrated.

The twenty-eight thought of themselves as a select group. They were all conscientious about their work and studies to the point of obsession. Instructors for the remote-controlled turret system of the P-51 Mustang were still wet behind the ears, fresh from factory training themselves. They knew little more about the system than their students. For three and a half months, students and instructors learned together, poring over schematics and wiring diagrams. They had been told that this system would go in a new secret bomber. The tempo had been set. When the six days on ended in one day off, they wanted that time as saturated with experiences as the ones preceding.

Denver offered no shortage of sights, smells and sounds. The wind either ushered in the resin-evergreen freshness from the mountains or the urea concentrate from distant stock yards. The latter brought back memories of nauseating odors that filtered into Maxson's. Robust winds often swept Denver skies clean, and a number of its well-manicured parks offered sweeping vistas of the front range and snow-capped Mt. Evans.

Jackie Fletcher nearly always accepted Bob's invitations to movies and dances. She was generous, spirited, unpredictable. And motherly, encouraging him to bring his uniforms to her parents' laundry and dry-cleaning business on Colfax Avenue. "It's the least we can do for our daughter's good friend," said Jackie's mother, who proceeded to treat him more like her son.

If diversity is the spice of life, Bob wanted his life seasoned with new faces and places. Dances were entertaining, but the Rocky Mountains called. One clear spring day, he rented a new Ford and with another new girl headed west on Highway 40, past the rusty gold mines and tailings that dotted the slopes sheltering Idaho Springs, turning onto the Echo Lake road and pushing higher and higher to Squaw Pass. The couple picnicked in the crisp, pungently scented air among lingering snow fields. When late afternoon chill settled down on them, they reluctantly repacked the car. Bob was shocked to discover the gas gauge read nearly empty. By the time they reached the long winding road to Bergen Park, he shut off the engine and coasted down, braking frequently to keep from careening off the curves. Every few miles he was forced to pull over and let the brakes cool. At Bergen Park, he put in just enough gas to get the car back to the city.

The next time Bob requested a rental car from the same agency, the manager was belligerent. "We don't need customers who burn out brakes on our new cars," he sniped, then offered some uncensored suggestions where else Bob might go.

Bob did take his business elsewhere. Another car and another date, this time a piano teacher whom he had met one Sunday at a Catholic box-lunch social. Bob asked the cute musician where she would like to go. Without hesitation, she chose Estes Park. At Bear Lake she pointed to a trail that wound through the conifers and broke into the open past timberline, then continued to Long's Peak, a "fourteener."

"Fourteener is the affectionate nickname climbers give peaks that summit above fourteen-thousand feet," she explained. "And *this* mountain climber can beat *you* to Chasm Lake." Without warning, she steamed uptrail.

Bob's spit-polished GI shoes weren't exactly what he would have chosen to run in, but they had miles ago contoured to his feet. He took off after his date and in minutes he had passed her. He raced up the switchbacks, past twisted, stunted trees to an overlook, where he waited for her to catch up.

"I didn't think a city boy could do that," she said, plunking herself down on a boulder.

He accepted her left-handed praise, and they leisurely picked their way over the steep, boulder-strewn slope that crowns Chasm Lake. For a long while they sat silently, surrounded by the crystalline water—like liquid smoky quartz—that was held captive by the sheer east face of Long's Peak. Marmots performed their staccato dance, appearing, then disappearing behind them, in front of them, darting in and out among the maze of crevices. Now and again the inquisitive creatures froze brazenly close and gazed in bewilderment at the two odd mammals who nuzzled contentedly as the sun danced behind the fine cirrus and disappeared over the peak.

It was often well past bed-check when Caron would finally sneak back into the barracks, if he got there at all. When he did, he seldom slept under the covers, much preferring, even on the coldest nights, to wrap himself in the warm quilt issued to him. The narrow bunks faced head-to-foot in sequence, and, conveniently for maintaining his ruse, his was head-in against the wall. Before the Charge of Quarters made his rounds, Caron's buddy would roll up his quilt and shove it under the blanket. If the CQ was ever wise to the deception, he didn't let on. The nearly ten-mile round-trip climb to Chasm Lake meant it was going to be one of those nights that Bob's bunk had no body.

There wasn't even peach fuzz on the second lieutenant's pretty-boy face. Fresh from West Point, the new drill instructor had in mind teaching his many squads—especially the unbridled twenty-eight-man armament squad—a thing or two about precision drilling. The squads practiced routines. "Right flank...*harch!*" "Left flank...*harch!*" Braiding in and out. The lieutenant was pleased with himself.

Each day he appointed a different squad leader to learn and practice calling drills. Corporal Caron's moment had arrived.

"About face...*harch!*" Bob spit out the command in his most authoritative voice. The men in the squad looked at each other for a split second of silent agreement. Then, like a covey of quail suddenly flushed by a shotgun blast, they scattered, laughing hysterically.

"HOOOOOLD it!" The squad-leader-for-a-day struggled to keep a straight face. He took a deep breath and belted out the command to halt. The playful squad froze.

"This is no time for levity," he reprimanded, tongue-in-cheek. "Don't you men know there's a war going on?"

The second lieutenant pressed his smooth jaw against his chest and looked sternly at the men. "Well done, Corporal Caron," he said, naively. "Well done."

His squad-leading capabilities firmly ensconced, Caron frequently marched the squad from the classroom to the drill field crowded with marching men. The moment the drill instructor turned his back, Caron called a right flank and marched his squad around the corner to the back of the base exchange, then right flank again up to the counter for Coca-Cola and malts. When field time was over, he ordered them into formation and marched them back. They had not been missed.

As the many squads marched past the Women's Army Corps area, their voices rose in unison to the familiar melody *Semper Fideles* cast with new disparaging lyrics about women in uniform. From barracks to barracks they echoed loudly, until they ricocheted into the ear of the commanding officer of the WAC detachment. By the next day, all male military personnel had read the new order: There would be no disrespectful references to service women at Lowry Field.

Caron was constantly amazed at this world within a world. The military environment compressed life into a storybook of experiences and personalities unique to it. A strange young man, heir to a fortune amassed from the family chain of mortuaries, had been assigned to one of the squads. Most everyone believed his family name, not his competency, impressed the psychiatric entrance examiner. Although the young man was scarcely able to make decisions affecting his daily life, he was an accomplished organist. In what he called his "full regalia"—the dashing garrison cap and regal shoulder braid, which he wore off base against regulation—the musician-for-an-afternoon would turn himself over to the ivories at a downtown church.

To get the regalia past the gate MPs, the obsessed young man suspended a string between the front and back of his belt and attached the garrison cap, letting it dangle awkwardly between his legs. The comedic garb covered by his overcoat, he strode past the guards, confident they had been fooled. Safely off the bus that shuttled GIs downtown from Aurora, the organ player donned the secreted cap and braid and strutted as proudly as a peacock to his sanctuary.

In the evening, the ritual was simply reversed. At the gate, MPs frisked returning GIs for half-pints of whiskey stashed in socks or boots. Inevitably, they "discovered" the dangling cap, shook their heads, buttoned up the young soldier as a mother bundles her child for school and watched him waddle toward his barracks as if he had a load in his pants.

Mile-high Denver had been a pleasant place to roost in the winter. As summer approached, Bob found its cooler temperatures and lower humidity a refreshing change from the hot, sticky East.

Socially, Caron played the field, sampling from the range of available single women who were looking for available single men.

The corporal met June on a day off. The sweetly girlish redhead from Grand Junction who worked downtown lived at the YWCA, as did many young women away from home. On one date, they devoted the entire day to the zoo, a picnic and, finally, a stroll through City Park. When nightfall turned the big oaks to silhouettes, June and Bob found a secluded hillside west of the museum and melted into the shadows.

A few days later, Bob called to see how Jackie Fletcher was doing. She was happy to hear from him and suggested that he join them for a family dinner and bring his laundry with him. Her mother was effusive. As usual, Jackie's father treated him more like a drinking buddy than his daughter's occasional date. Sometimes, while Jackie was out with someone else, her father would put his arm around his invited guest's shoulder, and they'd saunter over to the bar next door for a few beers.

Within the week, Bob called Jackie again to thank her and her mother for the delicious dinner. But Jackie was furious.

"What's the matter?" he asked, mystified.

"You know what's the matter," she lashed out at him. "Mother showed me the grass stains on the knees of your suntans."

Jackie had helped Bob learn another valuable lesson about women, and he added it to his mental guidebook to life. Since earliest childhood, every day was an exercise in discovery, and the methodical part of him looked for and noted the tidbits of wisdom that emerged.

From the long days of routing out problems in complicated turret systems came more valuable information. The student team helped formulate maintenance diagrams to go with the power turrets as they were installed in aircraft. So well had the team done their job that when the course ended the second week of June, the group commanding officer invited them to stay on as instructors. The program was to be expanded and numerous classes were to be added.

Half said they would stay. The remaining fourteen were contracted as military assistants to the Boeing factory in Wichita, Kansas. Slowly, Boeing turned out a few YB-29s. When Caron walked into the factory and laid eyes on his first B-29, he thought it was the biggest, most beautiful, most amazing airplane he had ever seen.

It was certainly big, and size more than technology put it in a class by itself. The behemoth's wings spanned more than one hundred forty-two feet, forty feet longer than the B-17's, and were supported by special web-like trusses. "Wingloading," which consumed seventeen hundred twenty-six square feet, threatened an impossibly high landing speed. To compensate for the problem, designers installed immense flaps that covered one-sixth of its wing area.

A lightweight aluminum alloy skin covered the plane's fuselage. To reduce drag, all external rivets had been countersunk. Advanced-design tricycle landing gear shifted the plane's center of gravity, increasing its stability on the ground as well as virtually eliminating the tendency to weathervane in a crosswind, as planes with a small wheel in the back, called taildraggers, were inclined to do.

Because its cabin was pressurized, the crew didn't need heavy sheepskin-lined flight suits or electrically heated flight coveralls. The B-29 had not been the first plane to be pressurized. That innovation belonged to the German Ju86R, which bombed England from forty thousand feet, and was pressurized to eight pounds per square inch. At thirty thousand feet, the much larger crew area of the B-29 could be kept as comfortable as flying at eight thousand feet.

Boeing designers divided the enormous fuselage into three pressurized areas—the nose, center fuselage, or waist, and tail—to eliminate the problem of sudden depressurization when its bomb-bay doors opened at high altitude. A twenty-eight-inch diameter tunnel connected the nose and waist. The tail was unconnected to the forward pressurized areas and received its oxygen from a four-inch umbilical tube to the waist.

Portable oxygen tanks were everywhere in the event of emergency, such as a blister blowing out or a combat hit that resulted in depressurization.

Major General Henry "Hap" Arnold first saw the need for a Very Long Range (VLR) bomber capable of reaching targets well beyond American shores in 1939. Major aircraft companies were authorized to design a heavy "intercontinental" bomber. In November 1940, Boeing had been granted a contract for two prototypes of its XB-29. On September 21, 1942, the first prototype, XB-29 Number One, took off on a seventy-five-minute flight from Seattle.

Each of the new bomber's four radial, eighteen-cylinder Wright R-3350 engines had two exhaust-driven turbo-superchargers. Fully loaded, the B-29 weighed nearly fifty-two tons and ate up seventy-two hundred feet of runway on takeoff. At the upper limits of its performance, the plane could reach an air speed of three hundred forty-two miles per hour. At a more economical cruising speed of two hundred twenty miles per hour, it could carry a maximum bomb load of ten tons.

The plane's armament consisted of four remote-controlled turrets, two above the forward fuselage and two hanging onto its underbelly like baby kangaroos. Each turret was domed by low-profile aluminum "blisters" and held .50 caliber machine guns. A tail turret was fitted with twin .50 caliber machine guns and a 20 mm cannon.

Innovative computers rapidly entered the business of war. Late in 1941, the General Electric Company introduced a small, state-of-the-art computer that enabled all gunners except the tail gunner to control the bomber's turrets. The tail gunner could only control his two guns and cannon. The bombardier in the nose had primary control of the two forward turrets. A gunner in control of more than one turret could engage them simultaneously and synchronously during an attack. All the guns were eventually fitted with interrupter gear to prevent them from accidentally blasting away great chunks of their own aircraft.

For all its boldness and power, the B-29 was continually troubled by operational difficulties from its engines to its turrets. Boeing sent out feelers for problem-solvers—civilian consultants and, on loan from the Army Air Force, fourteen armament experts.

Caron and the remaining trouble-shooters occupied a small, two-story wooden house apart from the mechanics, a short distance from the factory. The temporary quarters rented by Boeing for the task forces had sparsely outfitted kitchens. The armament crew bought enough utensils to prepare quick breakfasts. They lunched at the factory cafeteria, then returned late at night, if at all, to snore away the few remaining hours before the routine repeated itself.

The detachment of GIs was Colonel Harvey's responsibility. He had been assigned a staff car, and the enlisted men traveled to and from the plant in a six-by-six truck. Someone with a sense of humor designated the smallest of the armament men to be its official driver. Caron had to rob seat cushions from an airplane and shove them behind his back just to belly up to the steering wheel and reach the pedals. Once he mastered double down-shifting, he was issued a GI license. Driving the six-by-six truck was an experience far removed from cruising in his little convertible. It had its rewards. He and the rest of the men it shuttled soon discovered that, with the exception of a few GIs on pass from Fort Riley, theirs was often the lone GI truck in town and, for that reason, attracted at least as much attention from attractive young women as a classy convertible.

The team worked seven days a week at the plant, which hummed with three shifts of civilians. They worked one shift and part of another in a whirlwind of troubleshooting, disassembling, repairing, rewriting the manuals.

Only four of the prototype XB-29s had been built at Boeing's Seattle plant. One plane had been designated for static testing—determining the destruction of wings and strength of the airplane. The other three had been earmarked for use in test flights.

The XB-29's hydraulic gunnery system, built by Sperry Corporation, fired the tail-turret gun from the waist. There were two control consoles in the waist and one in the forward section. The gunner sat on a pedestal seat and looked through a viewfinder. His remote controls actuated the turrets and fired the guns. Orientation to find the target was not achieved through the periscope. In the blister and in the nose, the bombardier had a small spotting sight for aligning the target. His sight was connected to the console, which enabled the periscopic sight to pick up the target. The gunner would take it from there. The range-finding lighted reticles in his gun sight kept the target locked in.

Unfortunately, the system worked better in theory than in fact. The equipment continually leaked hydraulic fluid that spilled out onto the metal floor of the airplane. Walking without paying attention was an invitation to "go ass over tea kettle."

Colonel Paul Tibbets flew the first XB-29 from Seattle to the Boeing plant in Wichita on a stopover to the Eglin Field proving ground in Florida. While Caron didn't see its test pilot, he gave the plane a good once-over. Oddly, it had a tail gun but no place for the tail gunner. Its two .50 caliber guns and one 20 mm gun were fired by the gunner at the console in the pressurized waist.

The other experimental model, the YB-29, also had a pressurized forward section and a thirty-foot, wormlike tunnel over the bomb bay for crawling into the waist. Unlike the XB-29, its tail turret was surrounded by a small compartment for a tail gunner. To get into the tail hatch, the gunner crawled over a rack for a fixed belly camera, past the auxiliary power plant nicknamed the "put-put," over the tail skid gear and past two ammunitions cans. Inside, a gun sight was positioned toward the center of the Plexiglas windows. Beneath it, the turret protruded from the tail. An armor plate with a round hatch allowed access to the turret. Once the compartments were pressurized, the tail gunner was locked in. Pressure held the hatch shut.

The first YB-29 rolled out of the Wichita factory and onto the hardstand in mid June 1943, ready for its test flight. Three armament men were scheduled to assist on the first flight: two at the waist blisters as scanners to watch the engines, and one to operate the put-put. Over the intercom, scanners kept the pilot and flight engineer apprised of landing gear, ailerons, rudder and elevator operation. The put-put operator fired up the gasoline-driven generator, which provided power to start the Curtis-Wright engines. When the four-hundred amp generator ran at ten thousand revolutions per minute, it really howled.

The fourteen Army Air Force loaner armament specialists broke match sticks to select three scanners for the first flight. Caron drew for the second flight. Boeing released the plant's twenty-eight thousand employees to watch the YB-29 take off at Wichita's municipal airport, whose airfield was conveniently located across the road from the plant.

The test plane cleared the ground and retracted her landing gear. Everyone watched nervously as the plane they had bolted, soldered and riveted together gained altitude. Suddenly, smoke billowed from the number three engine. A collective gasp spread over the crowd. The YB-29's pilot made an flat, easy turn and slowly brought the plane around. As he taxied to the ramp area, the ground crew was already in motion. In short order, the crew discovered a blown rocker-box gasket was dumping oil onto the manifold. Notorious for throwing oil, the Curtis-Wright engines had spawned a standing quip: "When it's not throwing oil, worry."

Overnight the crew replaced the gasket. When the plane was airborne again, Caron flew right scanner position in the waist, calling the flap settings and keeping an eye on the temperamental engines. At the low altitudes of this test flight, there would be no need to pressurize the cabins and the interior hatches could remain open. From his position, he could see past the hatch, straight through to the tail, which shimmied with the synchronous vibration of the engine. Someone had forgotten to lock the tail gun sight, and it swung aggressively back and forth against the stop.

"I'm going back to lock the gun sight before it beats itself to death," Caron said to the left scanner. "Keep an eye on my engines." He unplugged his headset and crawled back to the tail. When he had latched the sight, he looked out over the countryside. The view from the tail was spectacular. He sat on the small folding seat and rode it out from a vantage point he'd never before experienced. Nor had anyone else.

All of a sudden he felt the thump as the landing gear locked down. Then the flaps came down, the nose went up and the tail started shaking like the fringe on a flapper.

Caron struggled to plug in his headset. "What the hell is going on?" his vocal chords yodeling the choked words.

"Who's that?" the pilot asked.

"Corporal Caron in the tail, Colonel."

"What the hell are you doing in the tail? Get the hell out of there, *now!* We're pulling full stalls."

Big "A" to Little "a"

Full "bird" colonels checked out in the B-29s as they came off the line. It took up to twenty-seven weeks to produce a pilot, fifteen to complete navigator's training and twelve to turn out a gunner. Each individual training component had to be mastered before a crew could be assembled. Once together, the crew trained on the B-29 itself, fine-tuning the intricacies of the Superfortress as well as their responses to her complex demands. Because of her long-range flying capability, the optimistic goal had been to train two crews for each plane.

A crewman either had the right stuff or he didn't. When a general discovered that two of the flight engineers trained for one of the planes were young privates, he objected vehemently. Only officers should be given that kind of responsibility, the general argued. Immediately, the two top-notch flight engineers were hustled off to the 58th Bomb Wing headquarters in Salina, Kansas, given a commission as flight officers and hustled back to Wichita.

A steady stream of check rides separated the wheat from the chaff. Most of the pilots whom intensive training hadn't scattered to the wind were first-rate flyers. In their capable hands the powerful B-29 was stretched to her limits.

During these flights, Caron rode the waist as scanner. All gun turrets remained idle. The armament crew was too busy getting the bugs out of them on the ground. Miles and miles of wiring harnesses ran from the pressurized section to an unpressurized section and back to the turrets. All electrical connections were created with Amphenol plugs. Each male was encoded with a capital or lower case letter (A-Z with exception of O, Q and I). Each female receiving socket was encoded with a corresponding letter. Male pin "A" fit into female socket "A." Or, "a" into "a."

Hour after hour, women assembly-line workers performed the tedious task of wiring and coding this elaborate electrical network, referring to color-coded mock-up boards or hefty service manuals. Occasionally a capital "A" was accidentally wired to lower case "a." When a turret malfunctioned, the crew communicated the problem with the cryptic diagnosis: "big 'A' to a little 'a.' " When an "E" met an "F" or an "H" met an "A," the mis-wired turret acted as though poltergeists were at the controls. It spun wildly or lurched up and down. Then the sleuthing began. Again and again, the armament team disassembled and resoldered the harnesses. As important as the troubleshooting was on the factory floor, it was secondary to teaching civilian workers checks and double checks for accurate installation.

When a plane was near completion, a ground crewman towed it to the firing butt, an embankment where turret guns were tested. If one didn't fire, the reason was usually a big "A" to little "a."

One day a civilian in the top turret position had been ordered to keep his hands off the guns until he received clearance to do otherwise. Caron climbed down the forward hatch and walked along the side of the airplane directly under the upper forward turret to inspect a malfunction. Suddenly, the impatient civilian released a burst of gunfire. The muzzle blast from the twin fifties slammed Caron against the airplane. Lightning bolts rumbled in his skull. When his hearing gradually returned the next day, he was relieved the injury hadn't caused permanent deafness.

Throughout summer 1943, crews delivered Superfortresses to four B-29 bases in Kansas: Pratt, Great Bend, Walker and Salina, which was headquarters. One base was nearly a carbon copy of the next: three runways; four hangars for the four squadrons all in line on the ramp; at the end, a depot hangar; barracks always in the same positions.

The pilot, with Caron flying scanner, had just delivered a plane to Pratt. Exactly fifty miles north lay Great Bend, looking for all the world like an identical twin, except its chapel was in a slightly different location. Unexpectedly, another B-29 dropped into Pratt's flight pattern. The crew on Caron's plane were puzzled. Why was a second B-29 being delivered to Pratt so soon? They watched as it taxied in and parked alongside its sister.

"What in hell are you doing here?" Kenneth Eidness, scrambling out of the waist hatch, asked Caron.

"I'll ask *you* the same thing," Caron said. "This is Pratt."

"No, this is Great Bend," he insisted. "I heard the tower describe the field and give us landing instructions."

The confusion was easily cleared up. The B-29 and its red-faced crew took off and landed where it was supposed to. The incident was one of many benign contretemps.

General Saunders of the 58th Bomb Wing at Pratt arrived on the flight line to check out the new B-29, while Caron conducted a turret orientation with members of the field crew. The general held his head so formally erect and thrust his chin so far forward that he appeared to look down on everyone.

He listened unanimated as Caron demonstrated harmonizing the turrets, leveling them so that their rotation was perfectly horizontal. Satisfied after a few minutes' observation that the complex B-29's armament specialist knew what he was doing, the general clicked his heels on the pavement with affected pageantry and paraded back to his staff car.

Engine mechanics wrenched off fittings and plugs during the day, which meant that trouble-shooting the turrets had to be done at night. Then, the huge silver bird was raised, supported at four jack points, two under each wing, one each under the nose and tail. Armament men inserted the jacks on the jack pads, careful to set them level and square.

Inside the propped-up plane, Caron showed the civilians how to adjust the turret ring so that it would rotate horizontally with the framework of the aircraft.

Suddenly, a loud pop echoed through the cavelike waist compartment. Then another.

Oh, my god, we're slipping off the jack pads. Visions of a half-million dollar airplane—that had never seen direct light of the sun—crinkling like foil right there in the hangar flashed before him. Then he heard a series of loud metallic raps and crunches. *How many lifetimes can they dock my pay?*

Pop. Ping. Crunch. Quickly, he scrambled out of the hatch. The jack pads were in place. The plane wasn't moving. Caron could breathe again. As he scanned the fuselage, lustrous in the brightness of the gigantic chamber, he realized what was happening. From seemingly everywhere, giant Kansas hard-shell beetles were swarming in the hangar. At first a few, then hundreds immolated themselves on the monstrous, sizzling ceiling lights. The crisped carcasses of the invading air force rained like flak onto the B-29's aluminum skin.

Late in August, the work at Boeing done, Caron received orders for Great Bend. In no time, the fourteen armament crewmen had packed their few belongings and loaded the gear into the back of a six-by-six. What little Midwest breeze stirred in the dripping heat fanned through the open windows onto the driver and his front-seat companion. The men in the enclosed rear swam in their own sweat and inhaled exhaust fumes and road dust throughout the one-hundred-mile journey.

At the 676th Squadron of the 444th Bomb Group, Caron found he had been assigned to one of the flight crews. Immediately, they got to work. Valuable air time concentrated on checking out much-needed pilots. Ground time enabled armament men to correct turret malfunctions.

After lights out, Caron often lay in his bunk and wondered how much longer he could avoid a flight physical and the accompanying eye exam. As a trouble-shooter with protracted assignments off base, he had been able to avert the dreaded procedure. Not since his enlistment had his vision been an issue. He wasn't ready for some doctor who knew nothing about his job to insist he couldn't do it. Following directions in the book, he had continued the daily exercises. They had strengthened his eye muscles and enhanced his focusing ability. He guessed vision in his right eye had improved to 20/30.

In Wichita he had purchased a pair of prescription sun goggles and often flew with them. They brought clearly into focus the many Kansas towns, which had taken on a distinct aerial personality of their own. He could recognize this one by the relationship of its swimming pool to its town hall, or another by its church in relationship to its grain elevator. Even navigators began to rely on the landmarks. Nevertheless, the bottom line was that without the glasses, his vision was less than perfect. The inevitable eye exam would prove it.

When the test was finally scheduled, he made a snap decision that surprised him. The night before the scheduled exam, he sneaked into the flight surgeon's office. Standing in front of the black and white chart, he repeated the sequence of increasingly smaller letters over and over until he could relate them by heart. The test would be pass or scrub. There would be no second chances. The high flyer had to make sure he wouldn't be grounded.

Four weeks later, Caron received orders to report to the 58th Bomb Wing at Marietta, Georgia, for "two weeks temporary duty for accelerated service testing of the B-29s." Duty near Atlanta sounded like a welcome change of scenery. He knew little of the South, except that Atlanta was a charming city with plenty of good restaurants, gardens, fine mansions, and, of course, sweet Southern belles with syrupy voices.

Fresh from their Lockheed assembly plant outside of Marietta, more B-29s were being shuttled to bases for testing. Caron assumed he would accompany them to spot and correct problems once at their new bases. Quartermaster issued him flying gear, including a luxurious sheepskin-lined leather flight suit and a parachute. The preparations made what was to come a surprise. Operations handed him a change of orders. He would be shipping out immediately to Eglin Air Force Base in Florida to join the B-29 Accelerated Services Testing Group. And he was to report to Colonel Paul W. Tibbets.

Caron questioned the sanity of hitching a ride to Florida in a plane that wheezed and rattled like the creaky, bag of bones DC-2. It fluttered through the air like a pregnant pelican with lunch in its gular pouch.

"Colonel Tibbets? You'll find him down on the flight line where the XB-29 is parked," said the boyish EM, pointing at a beige speck some distance away.

The beige speck grew larger and turned into a medium-height and build officer in suntans, his sleeves rolled up, collar unbuttoned.

"Colonel Tibbets, Corporal Caron reporting, sir."

The handsome officer wheeled and returned his new armament man's salute. Without pause, he stretched out his hand. His blue eyes flashed. "Welcome to the group," he said.

Sixteen years earlier, Paul Warfield Tibbets, Jr., climbed into the cockpit of a bi-plane. As bombardier, he was conscientious to execute the drop precisely on target. One by one, he launched his arsenal of rectangular projectiles. Caught in the plane's prop-wash, the objects on their tiny parachutes dispersed in all directions. The bombardier had rained Baby Ruth candy bars on an unsuspecting Miami. At that exhilarating moment, the thirteen-year-old felt shivers up his spine. Someday he was going to be a pilot.

The decision to walk away from medical school rocked his father. Enola Gay Tibbets, the red-haired daughter of an Iowa farmer, understood. Flying was in her son's blood. She saw it in his eyes after that first flight in Miami. She wasn't fearful of losing him. No matter where the Army Air Forces took him, he would come back to her. "Dress neatly and always tell the truth," she coached. "You'll be just fine."

And he was. In England, leading the first American B-17 daylight raid on Hitler's occupied Europe, venturing over North Africa, Enola Gay's calm assuredness and fiery tenacity were always with him in the cockpit.

Tibbets had worn the B-17 like a glove. Much like the XB-29s now parked on the hardstand at Eglin, the Fortress had been rushed from production lines with her paint barely dry. Never intended as a heavy bomber, the B-17 had been labeled "an offensive strategic weapon." In operation, she became dependent upon a support network provided by her sister aircraft. Furthermore, in the air she was altogether too vulnerable to nature's tempests. Her pilots knew her as a faded rose.

One of the best of her pilots, Tibbets was now concentrating his attention on the virtues and vices of the B-29. He was eager to prove that she could fly higher, faster and farther than any plane before her. Her innovations read like a Christmas wish list. A sophisticated firing system. Pneumatic bomb-bay doors that opened in one second and closed in three. Pressurized compartments. Enormous bomb capacity. Tricycle landing gear. But the technology was not without price. At a too steep bank or sudden movement of the controls, she threatened to stall. While the B-29 operated well at low altitude, it was difficult to control in the thin air of the troposphere. That made her a loner, unwilling to submit to tight formations that had been the forte of the B-17. Was it a character flaw that could be dealt with? Loners could be losers in the game of war.

If such non-conformity would make her a sitting duck for enemy fighters, Tibbets intended to find out. He pitted the B-29 against a captured enemy Zero, the deadly Mitsubishi A6M Reisen, a German Focke-Wulf FW-190, even a Messerschmidtt Me109 and the Republic P-47 Thunderbolt. Clumsy and heavy in appearance, the B-29 nevertheless out-maneuvered them at lower altitudes. At thirty-two thousand feet, she was out of harm's way. Flak couldn't touch her.

The bold test pilot's accomplishments impressed Caron less than his quiet self-assurance. He had no need to hang achievements on himself like a badge. As Tibbets introduced Caron to the crew chief and flight engineer, as well as the mechanics and four armament specialists who had already joined the Eglin group, the Colonel's manner was casual, his smile warm and sincere. The armament men, brought in from the Kansas B-29 bases Caron had come to know well, were cast in the Lowry Field mold, and he had worked beside a number of them at Boeing.

At one end of the base, Eglin families clustered in wooden apartment buildings. The WACs and civilian women employed by the maintenance depot quartered in separate barracks at the other end. The long, white clapboard buildings of the WAC detachment paralleled the north-south runway. At shift change, waves of female pedestrians gathered at the walkway and waited for incoming planes to land.

Just as the afternoon shift let out, twenty-six-year-old Captain Robert A. Lewis was bringing in one of the YB-29s that had recently been delivered to Eglin. Caron was flying nose, watching from the bombardier's seat rather than his usual scanner position. To get Lewis' attention, he reached behind him and knocked on the instrument panel, then pointed down to the ocean of women, whose faces turned skyward like whitecaps on breakers. Lewis grinned boyishly. Tipping one wing slightly, then the other, back and forth, he waved to them on the approach. The B-29 was still not horizontal when its landing gear met runway. The left wheel hit hard, and the fifty-ton plane bounced back and forth from one wheel to the other before it finally stopped rocking. Lewis had made an impression. Only it wasn't the one he intended.

Recognition and women were two things the Captain couldn't do without. Often, he got one from the other. Usually, there was plenty of both. At the controls, the first-rate test pilot's instincts took over, and he rarely made a bad call. His mind and body, peaked with adrenaline, performed flawlessly at thirty thousand feet. The closer he came to the ground, the more his testosterone took over. Tibbets worried that his daredevil stunts could threaten the welfare of his crew. If he was concerned about endangering them, it didn't show. He executed every maneuver confident that he knew his plane's limits and his own. Every man in his crew was important, none more than the next.

For Lewis, Charles Lindbergh's request to fly with him on a test run over the Gulf was a dream come true. Lindbergh observed how the B-29 responded to Lewis' touch. The famous aviator had a sixth sense about airplanes. And this time, it told him to caution his hero-worshipper about the tight turns he casually executed.

"Better dive and pick up that extra air speed first, or you'll stall," Lindbergh warned. Carelessness, mishandling, ignoring trim and attitude, could put the B-29 into an uncontrollable, deadly spin, he lectured Lewis.

Back at base, Caron was climbing out of the hatch when the crew chief informed him that they had a passenger up front during the test run.

"Yeah? Who?"

"Charles Lindbergh."

Caron had flown a fuselage-length from his boyhood idol. He wished he had known. But he wasn't one to brood over things that might have been.

Instead, he made a niche for himself among the new pilots, mechanics and armament men that augmented Tibbets' test crew. All day they flew—sometimes as many as three missions, landing only long enough to refuel and load more ammo. Half the night they worked on airplanes.

Tibbets assigned Caron the task of evaluating the performance of the General Electric firing systems of the YB-29—which he knew as intimately as a surgeon knows gall bladders—against the Sperry remote-controlled hydraulic system of the XB-29—of which he knew nothing. In fact, few people did, other than the Sperry technical representative.

On their first meeting, the representative was waiting for Caron at the flight line, manual in hand. Caron had given the system a quick, once-over the day Tibbets brought one of the XB-29s into Wichita. He recalled that the turrets were fired from a console in the forward section of the plane, near the navigator's desk. A gunner sat on a bicycle seat and peered through a periscope that raised and lowered. He actuated the turrets to follow the sight by rotating control handles. The lighted reticles in the sight had to align with the target. The gunner had to identify the target—gunners had to memorize the shapes and vital statistics of all enemy fighters—and then dial the plane's wingspan into the computer. Electronically, it calculated air speed, altitude and range and indicated how much to elevate the guns to compensate for the fall of the shell. If the gunner saw the target broadside, determining wing span was fairly simple. But a fighter was not likely to be so cooperative. The gunner had to make quick mental trigonometric calculations to adjust for variations in angle before he could dial in the reading.

In the waist another gunner sat at a second periscope sight from which he could coordinate the firing of either both upper or both lower turrets. The forward and waist gunners could share the turrets. To compensate for the lack of orientation on the target, additional linked sights had to be added. The bombardier in the nose had one, and the two waist gunners on the blisters had spotting sights. Once the ring and bead of their sights were on the target, the operator at the console had a view of it as well. He could then take over and track the target. The system had one major flaw. The periscope had a blind spot.

The tail turret was controlled by the waist gunner. That presented a problem. If a target approached dead center from the tail, spotters at the waist blisters would be unable to see him.

A target that could be picked up was at the mercy of two highly effective .50 caliber tail guns, which could fire seven-hundred rounds a minute, extracting shells from a belt and was forward into battery position, ready to fire. Unfortunately, as Caron later learned, the XB-29's 20 mm Swedish-designed cannon was dangerous and often malfunctioned. The cannon bolt was secured by a sear, a beveled plate that held it back out of battery. Once the bolt was shifted forward into battery, however, a shell immediately discharged.

On one test flight, its shell jammed and couldn't be released while in the air. When the plane landed, Caron warned the Sperry technical representative of the live round in the 20 mm gun and said he'd go into the turret and clear it. The representative insisted that he be the one to take care of it. Caron acquiesced and climbed down.

Behind the plane with the jammed shell, two men stood on the wing of a B-17, a dozen feet apart, holding a refueling hose. Beyond them was a twin-tail B-25 and, off the ramp farther in the distance, a storage shack.

The Sperry representative entered the tail, and instead of elevating the gun, as was standard safety procedure when one retained live ammunition, he eased himself into the turret. As he did so, his sleeve caught on the firing mechanism. Unexpectedly, the jammed shell discharged.

The two men refueling the B-17 dropped flat on their respective wings. Everyone else within earshot hit the dirt. When the excitement died down, Caron inserted a bore sight tool into the previously jammed gun to determine where the shell had hit. He focused the right-angle eyepiece and was amazed that the cross hairs centered between the two men on the B-17 wing nearby. The shell had whizzed past them, barely missing one of the vertical stabilizers of the B-25. Miraculously, it didn't hit the mechanic who had been in front of a storage shack well beyond the flight line. Caron jumped in a jeep and found the mechanic still shaking, the shell in the dirt not far from his feet.

The crew dubbed the close call its "Ramp Mission."

There were more differences between the pre-production XB-29 and YB-29 models than their armament systems. The XBs were designed with a three-bladed propeller. The YBs experimented with a four-bladed prop with self-starters on the engines. Caron hated start-up of the XB-29, which required engaging a heavy drill at the starter's outboard side location, several feet behind the prop and just forward of the exhaust stacks, and connecting it to a push-cart power unit. Just in case something went wrong, the crew stood by with fire extinguishers.

Its inboard engines were low enough for Caron to wield the heavy drill standing firmly footed. He inserted the drill and cranked the engines until the awesome propeller suddenly spun to life, revolving at eight hundred to one thousand rpm. In protest, the exhaust stack belched black smoke.

The XB-29's outboard engines were mounted higher. In order to crank them, Caron stood on tiptoe, wobbling unsteadily as he applied pressure to the starter. The tension and fear left him light-headed. He had visions of losing his balance...falling headfirst into those enormous blades.

Although the YB was more responsive and reliable than the XB, something in its turbo chargers, turrets, or harnesses was inevitably going haywire. The crew blamed gremlins who stole into the hangar at night for planting the recurring problems in their planes. Caron enjoyed solving problems on both models when his engineering skills could be involved. One such opportunity arose when armament specialists recognized that a harmonization system was needed to synchronize the various turret sights. Caron drew up a design and procedure for the synchronization, and another hurdle in the fine-tuning of the prototypes had been jumped. Other obstructions included blown vacuum tubes in the control boxes and faulty connections in the firing mechanism. The latter were usually traced to the Amphenol plugs. Often, the female connector had spread enough that it would lose contact with the male pin. It was one of the few problems that offered a little comic relief.

In many instances, in order for a plane to be ready for a morning test flight, repairs had to drag on throughout the night. Test flights on the two preproduction models served several purposes. As pilots and co-pilots were being checked out, they were given time to practice air and ground maneuvers. At the same time, performance of the engines and armament was evaluated and recommendations made for their modification.

Many of the flights cruised out over the open water of the Gulf of Mexico. One clear afternoon, Tibbets effortlessly skimmed the glassy surface like a giant white ibis, so close that the plane's shadow on the sparkling water was nearly identical in size to the B-29 itself. Caron, riding in the tail, called him on the intercom.

"Colonel this fun. I'm dangling my feet in the water."

"Then you better get them out, Sergeant. We need to pick up some speed."

Tibbets never lost control of his plane and seldom lost his temper. There were exceptions. Al Wheeler and Caron were fueling the YB-29, Wheeler on the left wing, Caron on the right. Caron clipped the static lines to the fuel hose to avoid a spark that could ignite the flowing gas, then topped off the tanks. As Tibbets headed out over the unruffled Gulf, Caron rode scanner and watched the engine. He blinked to refocus more clearly. There was the red semicircle of the filler cap, protruding from the wing.

"Colonel Tibbets, sir," he called to the pilot. "the inboard fuel cap is unlatched and standing up. It looks like it's vibrating loose."

"Keep your eye on it."

All of a sudden, the cap came off and dangled at the end of its twelve-inch chain, bouncing hard on the wing.

"Colonel, fuel is siphoning out."

With the turbo stack fires that had plagued the test flights, Tibbets could take no chances.

"We're going in," was all he said, then reported to the tower.

Fire engines, crash trucks and meat wagons—the name flight crews gave to ambulances—followed the B-29 down the runway.

"God dammit, Sergeant," unleashed Tibbets once his scanner was on the hardstand. "Your screw-up damned near got us all killed. Don't you *ever* forget to lock those caps again."

"Colonel," Wheeler piped up. "It wasn't Bob who fueled that side. It was me."

For an icy second, Tibbets stared at both men with penetrating blue eyes. Without another word, he walked away.

The open water of the Gulf gave gunners the practice using the remote-controlled firing system. They fired different colored ammunition at a towed sleeve target and kept track of their scores. The Goliath who always scored highest would never use his good aim at an enemy, however. He was too big and burly ever to fly in combat and had been relegated to join the ground crew.

Inside their streamlined, low-profile blisters, guns got hot fast. The built-up heat would "cook off" any shell left in battery and fire it at random. Cook-offs were unpredictable and potentially lethal. Firing the guns in relatively short bursts, pausing for a few seconds and firing again, helped to prevent overheating. Prolonged firing could actually burn out a barrel.

Thinking the target shooting looked like child's play, one test pilot had asked Caron, who had been shooting from the bombardier's position, to trade places and let him take aim. Caron explained the necessity of pausing after firing a few rounds. "No problem," the pilot assured him. Nevertheless, he immediately ignored the advice and leaned on the gun sight's firing button. Once he hit the target sleeve, he crawled back to his pilot's seat.

The gun's automatic stowing system had been designed so that once the dead-man's switch was released, the upper turrets lowered, lower turrets rose, and both stowed facing aft. On this day, just as the upper turret passed the number one engine, both guns cooked off in one thunderous explosion. One shell shot through the propeller arc. But the propeller still turned.

"I guess it missed," the pilot said, and landed the plane as usual.

"Hey, you guys got a bullet hole in your wing," announced an astonished ground crewman, pointing to a hole where the engine cell faired into the leading edge of the wing. The shell had buried itself in the main wing spar and cracked it. The plane was grounded. The pilot wasn't.

Before long, it became common knowledge that another officer at a Kansas base who had also wanted to test his aim fired the guns with a vengeance—until they jammed. As the overheated guns stowed facing aft, a sudden cook-off sent shells through the vertical dorsal fin and sheared off the tail gunner's head.

The incidents shook the military, and safety modifications were immediately introduced at the assembly plant. Planes in the field installed an armor plate under the skin in the dorsal fin at forty-five degrees to deflect any bullet that might be headed toward the tail gunner's compartment.

Working the kinks out of new planes was a trial and error process. At high altitudes, blisters for the waist gunners sometimes blew out, sucking unbelted scanners into the blue with them. One hapless scanner had enough presence of mind to free-fall until he reached an altitude that allowed him to deploy his chute. From then on, modification centers and the factory mounted blisters virtually blow-out proof with double the number of bolts.

Among ground and flight crews, it had become a standing joke. The XB-29 rarely returned from a test flight with all four engines running. The oil-slinging Wright-Cyclone engines required inordinate maintenance time. Armament men teamed with the mechanics whenever necessary to get them up and running. Cleanup meant stripping the protective metal cowlings from engine fronts and digging elbow deep into the tedious, greasy job.

Caron wasn't surprised to find his old friend Frank LaVista had taken a position at the factory inspecting the Wright reciprocating engines. And Caron wasn't surprised to hear LaVista's frustration with management's directive to rush them through inspection regardless of shortcomings. Pressed by military contracts with impossible deadlines, management was forced to move the engines out and let mechanics and technicians correct their problems in the field.

The XB-29's "Mickey Mouse" hydraulic system still turned the inside of the plane into a skating rink, as those who worked on them at Boeing had discovered. Then there was that inexplicable gunner periscope that defied logic. All tried the crews' patience.

In November 1943, the XB-29 Sperry computer went on the fritz. When the tech rep couldn't fix it, he conceded. It had to go back to the factory on Long Island. The crew borrowed one of the early B-26 twin-engine bombers with the too-short wing span that looked like it should have been melted into scrap. B-26s earned their reputation as "widow-makers" during training. Ironically, because the widow-makers' landing characteristics were so similar to that of the B-29s, pilots cut their teeth on them instead.

For aircraft commander Captain Lewis, whose parents lived in New Jersey, and his co-pilot and tail gunner, both from New York, the computer going on the blink was a good excuse to visit family. The tech rep came along.

By the time Captain Lewis brought the widow-maker down gently at Mitchell Field on Long Island, the sun had set. Off in the distance, New York sparkled like a crown of jewels.

The tech rep arranged for the factory to work on the computer overnight, and Caron called his parents from a pay phone not five miles from home. George and his son dropped Lewis off at the train station in Lynbrook. The next morning, when his train arrived on time, Caron and his parents were there to meet him. Hitching a ride on the return flight to Florida was a young sailor home on leave.

"Captain, how about flying below limits over my house?" Caron asked. The happy-go-lucky pilot brought the B-26 into a pattern of his own that circled the Caron back yard and the two people waving both arms at them. He tipped one wing, then the other and throttled for the climb.

The sailor riding in the waist with Caron was used to rough weather. But the turbulence that they encountered on this late fall flight south was more than they expected. "Put your chutes on," Lewis called back to the jostled pair. Caron fastened the harness on the sailor and coached him on how jump and when to pull the ripcord. Lewis dodged in and out of storms all the way to Birmingham, Alabama, where he requested landing instructions for a fuel stop. With a landing speed of one hundred thirty-five miles per hour, and an approach to a shorter-than-comfort-giving runway between two small mountains, the hot plane seemed determined to live up to its reputation.

"Let me take it in," offered the co-pilot, who had logged nearly as many test-flight hours as the aircraft commander.

"It's all yours," said the exhausted Lewis, hands in the air.

Through the combined efforts of the armament crew and the tech rep, the Sperry computer was reinstalled. It worked. But that was about all the crew had to say for it.

Machine gun ammunition was held together in a link roughly in the form of a figure three. As a shell was fired, the empty link was ejected out the other side of the gun. The guns on the upper turrets ejected links into a small, simple chute that dropped them into the bottom of the unpressurized gun well within the plane. Empty links from the lower and tail turrets, however, were ejected in the chute that sent them overboard. Links were frequently jamming in the upper turret chute at a curve intended to deflect them downward into the well. Once the chute was jammed, the gun couldn't take another round and stopped firing. A jammed gun was no defense in combat.

Its design puzzled Caron. He drafted some sketches and walked them to the depot. "Ought to work," Tibbets said and sent him to the sheet-metal shop foreman to make up the new chutes. When they cured the jamming problem, Caron shot his plans to the factory. The link-chute design was incorporated in successive modifications.

Out over the Gulf, from his right blister position, Caron watched the gull-wing Vought Corsair fighter move in closer.

"Colonel, there's an F4U at four o'clock, and he's curious."

"Keep your eye on him," Tibbets said.

"He can't figure us out and he's moving in for a better look."

"If he gets too close to our prop wash, he'll be in trouble."

"He's already pretty damned close."

"OK, Bob, I'll change course.

"Don't bother, Colonel. I'll take care of it."

There was no ammunition on board. The flight had been a routine engine test. Nevertheless, Caron turned on the power to the two lower turrets and aimed his sight and empty guns at the fighter. Its pilot could clearly see the two .50 caliber gun turrets converge on him. In a flash, he made a tight wing over and disappeared in the distance.

"He's gone Colonel."

"What'd you do, Bob? Scare him away?"

"You might say so, Colonel."

Although the crews worked day and night, their pay was always two or three months behind. Even if money burned a hole in their pockets, there was little time and only a few places to spend it.

Pensacola lay fifty miles west of Eglin and too far for exploring with only a few hours off. Just a few miles south of the base, however, the small fishing villages of Niceville and Valparaisio offered several quaint grocery stores and a couple popular bars. What appealed most to Caron was that the towns gazed out onto the Choctawhatchee Bay and beaches, where swimmers, strollers and daydreamers escaped from life or ran eagerly toward it, sought solitude or quiet company.

Juanita Louise wasn't looking for solitude. She was happy to befriend a New Yorker with whom she could vicariously walk up and down Fifth Avenue, or imagine the glitter of Manhattan. Alabama born, Juanita had moved in with her fisherman brother. When they weren't dancing on base, Bob would take the bus to Niceville, and they would sit for hours on the porch, smooching in between her seemingly endless stream of questions. When he was all storied out, Juanita, still giddy with the aura of Times Square, unconsciously pushed the swing with her toes, and he held her ever more tightly.

"Sergeant Caron, sir. You wanted to see me?"

"You didn't get that girl at the depot...what's her name?...Juanita Louise...in trouble did you?" Tibbets shot from over the paper he held in his hand.

"No, sir. I took her to several dances, and I've visited with her at her brother's house. We always stayed out on the porch swing..."

"Her boss is mad as hell. She's missed some days at work, and he thinks she's pregnant."

"That's highly unlikely, Colonel. And if she is, it isn't...."

"OK, OK, Bob. Just be careful."

A few Sundays later, Juanita invited Bob to join her for a "real Southern fish fry" on a remote section of beach. Her brother herded them into the back of his battered pick-up, and they bounced and tumbled down the miles of dirt road. The truck swerved right, then left, dodging potholes, pitching Bob and Juanita from one side of the pick-up bed to the other. Abruptly, the driver veered off to the weedy shoulder and twenty yards later pulled back onto the road. Undisturbed by the presence of a vehicle in its path, a bull consummated his procreative act with a nonchalant cow. Juanita flushed at the bucolic scene and was grateful when the truck thumped over another hill and dipped out of sight.

Far from the choking, sandy roads of Egypt, the palatial luxury that is Cairo welcomed Churchill, Chiang Kai-shek and the President of the United States. When on December 1, 1943, the triad had agreed upon and signed the Pacific Charter, they once again broached other pressing matters. Taking the defense against Japan, China was preparing bases to receive America's B-29 bombers.

Engine by engine, turret by turret, the B-29s were radically improving. Still, modification centers were handling planes like they were flipping burgers on a grill. Nothing came off medium or well done. Crews shuttled back and forth between Eglin and the mod centers revising manuals, running fingers over gaskets, relubricating seals, double-bolting weak spots.

No one ever doubted that Tibbets appreciated the hard work and detail. He was conscientious about relieving their stress with meaningful perks. Caron was promoted to staff sergeant, and his pay increased to ninety-six dollars per month, plus fifty percent flight pay. There were short breathers on the front or back of trips to mod centers, an excuse to RON, "remain overnight," with seven dollars per diem. Two at a time, crew members hopped northbound flights and jumped off in Atlanta for a night or two on the town.

A few days before the holiday, Tibbets called the crew together on the flight line. "We're all going to pile in a plane and spend Christmas in Atlanta," he announced. Caron wrote the young woman whom he had met one weekend there that he would be delighted to meet her family.

General K. B. Wolfe, commander of the 58th Bomb Wing, steamed when he heard the Colonel's plans. *Did Tibbets' men think this was a picnic? Christmas or not, there was a war going on!*

The officers and enlisted men were at evening chow when the crew chief raced in breathless.

"Hurry up and get into Class-A uniforms, pack your shaving kits...*we're going to Atlanta!*"

With food left on their trays, the men dashed for the barracks. To hell with a shower, Caron thought, and sped off to be first at the flight line. Tibbets was standing some distance from the tail of the YB-29, puffing peacefully, methodically on his pipe.

"What's up, Colonel?"

"We've got to go to the mod center in Marietta for repairs, and I've got the General's OK."

"What repairs?"

He pointed to the fabric in the rudder. There was a small tear. Caron figured a good piece of tape could have patched it in thirty seconds.

"You're not afraid to fly with me with that tear are you?"

"Colonel, if I get to go to Atlanta for Christmas, I'd fly with you on a carpet."

"That's what I thought." He poked the pipe between his teeth, shoved his hands in his pockets and waited for the crew. Flight crew. Ground crew. Men on holiday were jammed into every inch of floor space. Someone even volunteered for the tail. It was late when they finally stumbled off the elevator on the seventh floor of Atlanta's Wycoff Hotel. There was no per diem for their rooms, but Tibbets heard no complaints. The Deep-South hospitality of Caron's host family on Christmas day was unlike anything he'd ever experienced in New York.

Juanita Louise was sorry, but she couldn't go with Bob to the New Year's Eve party at the NCO Club. She had already called her family in southern Alabama, and they were expecting her. "See if you can get another date," she casually suggested. "Around here? That's a cinch," one of the crewmen assured Caron. He'd ask the WAC he was dating to bring a friend. Partying with a blind date sounded like more fun than sitting in the day room reading and listening to the radio on New Year's Eve.

The two spit-and-polished GIs waited for their WAC dates in the day room. As they entered Caron rose, instantly guessing which of the two was intended for the peewee tail gunner. *What a sweet couple they would make on the dance floor—Gulliver and the Lilliputian.* Self-consciously, the Amazon slouched through one dance, then encouraged Bob to sit out the rest. The evening had not been a disaster after all. They told Air Force tales, laughed over beer and kissed the old year good-bye.

The seventy-billion-dollar budget that the President submitted to Congress on January 10, 1944, was sharply reduced from last year, Roosevelt said in his radio speech. Two months earlier he told the nation that war was draining the United States by two hundred fifty million dollars per day. Opening the sixth War Loan Drive, the government announced that it needed to raise fourteen billion dollars. To Americans, it was a staggering sum beyond everyone's imagining.

On Valentine's Day, the senior statesman to the richest man in Japan spoke with a heavy heart. "I believe Japan has already lost the war," Prince Funimaro Konoye admitted with great sadness to his Emperor. "From the standpoint of maintaining Japan's Imperial system, that which we have most to fear is not defeat itself but, rather, the threat inherent in the possibility that a Communist revolution may accompany defeat." He waited for the Emperor to digest the import of his words. "With defeat staring us in the face, we shall simply be playing into the hands of the Communists if we elect to continue a war wherein there is no prospect of victory."

That their Emperor wished to avoid war did not deter the militarists from implementing their own self-interested plans. The Emperor had warned them that aggression would be met with aggression. But as usual his words were so much poetry in their ears.

How they had reveled in their early conquests. In the first six months of the war, their naval might had pushed Allied forces out of striking range to the Japanese homelands. It took two years for the Allies to position themselves for a full-scale air offensive against their enemy. As her warships sank, so, too, did her peace conspirators' hopes that Japan could command the terms of her surrender.

While the Superfortresses were still in their incubators, General Hap Arnold confidently assured his commanders that the new bombers would win the war. Outlining his "Air Plan for the Defeat of Japan" at the Quadrant Conference in Quebec, he saw victory emerge from south-central China, where strategic positions would stretch Allied reach to the southern Japanese island of Kyushu. As America's commander in chief saw a political advantage to shoring up China's Chiang Kai Shek, Arnold believed he had the makings of a *fait accompli*.

Kansas was waiting for its crocuses to pop up when Tibbets sent a team to Pratt. Trading Florida sunshine for Plains' winter doldrums heightened the urgency of their mission: to ready the 58th Bomb Wing's B-29s for India. General Arnold planned for the first wing to ferry supplies "over the hump" to China. From those bases, Japan would be reachable. He wanted the second wing on Saipan.

Together, the 58th and Tibbets' Trouble-Shooters waged war against time and equipment failure—a knock-down, drag-out that came to be called the Battle of Kansas. Boeing pitched in as well, dispatching its Tibbets' Trouble-Shooter-trained civilian employees, whom they lodged in ordinary barracks.

Despite the lack of creature comforts, the relationship between the two groups had been cemented by a common bond. Sensitive to the needs of brethren caught in a dry state, the Florida crew brought with them liquid relief—quarts of whiskey for which civilian workers gladly exchanged twenty-five dollars.

For civilians and military alike, grueling hours, frigid temperatures and peaked frustrations were incentive to work that much harder. Mechanics fine-tuned engines. Caron and other armament men tweaked the bugs out of turrets. As quickly as the B-29s were pronounced relatively sound, their crews flew them eastward across North Africa to India.

When the location of a firing system malfunction on the last plane defied detection, Tibbets held Caron and two other crewmen over to track it down. For thirty-seven straight hours in the drafty hangar, they worked, ate, took turns grabbing cat naps until, finally, they traced the one bad Amphenol plug—another big "A" to little "a" misconnect—in a curve along the forward pressure bulkhead, snugly wedged against the skin of the airplane. Finding it had been no small miracle. Repairing it had been an even larger one.

Big "A" to little "a." That was the story of the war, Caron said to one of his teammates when at last he held the offending wires in his hands.

Tibbets waited patiently, holding a Lockheed Hudson bomber ready to fly them back to Eglin Field. Giddy with exhilaration and exhaustion after their marathon diagnostic and surgical procedure, the tail gunner, who had eagerly awaited flying back in the nose, darted into the forward compartment. He heard his sleeve rip. A red-hot flash seared his nerves from his elbow to his shoulder as the sharp corner bracket tore into his flesh.

It was long after dark when Tibbets touched down in Wichita to have the gash properly bandaged. By then, the throbbing had sharpened Caron's senses. The first and only casualty of the Battle of Kansas, he had been careless and it cost him. But it had been a valuable lesson.

George Robert Caron's first encounter
with airplane, Brooklyn, N.Y.,
with parents, George and Anne.

Caron and 1940 Chevy, Colorado, 1944.

Katherine "Kay" Younger Caron,
Monarch Pass, 1944.

Kay, Wendover, Utah, 1944.

From left, Lt. Richard McNamara, Lt. Harold Rider, Lt. Stewart Williams, Capt. Lewis, Sgt. Duzenbury, Pfc. Nelson, Sgt. Shumard, S/Sgt. Stiborik, T/Sgt. Caron, at Wendover, Utah, June 1945, before flying No. 82 to Tinian. PHOTO: U.S. ARMY AIR FORCES

North Field looking southeast from 1,000 feet, summer 1945. PHOTO: KEN EIDNESS

From left, Lt. John Wright, Caron, Sgt. Ralph Bellamy (not on crew),
T/Sgt. Herbert Prout, cliff on east Tinian, late August 1945.
PHOTO: KEN EIDNESS

Lalo Point, southern tip of Tinian looking northwest at 1,000 feet;
Tinian Harbor at left.
PHOTO: KEN EIDNESS

Caron in tail of *Enola Gay*, August 1945.

Caron in tail of *Enola Gay* with Circle Arrow insignia.

Cpl. Mel Dahl, right, former next door neighbor, Lynbrook, N.Y., visiting Caron (Dodgers' cap) on Tinian from Saipan. PHOTO: KEN EIDNESS

Enola Gay taxiing to hardstand on North Field on return from Hiroshima, August 6, 1945.
PHOTO: U.S. ARMY AIR FORCES

Enola Gay with Circle Arrow insignia repainted on tail, North Field, Tinian,
late August 1945.
PHOTO: U.S. ARMY AIR FORCES

Caron on Tinian, late August 1945,
mess hall in background.
PHOTO: KEN EIDNESS

Standing: Major Thomas Ferebee, Capt. Theodore Van Kirk, Col. Paul Tibbets, Capt. Robert Lewis. Kneeling, T/Sgt. Caron, S/Sgt. Joseph Stiborik, Sgt. Robert Shumard, Pfc. Richard Nelson, Sgt. Wyatt Duzenbury, August 4, 1945, in front of Operations, Tinian. PHOTO: U.S. ARMY AIR FORCES

Crew of *Enola Gay*, August 6, 1945, prior to takeoff for Hiroshima. Standing: Capt. Van Kirk, navigator; Maj. Ferebee, bombardier; Col. Tibbets, pilot; Capt. Lewis, co-pilot; Lt. Jacob Beser, ECM officer. Kneeling: S/Sgt. Stiborik, radar operator; T/Sgt. Caron, tail gunner; Pfc. Nelson, radio operator; Sgt. Shumard, asst. flight engineer; Sgt. Duzenbury, flight engineer. Not pictured: Navy Capt. William Parsons; Lt. Morris Jeppson. PHOTO: U.S. ARMY AIR FORCES

Leaving hut for Hiroshima mission, from left, T/Sgt. Caron; Sgt. Duzenbury,
S/Sgt. Stiborik, Sgt. Shumard (obscured by flash), Pfc. Nelson.
PHOTO: YANK MAGAZINE

All enlisted men who participated in atomic bombing missions over Hiroshima and Nagasaki in Tinian Quonset on night of unofficial Japanese surrender. Seated from left: Sgt. Abe Spitzer, radio operator; Sgt. Raymond Gallagher, AM gunner; Sgt. Edward Buckley, special instruments operator; S/Sgt. Stiborik; T/Sgt. Caron; Sgt. Duzenbury; Sgt. Shumard; M/Sgt. John Kubarek, flight engineer; S/Sgt. Albert Debart, tail gunner; Cpl. Sidney Bellamy, special instruments; and Pfc. Nelson.
PHOTO: YANK MAGAZINE

Atomic bomb explosion over Hiroshima.
PHOTO: GEORGE CARON, U.S. ARMY AIR FORCES

August 6, 1945, interrogation of *Enola Gay* crew by General Carl Spaatz on return from Hiroshima in debriefing Quonset, Tinian. Caron in baseball cap.
PHOTO: U.S. ARMY AIR FORCES

XB-29 on test flight from Boeing, Seattle, 1942.
PHOTO: U.S. ARMY AIR FORCES

Caron, 1945.

Col. Caron, Colorado Wing, Confederate Air Force.

Caron and, right, Brig. Gen. Paul Tibbets (Ret.), 1994.

Col. Thomas Ferebee (Ret.), 1994.

Maj. Theodore Van Kirk, 1994.

Sgt. Richard Nelson (Ret.), 1994.

Wheat in the Tail Skid

A tribute to the men who were already overseas and those who were to follow came on March 3. No matter that winter held New England in an icy gridlock. Concert-goers turned out en force at Boston's Symphony Hall to see and hear thirty-four-year-old composer Samuel Barber dedicate the performance of his Symphony No. 2 to the Army Air Forces.

Before the trees blossomed, Brooklyn composer Aaron Copeland presented to eager audiences his "Appalachian Spring."

A quite different presentation was made to the Twentieth Bomber Command on April 15. General Arnold had one hundred fifty B-29s ready to leave their nest and fly on their own into spring.

Bectel, MacCone and Parsons modification center in Birmingham, Alabama, was receiving YB-29s straight from the factory and couldn't keep up with their turret malfunctions. Because Caron's dual MOS classified him as both a remote-controlled power turret gunner and mechanic, he was among the eight men Tibbets picked to troubleshoot their problems and train civilians, as he had done at Boeing. Armament officer Captain Robert Morrison was in charge.

Morrison scheduled the men for duty twelve hours a day, seven days a week. So that no one continually worked night shift, they broke into groups of four each, working a twelve-hour day shift for six days, then eighteen hours on the seventh day, bringing the night shift crew to days and the day shift crew to nights. Each trainer was assigned to a civilian trainee. Some of them were women drawn from the hundreds of "Rosie the Riveters." Caron's teammate was a man, and an arrogant one. Waving his paycheck under his instructor's nose, he sneered, "Read it and weep, sucker." It was an inexcusable *faux pas*. Caron looked him squarely in the eyes, shook his head, shoved his hands in his pockets to keep them out of the civilian's face and walked away.

Besides, he much preferred the company of redheads, especially file clerk Mary Tilger. He had just come off the eighteen-hour switch-over shift when he saw her at the Coca-Cola machine. As they were finishing their sodas, Tibbets happened by. Hesitating for a moment, he asked, "Bob, is that all you have to do?" Without waiting for an answer, he disappeared around a corner.

Captain Morrison was more than happy to give Caron a pass to spend the day with Mary's family in their gracious Southern mansion. He sat as their guest of honor at their long, elegant table, sparkling with crystal and silver. For hours after dinner, he entertained their questions about airplanes and flying and war and soldiering.

Morrison had an ulterior motive behind his generous pass. He was captivated with Mary's stunning friend Jinx and was buttering up Caron to arrange a double date.

Caron had just completed another marathon shift on their planned evening out. He raced to the downtown hotel that housed the crew, quickly showered and put on a fresh set of Class-A's. Morrison was waiting with the open-sided command car with the canvas top. Mary and Jinx were ready when their dates arrived. The two women raised their slim skirts and slid one silk-stockinged leg, then the other, into the vehicle's cramped foot space. That command cars were off limits to civilians had been conveniently ignored. The four sped off to the theater to see Frank Capra's *Arsenic and Old Lace* with Cary Grant and Priscilla Lane.

Caron wasn't surprised by Morrison's news later that month when they were finally back at Eglin. "Jinx and I are tying the knot," he crooned. "I want you to be my best man."

The man Britain's new scientific committee—code-named MAUD—wanted to supervise its nuclear research was G. P. Thomson, professor of physics at Imperial College in London. Britain's impressive experimental and developmental gains weren't wasted on Roosevelt. Gleaning a few benefits from a liaison was just what he had in mind when he suggested to Churchill that MAUD and America's Uranium Committee pool their resources in the United States. The idea appealed to Churchill. Such a move would ease Britain's battered finances, plus save the nascent British nuclear capability from Hitler's missiles. Churchill saw Roosevelt's proposal as a marriage made in heaven.

But the honeymoon was short-lived. After only a year under the sheets, the romance had lost much of its luster. America's leading universities were openly having affairs with expatriate physicists, enticing them into the boudoirs of academe. On January 13, 1943, Roosevelt broke the news to Britons (and to Canadians) that their relationship had cooled and needed space. The United States was taking the ring off. At most, Britain and Canada could look forward to an occasional tête-à-tête.

Churchill found the breakup disconcerting and was unwilling to concede divorce. In May 1943, the scowling, jowly statesman stormed into the President's office armed with irrefutable arguments. There was more to consider than Hitler. A flaccid Britain could not check Russian hegemony, he bellowed.

Roosevelt was half afraid that the red-faced prime minister would have a heart attack. Instead, the recomposed Churchill seduced his former partner to reconcile their differences. Both recommitted themselves to a relationship of trust and cooperation. Their counselor would be the Combined Policy Committee. The August 19 secret accord between the two world leaders at the Anglo-American summit conference in Quebec was genuinely unpatronizing and offered a fresh start.

Ironically, the nuclear advancements Britain had newly sown, Russia was about to reap. Soviet spy Klaus Fuchs was on his way from England to the United States. He had been invited to work on the secret atomic bomb project lavished with funds and many of the world's masterminds.

To Tibbets, the B-29's bomb-bay doors opened and closed too slowly. Boeing's Washington engineers had a solution. In April 1944, the Colonel picked Wyatt Duzenbury, who had recently joined the Eglin crew, to be his flight engineer, along with Caron and two other armament men as scanners and put-put operators, and delivered a YB-29 for revamping.

As earlier tests revealed one of the plane's upper turrets was malfunctioning, the armament crew would focus their attention on it while the engineers hyped the doors' hydraulics.

It was past noon when the plane finally took off for the Boeing factory in Renton, Washington, with a scheduled fuel stopover at Wichita. Caron marveled at the intensity of the skies high above Idaho and Montana.

By the time they reached the Cascade Range, thunderstorms crashed and boomed around them. Seattle was badly socked in.

Spying the signal beacon, Tibbets made the down-wind turn for the approach. From his right scanner position, Caron watched. They broke out of the clouds at five hundred feet. For this flight as for most, he had studied the charts and approaches. Test pilot Eddie Allen and his crew had been killed in one of the XB-29s when it crashed into a meat-packing plant on approach to Seattle. Caron knew the plant was off to the right somewhere, less than a quarter of a mile away. When the building came into view, Caron could see that its upper floors were still in shambles. Tibbets lined up with the runway and the B-29's wheels hydroplaned in the torrent of rain.

The new snap-action doors devised by Boeing's engineers became an open and shut case. Speed of operation was critical. Tibbets was pleased. During his stopover at Pratt, Kansas, he planned another test to determine how far the YB-29 could fly at altitude with the heaviest possible gross load. Base armament men loaded the bomb bays with dummy five-hundred-pound bombs. Caron and the two Eglin armament men filled all the ammunition cans. They refilled the fuel tanks until they couldn't squeeze in another drop.

Behind the stick of the overloaded plane, Tibbets began his race with the end of an eighty-five hundred foot runway. Kansas wheat waved its green blur as he built up ground speed. Where oncoming fields rose to meet her, the B-29's overburdened wheels reluctantly left the runway. Caron could breathe again. He swore that back at Eglin, he would find wheat stuck in the tail skid.

At altitude, the navigator charted her course due east to the Atlantic. Out over its pewter waters, they dropped the dummy bombs and headed south to Florida. Tibbets circled Eglin Field until the plane flew on vapor, then, eighteen hours after departure from the base, he set the big bird down as gently as a baby in a crib.

Silvery dolphins in small groups of four and six slipped through the mercuric waters below and glowed radiantly in the sun. Off the tip of the Florida Keys, Tibbets' crew watched the beautiful, spirited mammals in silent wonderment until they were mere glints of sunlight in the distance. The experience of flying over water was always thrilling, but this wasn't a joyride.

Tibbets was about to push the YB-29 to its outer limits. Caron had mounted a new gun heater on the General Electric turrets designed to keep the thin film of oil on their parts from freezing at high altitudes. The pilot climbed to twenty-eight thousand feet...thirty...thirty-four...finally, into the rarefied troposphere at thirty-eight thousand five hundred feet. The crew let out a whoop. They had just set a record for a four-engine plane.

As high-altitude sunlight prismed through the Plexiglas windows, the upper portion of the tail compartment warmed nicely. Sometimes, it even got hot. The icy air that settled in the dark, metal turret cubbyhole didn't stir, however. Heat channeled from a forward section through the four-inch tube to the tail had cooled by the time it reached Caron's feet, and they always felt cold. Rather than dwell on the discomfort during the twelve- to sixteen-hour flights, Caron enjoyed the view and smoked until stubs filled the five-inch round automobile dash ashtrays that Boeing had installed.

Two weeks temporary duty at Eglin Air Force Base stretched to a year and a half. In early June, with the accelerated service testing of the B-29s as complete as the demands of war permitted, Tibbets' group disbanded. Caron and Wheeler received orders for the 73rd Bomb Wing in Pratt as flight and ground instructors.

Caron enjoyed the flying instruction and trouble-shooting with students, but he wasn't much surprised to find standing in front of a classroom uncomfortable and confining. Classes were scheduled three days on, one day off with night flights worked in.

Officers were required to take only basics, but gunners and armament men had to complete the full course. One second lieutenant didn't much like the idea of being taught by a staff sergeant and was venting his discontent when an airplane commander overhead his heated resistance. "Lieutenant, you damned well better listen up and pay close attention to this instructor," the colonel flashed at him. "What he has to say might just save your life in combat."

For nearly two years, Caron had encountered every conceivable firing system malfunction. He would recreate those for his students to track down and correct. With masking tape, he marked relay contacts that he cross-wired to make the turrets do the crazy things he had observed at the factory. Eventually, the students discovered that it was easier to look for Sergeant Caron's tape than to laboriously check connectors within the elaborate wiring harnesses. Caron then had to resolder connections to make them harder to find.

The advertisement in the Sunday Pratt paper for the Harley 45 motorcycle caught Caron's eye. The two-hundred-dollar price was right, and the smaller Harley would fit Caron's short legs. Although he had never ridden a motorcycle, he figured there couldn't be much to it.

The unshaven owner was eager to demonstrate. He whipped onto Highway 50 toward Pratt and disappeared over a long hill. Caron listened to the Harley's small engine rev up as the buzz came toward him. To his surprise, when the bike whizzed past him, it looked like it had no rider. All of a sudden, its rider reappeared, swinging himself onto the seat from the left side where he had hung, balancing close to the pavement.

"I don't advise you to try that," said the owner, admitting he earned his living as a trick rider. The thought had never entered Caron's mind. The only trick he cared about was keeping the thing running. He soon discovered that the bargain bike slung oil up past the buddy seat, leaving a streak along the back of his suntans. When Caron couldn't stop the leaks, he simply rode in coveralls.

The young Anne Westrick found few activities more thrilling than swooshing past the countryside in the buddy seat of a motorcycle, fingers of wind raking through her hair. As motherhood mellowed her thrill-seeking, she began to fear the fast bikes that offered no buffer between unprotected riders and foreign objects.

"I hope you never get one of those dangerous things," she said to her son every time she read about another maimed or killed cyclist.

While many of the enlisted men had motorcycles, without insurance they weren't allowed to bring them on base. Since Caron couldn't afford insurance either, he parked the Harley near the entrance gate where the MPs watched it. And since he didn't trust it not to leave him stranded in Wichita, on his days off he would hitch-hike the eighty miles to town or take the bus.

Which is what he did one hot Sunday in mid July. A friend from base had planned to meet him at the municipal pool. As he waited, Caron swam laps, practicing racing turns against the edge. On one turn he noticed that the feet dangling in the water in front of him were attached to the shapely, long legs of the slim sunbather in a bright blue suit. Casually, the sunbather tossed her long, curly jet hair away from her face, and the glittering water reflected in her dark eyes.

After a few more laps, Caron tired, or so he told himself, and rested his elbows on the rim beside the dangling feet.

"You're splashing me," she said.

"Why don't you get in the water and swim?"

"I don't swim, and I don't like to go in the water. I only like to get my feet wet."

"That's a pretty hairdo."

That was a strange leap, she thought. "Thank you."

"Can I walk through it in my bare feet?"

"What?"

"I'm just kidding. You do have beautiful hair." He raised himself to the edge and sat beside her.

"Where are you stationed?" she asked, noticing his dog tags.

Pratt, where he was an instructor, he explained. She was from Dodge City, she said, but worked for the Internal Revenue Service in Wichita and lived at the YWCA. At a bench in the picnic area, they talked as easily as old friends. When Caron's base mate arrived with his date, the foursome agreed to prolong the day with dinner at a quiet restaurant.

The enamored instructor asked Katherine Marie if he could see her again. "Yes," she said, "but call me Kay."

The dedicated bachelor wasn't thinking about love at first. He simply lost interest in everyone else. Kay became his constant companion at movies, or at the USO and "Y," where he thrilled to the nearness of this trim, well-dressed woman as they danced fox-trots or waltzes. "That Old Black Magic" had them both in its spell and became their song. Sometimes they would leave the music behind and stroll through the deep stillness of the park and make a little magic of their own.

To stretch his time with her, he stayed overnight in Wichita with a couple he had befriended while at Boeing. Spending extra moments with Kay made getting up at dawn to catch the 6 A.M. bus for Pratt worthwhile. Often the two couples double dated at local clubs, bringing their own bottle in a plain brown paper bag that they kept hidden under the table. Neither Kay nor Bob cared much for mixed drinks, but everyone brown-bagged, and it seemed like the thing to do.

Before long, marriage also seemed like the thing to do.

Kay saved her fiancé's life. She had invited him to spend a weekend with her parents at their wheat farm outside Dodge City, eighty miles west of Pratt. Bob looked forward to the occasion and had already obtained an overnight pass when someone accidentally put his name on a flight schedule for that same weekend. Switching flight assignments with the camera gunnery instructor was no problem, said his commanding officer. Bob caught a bus to Dodge City and checked into a little hotel in the heart of town. Kay's parents picked him up in a rusty Chevy, brought him to the farm for supper and drove him back to the hotel that evening. The next day his future in-laws took him on the grand tour of Dodge City, driving him up and down the patchwork of roads that stitched together neighboring farms, then deposited him at the bus stop.

When he arrived at his barracks, the men lolled about in their bunks. The cold silence crushed him. No one played poker or black Jack. No one arm wrestled or told off-color jokes. No one even looked at him.

"What is this, a morgue?" his stultified lightness landing heavily in the hollowness of the long space.

"Yeah, something like that," a tech sergeant scoffed. Then, mellowing, he explained that just outside Dallas the pilot of the plane Caron had been scheduled to fly lost control, and the B-29 went into a spin, then plunged into an oil tank. Everyone was killed. The irony, the sergeant said, was the morning of takeoff, when the charge of quarters came around to wake the enlisted men, the camera gunner who was to switch with Caron refused to go. Eventually, he was ordered to fly. He must have had a sense about that flight, the tech sergeant said.

Nobody had to tell Caron what the men were thinking. It was written in their faces; the unspoken words hung heavily in the eerie silence.

He laid his shaving kit on his bunk and opened the official-looking letter that waited for his return. The paper exaggerated the trembling in his usually steady hands. Briefly, the notice informed him that because of his exceptional organizational skills and the respect he had earned within his unit, he was being given the added responsibility of barracks' chief. In the face of tragedy, the order struck Caron as ironic.

"Unless I completely misjudge the psychology of the Germans," wrote Lord Cherwell during that summer of 1944, "they ought to be making now one or two bombs a month." Churchill's scientific adviser *had* misjudged. Nevertheless, a chain reaction was about to begin. Whether or not it could be stopped, perhaps only the gods would know.

It was a pale, drawn Roosevelt who welcomed Churchill on Monday, September 18. Even the usually invigorating atmosphere of the President's estate in Hyde Park, New York, hadn't revived him fully. Fatigue was to be expected after the rigors of the campaign trail. There was the pressing matter of using the bomb on Japan to discuss with his favorite English statesman. Roosevelt felt good about their progress, although, in an *aide-mémoire*, they agreed that the decision would be considered further as the weapon neared completion.

The St. Louis Cardinals were cheered by their progress, too. They took the 1944 World Series pennant, defeating the St. Louis Browns four games to two. Yet their glory was not in the winning, but in the playing. Both teams had been assembled from over-aged athletes, including some with physical defects. Most able-bodied ballplayers were in the armed forces, serving their country.

Cruising over a sea of white sand, Tibbets paralleled the San Andres Mountains rising to his west. As usual, he had hoped this test flight would reveal another of the B-29's idiosyncrasies that made her so unpredictable. The pilot had been assigned to the Alamogordo airfield to help Dr. E. J. Workman, physics professor at the University of New Mexico at Albuquerque, iron out some of the B-29's wrinkles. Through simulated combat, he could determine the plane's vulnerability to attack. One day, when the fully equipped B-29 he expected to fly wasn't available, Tibbets resorted to a loaner from Grand Island, Nebraska. Stripped of its armament, except for its tail guns, the Superfortress was nearly four tons lighter. Tibbets discovered it maneuvered significantly better and readily climbed four thousand feet higher.

Later, over coffee, he shared the discovery with Workman. Clearly, the stripped-down plane out-performed any he had flown. He recommended more tests.

General Uzal G. Ent had other plans for Tibbets' time. There was no mistaking the urgency in his call to meet at United States Army Second Air Force Headquarters in Colorado Springs on September 1. When Tibbets entered the meeting room, it looked like a summit conference was about to take place. And, indeed, it was. National defense matters of utmost secrecy were about to be laid on the table. The Colonel could not have guessed that the men who now addressed him had selected the twenty-nine-year-old pilot for his biggest test flight yet.

General Ent, commander of the Second Air Force; Lieutenant Colonel Jack Lansdale, security officer for the "Manhattan District;" Naval Officer Captain William Parsons; and a civilian from Columbia University, Dr. Norman Ramsey, had brought Tibbets to Colorado Springs to enlist his help in winning the war. They were ready to show him the ace up the military's sleeve.

Parsons and Ramsey unfolded their fantastic story. Physicists, some recipients of Nobel Prizes, were developing a top-secret weapon, a new type of explosive so powerful that its potential was yet unknown. Even as they spoke, the Manhattan Project—first the "Manhattan District" and "S-1"—was underway at Los Alamos, New Mexico, to create a bomb using atomic fission. Its raw materials, uranium and plutonium, were being produced at enormous plants at Oak Ridge, Tennessee, and Hanford, Washington.

Tibbets got the picture. The Army Air Forces needed a delivery system. His mission would be to organize a combat force capable of dropping a nuclear weapon on a target that was yet to be determined.

To accomplish his task in secrecy, he would need a leak-proof, self-contained organization. Pilots, ordnance and maintenance crews, engineers, technical units, military police, medical specialists, even troop transport aircraft. They would all be made available, General Ent assured him. His organization would operate under a bogus name, the 509th Composite Group. Furthermore, the general already had eyed the competent 393rd Bomb Squadron at Fairmount Air Field in Harvard, Nebraska, as the core for Tibbets' group—if he wanted them. And why wouldn't he? The 393rd's fifteen precision-trained bomber crews were hot to exercise their bravura overseas.

Tibbets could pick the training site. The general offered Great Bend, Kansas, Mountain Home, Idaho, or Wendover, Utah. Tibbets chose Utah—code named Kingman—for its remoteness. It would prove that and more.

The yet-to-be-built bomb was expected to weigh about five tons. Although that was a normal bomb-carrying load for the B-29, the future weapon would assume a pumpkinlike shape and, therefore, require special airplane hoists and modified carrier assembly and release systems.

"By the way," Dr. Ramsey said, "there is one more thing." No one was certain if the shock wave would cause structural damage to the plane and render it uncontrollable. Bomber training would involve more than just dropping the new weapon on target. It meant living to tell about it.

The Colonel's cup ran over. His mind raced. He was already conceiving an intensive training program. The test pilot had arrived in Colorado Springs with one B-29. Now, he was leaving with "Tibbets' Individual Air Force."

"If you run into log jams," General Ent added, "unblock them with the code word 'Silverplate.' "

Exactly one week later, Tibbets set up headquarters at Wendover without silverplating anything. Flight and ground crews for fifteen B-29s from the 393rd Bomb Squadron arrived from Nebraska three days later. The leader of the contrived 509th Composite Group entrusted squadron commander Lieutenant Colonel Tom Classen to take over as his chief deputy, maintaining strict regimens when the helmsman was away.

The skeletal six-footer at the Los Alamos helm, the brilliant theoretician with eyes the color of the Atlantic and just as bottomless, dedicated his thirty-eight years to overcome his imagined shortcomings. He had little cause to feel inadequate. At twelve, J. Robert Oppenheimer had lectured before the New York Mineralogical Club. Then he took Harvard by storm. Nevertheless, the tempest of doubt continued to rage within him. When the in-turned young man finally opened his eyes to the world, he discovered there a need greater than his own. In March 1943, the Federal Bureau of Investigation placed the new member of the communist party under military surveillance. His ardor was short-lived, however. Oppenheimer was soon a man possessed by a most potent force.

The former student at the Los Alamos Ranch School for Boys was about to turn over his old classrooms to the eminent minds of Enrico

Fermi, Edward Teller, Niels Bohr and scores of other scientists impassioned by his eloquent appeal to develop a nuclear weapon before Hitler's scientists did.

Physicists—theoretical and experimental—chemists and metallurgists figured out how to make a bomb. The head of the Ordnance Division, Captain William Parsons, figured out how to make it useful. Groves charged the forty-four-year-old finest gunnery engineer in the Navy with directing developing design for the various bomb components and making them deliverable. At sixteen Parsons had received an appointment to Annapolis. Groves had no doubt that the unflappable, cool-tempered Captain would be a perfect complement to Oppenheimer and a competent stand-in.

Parsons' perfectionism was matched by Tibbets', to whom had been entrusted nearly eighteen hundred military personnel and millions of tax-payers' dollars in hardware.

When Tibbets learned that the Captain would attend to the bomb during the mission like a nurse to her baby, he took liberty with levity.

"Good," he fired at the weapons expert. "Then if anything goes wrong, Captain, I can blame you."

"If anything goes wrong, " Parsons flippantly returned, "neither of us will be around to be blamed."

Site "Y" was as obscure as the Manhattan Project was secret. To Tibbets, the Los Alamos microcosm—home to seven thousand scientists, technicians and their families—was not very "factorylike." He wondered what kind of a fuse would need to be lit under the idealists and theorists if their brainchild was to be delivered on time to win the war. The sense of purpose and urgency that had brought many of them together before they were officially the Manhattan Project now seemed secondary to the quest itself.

Even the magnificent mesa on which they settled had become a storm of gritty debate. Too much of nothingness. Too little to do. Too few amenities. Too few tubs. Too little water to fill them had they been available. Barbed wire and armed guards made the army prefabricated houses with thin walls feel more like a labor camp than a center for scientific exploration and expansiveness of thought. By necessity, self-censorship festered within the sacred circle that longed for open discourse with the scientific world outside its restrictive barbed wire. The ability to tolerate the oppressive isolation and the devilish pace became a matter of moxie. Material inconveniences were small splinters under the quick. Administrator Oppenheimer discovered his expanded role as therapist Oppenheimer. War was hell.

Every man on a battlefield knew that. On D-Day, June 6, 1944, Allied troops had swarmed Omaha, Utah and other Normandy beaches like armies of fiddler crabs. General Dwight D. Eisenhower, who had commanded the one hundred seventy-six thousand troops to begin the liberation of France, was doing everything he could to make war hell for the Axis.

Strategically, the Marianas Islands in the Pacific were the key to caging Japan. Discovered and named Ladrones, "Thieves," in 1521 by Magellan, the islands were later renamed by the Jesuits. In what came to be known as the June 16 "Great Marianas Turkey Shoot," B-29s cast their first shadows on Saipan. On July 9, Americans wrenched the island from Japan, which held it for thirty years. At the end of the twenty-three-day battle, thirty-one thousand Japanese soldiers and sailors and fifteen thousand civilians had martyred themselves. Many hundreds took their children with them over the cliffs on the island's northern tip in the ritual suicide *seppuku*.

Conquest of the island marked a turning point in the war. While it placed an Allied springboard to the enemy, its value was not entirely a matter of geography. Losing more than four hundred planes and nearly that many flyers, Japan forfeited its viability as an air power. Nearly as important, the defeat was a decisive blow to Japanese morale.

The United States Army Air Forces had nearly eighty thousand aircraft and almost two and one-half million men positioned at its various fronts by July 20, 1944, when an assassination attempt against the Führer failed to loosen his controlling hand on the Wehrmacht.

On August 4, Gestapo routing in Amsterdam discovered a fifteen-year-old German-Jewish girl and her family in hiding. For more than two years, Anne Frank infused life into her secret world through her diary. With hope, she would "...keep on trying to find a way of becoming what I would so like to be, and could be, if...."

A Slip of the Lip
Could Sink a Ship

"**L**ewis is back. Sweeney, too, as well as others from the old test group." Caron reread Tibbets' letter. The Colonel was forming a new group to go overseas and would like to get as many of the old group back as possible. "Would you and Al Wheeler be interested?"

"Hell, no," Wheeler bellowed. "I like it here. I'm going to get married."

"Me, too." But Caron dashed over to the TWX office, anyway, and wired Tibbets: "Count me in. Count Al out. Letter follows."

In his precise, draftsmanlike script, Caron wrote: "Kay and I plan to be married on my birthday, October 31. Could I report after that?"

No, Tibbets flashed back. "Report to Wendover first, then I'll get you a furlough to get married."

Kay wasn't happy about her future husband going overseas, no matter how often he tried to explain why it was important.

"What will I tell our children if I don't go?"

Orders for transfer to Wendover arrived in October. Tibbets' Individual Air Force was getting off the ground.

"**N**othing going that far West from Pratt," the sergeant at operations said discouragingly when Tibbets' new gunnery sergeant checked about hitching a ride. Caron was told, however, that he could take a B-17 as far as Lowry Air Force Base in Denver. He crawled into the plane's cramped tail gunner compartment and straddled the bicycle seat. The spectacular view made up for the pain in his groin. In Denver he caught a trolley to Union Station and hopped on a 5 P.M. Zephyr for Salt Lake City. By early morning, it rolled into the quiet depot, where a six-by-six waited to transport incoming GIs to Wendover.

Two-day-old stubble shadowed Caron's jaw and he had vainly resisted taking off his prized leather A-2 flight jacket, despite regulations against wearing it off the flight line. At this point, he just didn't give a damn. Hours ago he had unbuttoned his shirt collar and loosened his tie. At the gate, the MP scanned the disheveled airman, shook his head and made a sucking sound with his lips. "Jeep's on its way," he said, reserving Caron's dress-down for someone with more rank.

As clouds of dust boiled behind the jeep, Caron wondered where in the East could anyone find such expansive, intense skies. The thought brought back memories of Coney Island, where skies seldom achieved a hue more appealing than pale tourmaline, like the ring his mother wore. Here, the zenith was purple. He had begun to notice the change somewhere in the mountains of Colorado. Would it be different...high flying in these western skies?

The day that most of Tibbets' crews arrived at Wendover, the Colonel had staged an impressive speech from atop a sound truck. He told the assembled men that the 509th Composite Group would be unlike any other—totally self-contained. A lot would be demanded of them, he cautioned. How well they did their jobs could affect the outcome of the war. No loose talk would be allowed. No speculating. Anyone who didn't want to stay under those conditions could transfer out, *now*. He repeated to the men the warning posted at Wendover's gate. It was the message that had gotten Caron's attention a few moments earlier:

> What You Hear Here, What You See Here,
> When You Leave Here, Let It Stay Here.

The driver wheeled the jeep around a corner and the black letters before Caron puzzled him: "Tech Area 'C'. Most Restricted." He smiled, contemplating what earthly difference there might be between "restricted" and "most restricted."

That Intelligence gave any consideration to semantics when they ordered the superlative with the adjective was doubtful. Security was their number one priority. And preventing security leaks drove them to great surreptitious lengths. At any one time, thirty or more agents in the guise of ground crewmen, telephone operators, cooks, plumbers and electricians peeked in, under, around and over the 393rd squadron's shoulders, bunks, stalls and mess trays. Intelligence prided itself on compiling a dossier on everyone. To the MP squadron was relegated the less glamorous task of extinguishing brouhahas. Censors opened letters to wives and lovers, friends and mothers, sliced out sensitive lines, stamped envelopes with their rectangular seal of approval and sent them on their way. Unknown ears listened in on telephone conversations. Tiny tape recorders bugged hotel bedrooms. Cloaked figures shadowed braggarts. In a short time, those who didn't pass muster suddenly found themselves in the company of polar bears and icebergs.

Inside the top-secret compound, Quonsets crouched close to the ground as though pressed downward by the weight of that all-pervasive sky. At headquarters, Caron dropped his dusty B-4 bag on the scuffed wood floor. Another sign reminded, "A slip of the lip can sink a ship." He handed his orders to the sergeant behind the desk. Before Caron could speak, the sergeant discharged both barrels at him. Midway between "disheveled" and "out of uniform," a familiar voice from the next room interrupted.

"Is that you, Bob?"

"Sure is, Colonel."

"C'mon in and shut the door."

As he trotted past the red-faced sergeant into Tibbets' office, Caron beamed.

"I'm glad you decided to join us," Tibbets said, firmly shaking the sergeant's hand as robustly as their first meeting at Eglin. "All I can tell you is that we have a chance to end the war. Everything you do here will be top-secret. Don't ask questions. You'll only be told what you need to know. I know you can keep your mouth shut."

"Colonel?"

"What is it, Bob?"

"With all due respects, sir, you broke up my wedding plans...."

"And I promised you a furlough once you reported to Wendover. You've got two weeks."

Tibbets told Caron that he was flying to Colorado Springs in the morning on his way to Washington. He would drop his old armament specialist in Wichita in time for the wedding.

"Check into your outfit and be out at the flight line at six in the morning."

"Y ou and everyone else," declared the sergeant when Bob told him he needed a two-week pass. "There's a six-month waiting list for those things."

"Colonel Tibbets just approved it."

"Sure he did," the sergeant mocked, already a half-dozen paces into his Captain's office.

"I see, Colonel. Yes, sir." The Captain slammed his phone in its cradle with enough force to make it jingle. His call to Tibbets hadn't turned out quite as he expected.

Amused, Caron pretended to read the bulletin board.

"Give that sergeant his god-damned furlough," the Captain roared.

At Colorado Springs Tibbets told the anxious bride-groom-to-be to wait for him in operations. Caron read every magazine on the table. Darkness had quieted down the offices. Finally, the Colonel stepped back into the waiting room.

"Looks like I'm going to be stuck here a few days," he said straightforwardly. "I'll see if I can get you a flight to Wichita."

Caron wasn't surprised that available pilots suddenly weren't once they heard an enlisted man needed a chauffeur to Kansas.

"What's next?" asked Tibbets.

"The train station."

Tibbets ordered a staff car to take him to his downtown hotel and told the driver to stop at the depot. Then he introduced Sergeant Caron to the disgruntled major with the official-looking briefcase who would be riding with them to the hotel.

The depot was nearly deserted. Caron asked if Tibbets would mind waiting while he checked the schedule. The Major fumed. Why an officer would cater to an enlisted man was beyond his understanding.

"No train until tomorrow afternoon," the enlisted man reported, hopping back in the front seat. "How about we try the bus station."

The driver assured Tibbets he knew where it was.

"No luck," Caron said, peeking his head back in the staff car. "That's it, Colonel."

"How are you going to get to Wichita in time for your wedding?" Tibbets asked with genuine concern.

Caron held up his thumb.

"Can you drive me to the edge of town so I can hitch a ride?" The Major groaned and folded his arms across his chest. The staff car turned on its windshield wipers and headed south on Highway 85. "This looks like as good a place as any." The hitch-hiker stepped into the drizzle and surveyed the corner, well-lighted with several gas stations and a small store.

"Good luck, Bob," Tibbets said, and extended his hand with genuine sincerity. Caron watched the staff car's tail lights disappear into the mist.

"Hold everything. I'm on my way." Bob shouted into the receiver and hoped that his soon-to-be-sister-in-law could hear him. The scanty protection of the glass telephone booth barely dampened the din of the highway.

He hustled along the highway shoulder, turning and walking briskly backwards to face approaching cars with raised right thumb. Buses and trucks whooshed past, sucking him into their slip stream. A half-dozen miles from Dodge City, a hay wagon pulled over and waited for him to catch up.

Katherine Marie Younger also waited. When Bob finally arrived, he was delighted to see her in blue, the color she wore when they first met. A single rose corsage lifted the moonstone glow in her narrow face. In the spirit of the moment, the blithe Irish monsignor tackled the sacrament of holy wedlock as though time were of the essence. And, indeed, it was. The small group sampled day-old wedding cake, and the bride and groom scuttled off to the depot.

The porter offered Kay his plump hand to help her into the car. Even without "Just Married" chalked on the top of her suitcase, hastily added by a wedding guest, he would have known. "Only two upper berths left, sir," he said genuinely apologetic. "But that's no way to spend your honeymoon. Why don't you nice young folks put your luggage in this berth and take the other for yourselves?" He chortled, then left the marriage bed logistics to his grateful passengers.

By the time the train pulled into Chicago the next morning, Bob had told Kay nearly as much about his parents as he had written them about her. Only coach seats remained on the over-nighter to New York, a long, jostling, upright night away from George and Anne, who would be waiting anxiously at Penn Station to meet the "charming creature" they had read so much about.

"That's regulation," persisted the woman at the New York rationing board. "I can't give you additional gas coupons without *something* from your commanding officer telling me that he's approved your bringing a car to...where is it?"

Bob's "A" sticker—good for about five gallons of gasoline a week—was barely enough for errands in Lynbrook. He needed to get from New York to one hundred twenty-five miles west of Salt Lake City, with a slight detour through Dodge City to pick up a few of Kay's belongings at the farm.

Although Tibbets had already given Caron permission to bring the Chevy to Wendover, the rationing board demanded it in writing. Caron wired Utah. Shortly after noon the next day, he received a lengthy wire from the Pentagon, which he smugly shoved under the nose of the stodgy board clerk. Later he learned that a not-so-stodgy clerk at Wendover had interrupted the Colonel with his gunnery-sergeant's dilemma in the midst of his meeting at the Pentagon.

To the Kansas farm girl, the Rocky Mountains of northern Colorado were a sensory adventure. The air at Monarch Pass, so thin and crisp that it seemed almost brittle, fractured into zillions of minute prisms, sparkling rainbow colors with every breath. Bob fished the camera out of the Chevy and posed his new bride amid the splendor of Engelmann spruce and the sweet, piquant smell of resin.

Over their shoulder, the next evening's sinking sun draped Utah's snow-capped Wasatch range in rose. The unmistakable thump, thump, wobble, wobble came as an unwelcome intrusion into their serenity. Bob unloaded the over-full trunk to access the spare, and the Chevy limped into American Forks for the night.

The stark, expansive landscape west of Salt Lake sharply contrasted with the embracing, cloaked mountains to the east. Peaks arrogantly pried their way out of the desert floor, and the long, black straight-of-way they traveled replicated itself in shimmering waves that defied the senses.

Bob and Kay hiked their suitcases to the lobby of the dowdy State Line Hotel, just a boot print into Nevada. It would be home for a week. Had there been space for belongings in their Spartan room just off the noisy main gambling hall, Kay still would have insisted that they "store" them in the car. Out on the street, at least, they would be safe from invading cockroaches.

An invasion took place after all, but roaches were not to blame. When the newlyweds came down for breakfast the next morning, the Chevy's convertible top had been slashed. And appearing as though Hansel and Gretel had scattered crumbs to mark their path, a comical trail of cosmetics trickled nearly all the way to the Wendover gate. There, MPs were sobering up a lieutenant who refused to turn over Kay's cosmetic case, which he clutched tightly to his chest like a frightened child clings to his security blanket.

One-hundred people populated Wendover. That was thriving. Occasionally the town swelled with a few lonely GIs. The preceding winter, when Wendover was the training site for a P-47 fighter group, visiting comedian Bob Hope dubbed it "Leftover Field." With the reassignment of the fighter planes, crews and commanders, the base looked ever more "passed over."

Caron requested permission to live off base. The rows of cement block apartments were mainly for permanent base personnel and officers. There seemed little sense in being put at the bottom of a waiting list six months' long. There were a few dormitory apartments, and Wyatt Duzenbury and Robert Shumard had settled in there.

An opportune meeting at the Non-Commissioned Officer's Club with a young medic opened one closed door. His unit was shipping out, and he was sending his family home. Caron could have their apartment if he wanted it. "Don't worry about the waiting list," reassured the medic, explaining that he sublet from the man who ran a junkyard, a graveyard for the rusting carcasses of B-24s. The old man was partial to enlisted men. "Not that he had anything against officers, mind you." The medic winked.

"Oh, sure. You can have it." The words fell out of the junkman's mouth between well-masticated mouthfuls of bologna sandwich. A torn undershirt displaying last month's sweat and grease tented over his mountainous belly. Bob doubted that he had ever seen a scroungier fellow.

The thin man and fat man made small talk outside the fat man's ramshackle trailer. It was impossible to tell where the junkyard began and ended.

"You 'n the 'lil mizzuz kin have it fer forty dollars a month," he beamed over the bargain he was offering. He explained that the base allocated the apartment to him, but he didn't need it. He had a place to live, motioning to the ratty trailer.

"One more thing, though."

Bob waited.

"You gotta keep one bedroom fer my wife ta store stuff...when she comes up from Salt Lake City." He paused, as though he had to think hard about what he was going to say next. "...'n maybe once 'n a while I'll wanna come over'n use yer show'r."

Bob would have wagered Hell would freeze over first. "You've got a deal."

The little cement block row apartment was officially theirs, he announced to a jubilant Kay. Since a medic and his family occupied it before them, it needed little scrubbing. A sturdy wooden card table with two folding chairs were among the few pieces of furniture that had been left behind, along with a handful of dishes, a pot and skillet.

If the Internal Revenue Service could get blood out of a stone, Kay, who had learned much from that venerable institution, could use her considerable ingenuity and practice with a coal stove to transform a can of SPAM into a memorable first meal in their first home. In the following months, as often as Bob filled the kitchen coal scuttle, Kay invented variations on the theme.

As she worked, she sang. The cord to Kay's little kitchen radio was her lifeline to the outside world. The couple had crossed over a threshold and there was no turning back.

Sergeant and Mrs. Caron had settled in at the opposite end of the row from Colonel and Mrs. Tibbets. One Saturday Tibbets was prudently washing his car with a lone bucket of water when Caron strolled past.

"Hi, Colonel."

"Bob! What are you doing up here?"

"I live here."

"You have one of these apartments? How did you ever get it?"

"Hell, Colonel, we enlisted men stick together, too."

"Good for you, Bob," and he re-immersed himself in his ritual.

The weight of war pressed heavily on Tibbets' shoulders, lightened not at all by the frequency with which he was suspended—at altitudes exceeding twenty-five thousand feet—somewhere in the triangle between Wendover, Washington and Los Alamos. The secrecy unnerved Lucie, and she clung to their two sons, Paul Jr. and Gene, as duty tugged at her husband and he slipped from her grasp. Sometimes, when the loneliness overwhelmed her, the quiet Georgia belle welcomed the ritual comfort of Mass with the obliging young couple at the end of the row.

As Tibbets watched the new team players he had inherited from the 393rd, his confidence in them grew. Intuition told him as much about them as his circumspect eye. The Colonel hand-picked the men who would work most closely with him from among the best in the Air Force.

Like most of the officers, Major Thomas W. Ferebee was in his mid-twenties. Tibbets' bombardier over France and North Africa, he could have been cast in a film as the dashing river-boat gambler. The Mocksville, North Carolinian earned his Southern charm by birth, and a way with women and cards had been part of his education. A "wheeler dealer," Major Bud Uanna, head of security, called him, not at all affectionately. Yet, compared to Lewis, Uanna confided to Tibbets, he looks "like Shirley Temple." Even with his escapades that kept security on its toes, his value to Tibbets was undisputed. As a teacher of precision bombing techniques he was right on target.

Captain Theodore J. Van Kirk and Ferebee were a natural team, on duty and off. Van Kirk let things roll off his back as easily as the morning Pennsylvania mist rolled off the Northumberland highlands that was home. It was more than his positive attitude that made Tibbets want his old navigator to be a part of the forthcoming mission. Van Kirk was a perfectionist.

The warm-hearted Captain Robert Lewis could be overbearing one minute and deferential, even a pussycat, the next. Tibbets understood Lewis' resentment whenever the Colonel had to bump him out of the pilot's seat. Lewis had considerable natural talents as pilot. But his mischievousness was potentially dangerous, and that worried Tibbets.

One man understood the new technology called electronic countermeasures better than anyone—Lieutenant Jacob Beser. He had studied engineering at Johns Hopkins University and taught radio and electronics in Florida. Now Beser was mastering the nuances of the monitoring system that would prevent enemy radar from jamming or detonating the complex firing mechanism of the new bomb, which would contain its own built-in radar. There was mutual respect between him and Tibbets. Many of the officers and enlisted men found they had little in common with the strongly opinionated lieutenant. They called him a "longhair," as they did the civilians who frequented Wendover, although few knew how these visitors from Los Alamos figured in ending the war.

Tibbets held Captain William "Deak" Parsons, the Navy weapons specialist and his ordnance officer, in the highest regard. He had little doubt that a brilliant mind was housed behind that great forehead.

Assistant weaponeer Morris Jeppson worked well with everyone. As ordnance specialist, his physics training from Yale, Harvard and MIT would be put to use under Parsons' guidance. Strong religious convictions guided the second lieutenant's thoughts and actions, though he never pressed them on others or sat in judgment.

Poker was one of Sergeant Wyatt Duzenbury's favorite pastimes, although he was a more passive player than most. When the flight engineer was at his instrument panel, however, he was no gambler. Every crew member, including Tibbets himself, knew they were flying "Duze's" plane, with "Duze's" engines. He was quick, eager to learn, and Tibbets admired that.

Easy-going Sergeant Robert Shumard smiled frequently and was always eager to please. At six feet, four inches, the assistant flight engineer who usually flew scanner position towered over Caron. Off duty, Shumard and radio operator Private Richard "Junior" Nelson were inseparable.

Sergeant Joseph E. Stiborik, radar operator, had a dry sense of humor, although he usually kept it under wraps. He was a quiet man who preferred solitary time to carousing with the crew.

The 509th was truly a composite group. Working as tool- and die-makers were a murderer, three men guilty of manslaughter and several lesser felons. All had escaped from prison. And all were experts at their jobs.

Tibbets took each criminal aside. He stared hard at them with eyes that flashed confidence and steely control. "Do your job, don't cause any trouble, and when the war's over, I'll give you your file and a match."

Murder and mayhem were not on the minds of the other fifteen hundred and forty-two enlisted men and two hundred twenty-five officers of Tibbets' Individual Air Force. They were too busy perfecting flying and bomb-dropping techniques by day and making babies by night.

Paramount Picture's "Eyes and Ears of the World" flickered its news reels into movie houses across the country: "As the eyes of the world turn to the Pacific, the pilots and crews of American bombers carry the mail over Japanese-held islands with monotonous regularity. ... American wings are regaining the Pacific and clearing the skyway to Japan."

Those wings on November 24, 1944, belonged to B-29s, and from Saipan they launched the first aerial strike on Tokyo. On that same day, the 393rd Bomb Wing at Wendover received its fifteenth B-29, a plane the crew would also strip of its armor plating and all but two guns in the tail, making it lighter and more maneuverable. Mechanics christened the first emasculated planes "Sitting Target One" and "Two."

Eight days before Christmas, appropriately near the forty-first anniversary of the Wright brothers' inaugural powered aircraft flight at Kitty Hawk, the 509th Composite Group received its official activation papers. At Los Alamos, two days later, General Leslie Groves and Robert Oppenheimer agreed that the gun-type firing mechanism seemed the best method to detonate the new uranium bomb. Confident the firing system was reliable, they could dispense with a test that would waste the precious little isotope that had been produced.

The limited quantity of U^{235} available had Germany's name on it, Roosevelt said to Groves during December's Battle of the Bulge. Groves explained why he thought that hitting Germany with an untried weapon was a bad idea. If America's new atomic bomb failed to explode, the Germans might glean from it production methods to assemble a bomb of their own. He had no such confidence in Japan's ability. Besides, a bomb ear-marked for Japan, where the majority of its buildings were wooden, could wreak far more havoc.

As the scientists rushed to have a bomb ready, Hitler's troops smashed deeply into Russia. At home, Americans were as weary of war as were their fighting men on scattered fronts. Yet, as 1944 drew to a close, citizens were heartened. In the past year they had more money in their pockets than in the many years before. And they spent it readily on items that previously had been trimmed from their budgets. There was more fresh meat on their tables, in part because execrable crime bosses had created a lucrative black market. For the first time, consumers were seeing red—plus yellow and cyan—in Kodacolor photographs, Eastman Kodak's new color negative film.

On Friday and Saturday evenings, Americans flocked to dark theaters, eager to be swept away from the gravity of headlines through laughter and lightheartedness or passion and fury. Otto Preminger brought them *Lara*, with Clifton Webb, Gene Tierney and Dana Andrews. The refreshing, extraordinary beauty of Elizabeth Taylor warmed their hearts in Clarence Brown's *National Velvet*. They searched for *The Way Ahead* with David Niven, Peter Ustinov, Stanley Holloway and Trevor Howard. They tapped their toes with Rita Hayworth and Gene Kelly to Jerome Kern and Ira Gershwin's *Cover Girl*.

To the voice of "Chiquita Banana," they rumbaed in their living rooms. Children of all ages thrilled to the hearty "Hi-ho, Silver," as The Lone Ranger and Tonto galloped across their imaginations. On dance floors Americans swayed and swooned to "Twilight Time," longed for "Moonlight in Vermont," or a "Sentimental Journey." Life had shown them "It Could Happen To You" and "You Always Hurt the One You Love." They stropped their wits on *The Razor's Edge*, by Somerset Maugham, and were ultimately brought face to face with war through novelist Harry Peter M'Nab Brown's *A Walk in the Sun*.

Americans gave their incumbent president fifty-three percent of their vote and confidently reseated him in his Oval Office for a fourth term, dumping his surprised Republican opponent, New York Governor Thomas E. Dewey. But it was a time for dumping and a time for surprises. While Roosevelt faltered at the starting gate, he took the lead with his unexpected vice presidential running mate. Harry S. Truman and his watchdog committee to investigate profiteering on national defense projects had been making the news.

The atomic-bomb secret had nearly exploded on the floor of the House, detonated by this overzealous member of its Appropriations

Committee. What, Truman demanded to know, was this damn-expensive project that was dragging its backside in the sand? He wasn't about to see good money thrown after bad on some cockamamie, farfetched government scheme. He put his foot down and threatened to spill the few beans in his pocket unless he got answers, fast. His meddling in the Manhattan Project was both a nuisance and a security risk. To quell the roar, General George C. Marshall, Army chief of staff, agreed to meet with Truman's committee in a secret session. One by one, Marshall lassoed the mooing herd and told them that if they wanted to see a quick end to the war, they heard nothing, saw nothing and said nothing. Stunned and still in the dark, the committee butted out. Roosevelt covertly channeled funds to the project.

The same "see nothing, hear nothing, say nothing" code imposed itself on workers across the country. As far as WAC Alene Carter, a patent draftsman stationed at the Army's secret atomic bomb testing grounds, was concerned, there were two reasons why no one involved in the mysterious goings-on at the New Mexico base breached security. "In the first place, we were afraid to," she said. "And in the second place, no one would have believed us."

In the midst of sand, salt and sun, there was no such thing as a Christmas tree. The quest took Bob and Kay west, to the nearest Nevada town of Elko.

Six weeks before Bob was born, on a winding mountain road a stone's throw northwest of Elko, a half-crippled sixty-year-old geologist stooped painfully and palmed a lumpy rock. To anyone else, it might have seemed a wasted effort. To his trained eye, the chunk of ore held the promise of an empire, and he its copper baron. Could he have foreseen that the pulse of a world at war would course through miles upon miles of its finely drawn wires?

Even in this tiny town, far from the war-torn cities of Europe, Christmas was not an easy time. It was a short tree that the young couple finally found, but fresh and pungent, nevertheless. They purchased a box of cardboard ornaments covered with colored foil. Bob set up the tree in the living room and Kay strung popcorn as her family had done on farm Christmases past. The tinny-sounding little kitchen radio crackled out carols from Salt Lake City. Kay put on her best blue dress, and the newlyweds mingled with other displaced people at an NCO Club party.

Captain Chuck Sweeney and his wife joined the Carons for midnight Mass. The only way to stuff the tall, well-built pilot in the cozy convertible was to drop the top. Sardined in the seat, Sweeney scrunched his knees to his chin and Caron closed the top over him.

Father Time had taken with him ambivalence and doubt. It was to be a productive year ahead. Cooperative Anglo-American research would see its labors rewarded, not only in the final assembly of a nuclear bomb, but also through the mass production of life-saving penicillin and streptomycin.

Box offices would be besieged by those eager to see Laurence Olivier deliver *Henry V*. Ray Milland and Jane Wyman would try to discover *The Lost Weekend*, while Raoul Walsh would charge Erroll Flynn with one *Objective, Burma!* Alfred Hitchcock, with the help of Ingrid Bergman and Gregory Peck, would hold moviegoers *Spellbound*.

National morale and prosperity were not of interest to General Groves. His immediate concern was for the productivity of a cotillion of super minds at a Los Alamos think tank and a handful of hotshot pilots at a remote air base two thousand miles from his Washington office. Tibbets delivered half the news he wanted to hear. The man in the driver's seat of the 509th confidently assured the general that his flyers would be ready to deliver the bomb on June 15.

Outside of closed-door meetings with scientists and Pentagon brass, the words "atomic bomb" never flowed from Tibbets mouth. The crews knew that their extensive training to drop a single bomb and the complex evasive maneuver spelled something different, something new. What they could not have imagined was at that very moment the something new was an earth-shaking weapon that might not only end the present war, but deter global warfare for all time.

Coast to coast, several hundred thousand military, civilian and scientific personnel were spinning filaments of an elaborate web. Ironically, the web itself remained invisible to millions of Americans until a blinding light revealed it one August dawn.

The tail gunner assigned to Captain Robert Lewis' crew sensed that whenever they were ready for the "big one," Tibbets would take over as aircraft commander. Although the helmsman of the 509th was frequently spirited away to heaven knows where via the most circuitous routes, he had a sixth sense about the huge bomber, her responsiveness in his hands, the power of its engines. Caron had not forgotten that when he had received Tibbets' telegram for the rationing board, his Colonel was at the Pentagon. Whatever the big one was, it belonged to Tibbets.

Winter at Wendover could have been worse. Monstrous cumulo-nimbus clouds crescendoed on the Pequop Mountains to the west and there lost much of their enthusiasm for blanketing the lowlands. To the north, ten-thousand-foot Pilot Peak received a sugary icing. Wendover might more appropriately have been named Windover. Savage air currents spiraled off the mountains and slapped the open flats, hurling handfuls of sand into faces, indiscriminately permeating the movable and immovable with equal ferocity.

When the weather and tedium drove women and men inside, they worked out in the gym or, like Caron and radio man Abe Spitzer, played handball until their pent-up energy had been spent.

Wendover had become a country unto itself. And the 509th developed a unique self-image as one of the most individually dressed, best-fed and best-trained units in the service.

Designers of the Superfortress promised a cruising speed of three hundred fifty miles per hour for distances up to thirty-five hundred miles at an altitude of thirty-eight thousand feet. But aeronautical engineers didn't have to fly them. The higher the B-29s got, the more unstable they were. Their crews came to expect severe mechanical problems above thirty thousand feet. The B-29s delivered.

The well-used planes that served the 509th's fifteen flight crews were no exception. Mechanics, often assisted by armament men, constantly pampered their engines. As long as her temperamental Wrights held up under the strain, a B-29 could out-maneuver the enemy. If they didn't, all the protective armor the factory could install wasn't worth a damn.

Based on Tibbets' early performance tests, and to avoid overstressing the engines, armament men had lightened the 509th's planes. They ripped out nonessentials. Among the equipment that went were the two top and two bottom turrets, along with their gun sights, all the electronic black boxes, wiring harnesses, their micro switches, Alnico magnets, nuts and bolts—everything that held the works together and had weight. That left the tail guns. By default the tail gunner ended up the sole defender of the plane. Armament specialist Caron now officially filled that position. He called himself the sandbag.

On most training flights, however, after firing test rounds from the tail, Caron rode scanner with Bob Shumard. Tibbets quickened the pace and increased the number of flights. Bomb runs were often practiced over the nothingness of the southern California desert and the reflective waters of the Salton Sea.

Pilots practiced Tibbets' evasive maneuver. The one hundred fifty-five degree dive turn had been calculated to provide maximum diagonal distance between the plane and the point of detonation. Washington and Los Alamos hoped that would put a "safe" distance between the plane and the unpredictable shock waves from the bomb blast. Like the scientists who were furiously readying the "gimmick," Tibbets was flying into unknown territory. How far would be far enough from a blast that *might* be expected to equal the force of twenty thousand tons of TNT? No one could be sure. Still, he pushed his pilots and they, in turn, pushed their planes to outer limits. Failure to execute a proper turn temporarily grounded a pilot. Tibbets' dogged persistence that crews achieve perfection focused on eliminating variables. And there were already too many of those. Successful delivery of the explosive—about which the group was not even permitted to speculate—and escape from it would depend on skill, teamwork and luck.

From six miles up, bombardiers strained to drop dummy bombs on a seven-hundred-foot bombing circle, which gradually grew smaller and smaller. Pilots and flight engineers steadied the plane and maintained a uniform speed to provide the bombardier with a stable platform for the drop. Once the bombardier spotted his critical initial point and aiming point for lining up the drop, the radar operator served as a double-check.

Believing that most of the flight crews would benefit from a brief respite from winter, Tibbets assigned them several weeks of training nearer the Equator. Over the Gulf of Mexico they could learn the intricacies of long-distance navigation, made more challenging by expanses of open sea flown in the inky black of night. Captain Claude Eatherly was the first to fly his B-29 to Batista Field, twelve miles from Havana, Cuba. Pilots and crews practiced identifying IP and AP and precision bombing from thirty thousand feet.

In February's sub-freezing Crimea, a colorless Roosevelt and rosy-cheeked Churchill threw dice with Stalin over the gameboard of Japan. Stalin assured his partners that the Red Army would be ready to launch its offensive against the country that had caused it such grief three months after the defeat of Germany. "That is," he continued, his caveat not wholly unexpected, "as long as the United States provided supplies."

Roosevelt's military advisers had estimated that it could take as long as eighteen months to bridle Japan. He and Churchill would have to wait and see how fortuitous was this Yalta Conference agreement with Russia to declare war on Japan. Stalin's assistance would not come without cost. Stalin had already been blunt about that. In addition to supplies for the offensive, his price tag included assurance that the Allies would return to Russia territories she had lost to Japan in the 1905 war.

Thousands of miles in the direction of the jet stream, Utah's warming days came and went with morning briefings, bomb practices, lunches and more bomb practices. As target circles shrank, so did the group's days in the States. In May, Tibbets ordered the 509th overseas.

During the months of training, reliable transports had shuttled scientists and matériel between New Mexico and Utah. For the coming long haul over the Pacific, however, Tibbets needed planes with really cavernous spaces. When the Curtis Commander C-46s arrived, Caron whistled his amazement. "You could make bowling alleys out of these, Colonel." Tibbets put his hands on his hips and shook his head. Nope, he wasn't going to make one damned thing out of those tail draggers. They were going back. What he needed to transport the 509th's equipment over thousands of miles of open ocean were more C-54s.

While the 509th rehearsed for the "big one," intrepid pilots flew sorties in the Pacific. The danger of missions was increased by the unreliability of the B-29s' engines, which overheated on long flights with heavy loads. General Curtis LeMay, commander of the 20th Air Force, which enfolded the 509th Composite Group, was discovering that the

Superfortress was not cut from the same cloth as the B-17, which at high altitudes sought solace in the bosom of her sisters. Not the B-29, as Tibbets had learned from his early test flights. At thirty thousand feet, the big bomber was picky about her wing-tip space and elbowed her way out of formation.

That quirk muddied LeMay's tactical decisions. His strategy had been to deploy formations of B-29s for daylight bombings from altitudes where they were invulnerable to flak. The general was deeply troubled by the number of missions that had to be aborted for a myriad of reasons, especially engine trouble. Worse, crews and aircraft overloaded with bombs and fuel for the long flights had been consumed in fiery infernos at the ends of runways.

Tibbets suggested LeMay lighten his planes by stripping them down. Excising just one fuel tank from the bomb bay and some armament could trim the weight of each aircraft by six thousand pounds. The modifications would not only enhance maneuverability, Tibbets explained, but would also extend engine life, and perhaps human life.

On March 9 and 10, 1945, the drone in the sky and the deafening sirens sent a panicked Tokyo running for cover. LeMay's Superfortresses rained incendiaries on the expectant city. The firestorm and the windstorm that followed whipped the ashes of one hundred twenty-four thousand souls into the scorched air.

Japan reeled as LeMay again brought down his "bludgeon of air power." During the May 24 raid, five hundred sixty-two B-29s dropped bombs on Tokyo. Three-quarters were incendiaries. Of these, the M76 "pyrotechnic gel" bomb was the most deadly. Five-hundred pounds of jellied oil, heavy oil, petroleum, magnesium powder and sodium nitrate created a fire that was virtually impossible to extinguish. Within a month, B-29s' crushing blows to the shoulders of Tokyo, Nagoya, Yokohama, Kobe, Osaka and Kawasaki left them crippled and senseless.

When their military leaders, their technology and their politicians could not save them, the Japanese people prayed to the spirits of iridescent goldfish for the miracle of deliverance. To ward off evil, they ate magic pickled scallions.

More substantial food was in short supply, as were fuel, munitions and clothing. Distribution of the few available commodities had been severely hampered. American and British gun ships had frayed

Japan's coast. Her six largest cities lay flailed and raw. Still, Imperial warlords, steeped like green tea leaves in ceremony and tradition, longed for the glorious death of the samurai warrior. If not death at the hands of the enemy, then at one's own hand. In one swift, bittersweet kiss, *hara-kiri* relieved melancholic souls from the agony of dishonor.

From her ranks swollen with boys and men well past their prime, Japan replenished her fallen in a bleak cycle of death. The beleaguered country prayed for victory. Yet it did not come. Driven by the military, civilians prepared for a land invasion. They carved bamboo spears, cleaned musty muskets, sharpened sickles and, to take the place of ammunition, recruited their crippled and maimed for suicide squadrons. While much of the Imperial Navy lay paralyzed—or leagues beneath the sea—thousands of small, civilian craft were transformed into human torpedoes. Packed with explosives, small suicide destroyer escorts and torpedo boats were prepared to crash into Allied troop carriers as they approached the beaches. Every conceivable defense was being readied for the expected invaders. *Kami* (divine) and *kaze* (wind), which drew their name and strength from the legendary 1281 typhoon that saved Japan by destroying the Mongol navy, prayed the divine wind would save their country once again.

Had he heard correctly? To Kantaro Suzuki it was madness. Militarists had pledged to fight until *all* Japanese were killed. In such death, there was no defeat, they had said. *Blind fools.*

Once again the seventy-eight-year-old admiral bowed to the whims of Fate. This time, reluctantly. In early April 1945 the venerated war hero had agreed to serve as prime minister only out of love for his country. Age was playing tricks on him. He could no longer hear the many beautiful song birds in the garden, or the distant crickets in the night. Yet the voice of his Emperor rang in his ears. As did the mad promises and predictions of the Imperial Army. His supreme—perhaps impossible—task would be to temper the impatience of warmongers for victory with the unconscionable prescriptions of the peacemakers. It called for *haragei*. And speaking out of both sides of his mouth was distasteful to the old samurai. When the insanity of this new kind of war overwhelmed him, he retreated to a quiet place and looked for wisdom in the Tao.

General Korechika Anami, war minister in Suzuki'a cabinet, held out no false hope. Japan had lost the war. There was little time left to salvage a peace and a culture before both were no more than divine wind. Sadly, he recognized the flames of war had been fanned not by loyalty to the Emperor, but by industrial profiteering. He had seen for himself how his officers had been corrupted with black-market luxuries like eggs, sugar and sake. Now, their misguided allegiances were obstacles in his path to rescuing Japan from the jaws of defeat with its honor intact. *Bakayaro*. The stupid bastards. He did not see *yamatodamashi*, the living Japanese spirit, as it appeared in the eyes of the simple man. What he saw was an insuperable quest for glory, at a price Japan could not afford to pay.

Like Suzuki, he faced a two-edged sword. If the conditions of surrender were to be Japan's, she must exercise restraint, wait for the enemy to come to her. Then, with all of her forces, she would pounce. Wielding such power, she could write her own conditions for peace. Anami tried to convince himself the plan was sound. Yet it stuck in his throat. To prolong war was to assure blossoms would fall too early from the trees only to be trampled into the bloody earth.

If spring strengthens a man's soul, it did little for President Roosevelt's failing body. As peach trees bloomed in Warm Springs, Georgia, the President slipped out from under the heady responsibility of a nation at war and passed that yoke to an unsuspecting farm boy from Independence, Missouri. At 5:25 P.M., April 12, 1945, Eleanor Roosevelt called the vice president to her second floor study. "The President," Eleanor announced forthrightly, "died at 3:35 P.M. today." She let the gravity of her words settle on Truman's shoulders, then began again.

"Harry," her sympathetic outpouring genuine, "is there anything we can do for you? *You* are the one in trouble now."

At 7:09 P.M., in the Cabinet Room of the house on 16 Pennsylvania Avenue, Harry S. Truman, his twang a little lower-pitched than usual, swore on a Bible that he would faithfully execute the office of President of the United States and to the best of his ability "preserve, protect and defend the Constitution of the United States."

The 509th Composite Group was at mess when the 5:49 P.M. radio flash reverberated off the walls. The President had been posing for his portrait with Madame Elizabeth Shoumatoff when he suffered a sudden cerebral hemorrhage, the announcer said. Immediately, the order was issued: until the President was buried, there would be no drinking or gambling in the officers' or enlisted men's clubs. On hearing the shattering news, Captain Claude Eatherly, the rakish pilot whose carefully cultivated reputation for self-indulgence in whiskey, women and cards was well-known, had been the first to agree that abstinence was a fitting tribute to the former commander in chief.

Exactly twelve years and one month earlier, Roosevelt had begun his fabled fireside chats. "My friends," he always began, allaying fears, effortlessly sliding into the casual assurances the way one eases into cozy fleece-lined slippers.

In February, at the Yalta Conference, he had pledged "unity of purpose and of action" with superpower leaders Churchill and Stalin. Now, at 63, wrote Walter Lippman, journalist for the *New York Herald Tribune*, "Roosevelt is Gone. The final test of a leader is that he leaves behind him in other men the conviction and the will to carry on.... The genius of a good leader is to leave behind him a situation which common sense, without the grace of genius, can deal with successfully."

The same year Sergeant George Robert Caron was born, a plain-speaking young man from rural Missouri exchanged vows with Elizabeth Virginia Wallace. Fresh from a world war, Harry Truman tried his hand at politicking and found it to his liking. Apparently his constituents liked it, too, and respected his brash, forth-right manner, because they gave him a United States Senate seat and packed him off to Washington. When the round-faced man whose words sprung through the gap in his teeth clambered into the position of chairman of the committee to investigate government spending, not just the folks back home sat up and took notice. The updraft he created swept him into the vice presidency. He had barely warmed his seat when the living legend FDR turned the world upside down by leaving it.

The Secretary of War had reservations about the political savvy of Roosevelt's simple, almost shy replacement. He had, reports stated, consorted with the corrupt political machine of Jackson County, Missouri, the rogue Tom Pendergast. They said Pendergast had bought Truman's senatorial seat and pretty much everything else that suited his purposes. To Truman, who was too honest and too impoverished to buy his way into or out of a paper bag, Pendergast was a little below the angels. The young politician reckoned that men like Pendergast took power because others relinquished it. Excluding himself, he could pin that blame on feckless, "sniveling church members who weep on Sunday, play with whores on Monday, drink on Tuesday, sell out to the Boss on Wednesday, repent about Friday and then start over on Sunday."

In odd contrast to his picaresque association with Pendergast, Truman voraciously gobbled up the storied strengths of selfless heroes. Extraordinary, thought Stimson. The man who demonstrated seemingly little depth and no confidence—and who hadn't even wanted to be vice president—was taking the oath for the highest office of the United States. Stimson sorely hoped that the best of Truman's "ability" was considerable. No one quite knew what to expect from the modest man whose efforts always seemed geared to proving that he wasn't—as he feared—a failure. Here in the Oval Office now sat the self-deprecating, Pendergast-made man whose taste in neckwear left something to be desired. No one knew how he would deal with power. Least of all the new President.

Stimson had become aide-de-camp to the man West Point rejected because he couldn't see. To the Secretary now fell the task of opening his eyes to the most fantastic weapon ever envisioned by man. It appeared to Stimson that, regarding prior knowledge of the atomic bomb, the President's mind was a blank slate. He wondered where to begin.

If the new president was an enigma to the Secretary of War, the distinguished Stimson, himself a complexity of characters, was a mystery to others. His starched primness gave the impression that he was staid and inflexible. Yet his policies were anything but. Stimson personified the classic situationalist. As evidence unfolded to prove a cause or position he staunchly advocated unworthy of further support, he merely abandoned it and took up another. If saving his country meant hard strokes, the taskmaster was unafraid to administer them. A veteran of two wars and graduate of both Yale and Harvard, Stimson's desire to be a man of the cloth early had been subrogated to his father's dream of seeing him a barrister. In early summer 1940, Roosevelt called the never-ordained "clergyman" out of retirement to embark on a world crusade. He would now share his pulpit with the thirty-third President of the United States, a thirty-two-degree Mason whose overzealous Senate probe into the hush-hush Manhattan Project ironically Stimson had personally quashed. It was, indeed, a strange world.

Truman wasn't mincing words. In a scant twenty minutes, he outlined to a still-stunned radio audience terms for Japan's unconditional surrender, punishment for war criminals and the pattern for a universal body to maintain world peace.

When his predecessor died, it was already Friday the 13th in Japan. The omen had not been missed. Over Tokyo, one hundred sixty B-29s rained incendiaries. Caught in the blaze at the Research Institute was Building Number 49, the heart of Japan's nuclear research.

On April 25, Stimson labored with a seven-hundred word memorandum on the status of nuclear research entrusted to the Manhattan Project. "Within four months," he maintained, "we shall in all probability have completed the most terrible weapon ever known in human history, one bomb which could destroy a whole city."

That ugly prospect was precisely what stuck in the craw of the Metlab scientists, who had come to fear the bomb might work too well. A demonstration of its power should be sufficient, they argued, to underscore the power of this awesome weapon to force negotiation. So convinced were they of the merits of demonstration over use that they added their names to a petition circulated by Szilard. If Groves was surprised by Szilard's about-face, he was more perplexed by the lack of confidence the bomb inspired in select top brass within the inner circle. His own scarcely whispered misgivings set the odds of successful detonation and resulting conclusion of the war at only a sixty-forty.

Wishful Japanese were wagering on the war's outcome as well. With one ten-yen government lottery ticket, they hoped to fulfill their dreams of victory and wealth. The fund-raising scheme was one of many the military had hoped would shift the fulcrum in this out-of-kilter war. It had played most of its cards. The wild card that it tossed on its strategists' table was the people's "volunteer" corps, which conscripted everyone age sixty and younger.

"Every man, woman and child is a warrior," its leaders rallied townspeople. And the warriors—able or not—laid aside the pastimes of peace and took up the shields of nationalism. Wheelchair patients assembled booby traps to slow the invading enemy. Children learned to assemble and lob gasoline bombs. Thirty thousand adults and eleven thousand students between the ages of eleven and seventeen had been drafted into labor battalions to clear fire breaks.

Hiroshima—like the wolf that chewed off its leg rather than die in a trap—set about the demoralizing task of self-preservation through self-destruction. From shortly after dawn and long into evening, wooden roofs and walls collapsed, slapping the strained earth, suspending swirls of dust in the humid sea air. Demolition crews of the young and old, many of them secondary school girls excused from their classes—bent on ensuring their city's salvation—ripped apart their own and others' homes, shops, trees and fences. Anything that could fuel a fire storm toppled to the ground.

All the while troops poured into Hiroshima. Outside headquarters and in the streets, the Second General Army, under the command of Marshal Shunroku Hata, drilled. As the troops marched past, rigid and unseeing, civilians stood aside. Strangely, Hata's army only made the people of Hiroshima feel more insecure.

Propaganda flowed like the city's rivers, thick and muddy. "We believe that people win wars," faceless radio voices chimed, the words increasingly perceived as so much dross. Nevertheless, as Hiroshimans waited in quiet desperation for the best, they prepared for the worst. When the air-raid sirens wailed, the people of the sun took refuge in earth-covered shelters.

Good for a Single

A lthough the April order to send families home had been expected, the women's absence from the base touched nearly everyone's sensibilities. With Kay gone, even the new spring days felt long, the nights longer. The apartment where Bob and his spirited, dark-haired bride laughed and loved seemed hollow. Walls echoed the clap of his heels on the cold floor. Sunlight that had once warmed her place at the table (and had compelled him to photograph her bathed in its glow), now searched for her in the empty chair. No steaming pots promised a hearty farm supper. The beribboned shocks of delicate dried weeds (these would do nicely, she said) that had graced the table as grandly as a spring bouquet crumbled and scattered their tiny seed heads on the sandy surface. Bob followed the contours of the little kitchen with his eyes, then locked the door behind him.

The order meant that the 509th would soon be going overseas. Tibbets gave Caron a one-week furlough. It was barely enough time to help a mother-to-be resettle at her family's farm.

The newlyweds' short time together made the bachelorhood of the barracks—where he had shifted his few belongings—seem strange. On duty, everyone immersed himself in his tasks. Off duty, Caron retreated to the library. Anything on flight and physics came off the stacks, and he lost himself in them. He recalled an article written before the war on a fantastic machine called a cyclotron and the physicist who created it. Now, in the middle of nowhere, he again tripped over information on atomic energy.

The material read like science fiction. Caron synthesized it, making it visual. *A unit of matter is loosely analogous to a miniature solar system. System implies components. Minute electron planets revolve around a center—such as earth's sun—called a nucleus. Inside the nucleus are protons and neutrons. Neutrons carry a neutral charge. The attraction of negatively charged electrons for positively charged protons keeps the miniature system from falling apart. When the force that holds it all together is released, a miniature cataclysm results. Particles crash violently against other particles until the entire system breaks up...in one-millionth of a second. Creating a deliberate, "controlled" cataclysm is easy—in theory. Atoms make up all things. But all things are not tightly packed with atoms. Like the stars and planets that dot the solar system, protons, neutrons and electrons have lots of deep space to roam around.*

The congenial Einstein, in his own inimitable way, compared the challenge of smashing atoms to shooting ducks on a very dark night in a place where ducks are rare.

The premier atom smasher was Lawrence's at Berkeley. The element that had long eluded physicists as key to the process was uranium, specifically its light isotope 235. Bombarded with initial neutrons, the uranium submitted to fission, the splitting of the atomic nucleus. As the atom split, the neutrons thrown off bombarded other atoms. They, too, shattered, releasing other neutrons, which then shattered still more atoms, and so on. The "so on" was referred to as a chain reaction.

To create an atomic explosion, several pieces of fissionable material that were as pure as possible had to be united as quickly as possible. The trick was to figure out how much was "enough" for the mass to become "critical." Too little and nothing happened. Enough and a chain reaction began, developing so rapidly that the material exploded.

Over the weeks that Caron read about chain reactions, Los Alamos physicists were creating them. The scientists and Parsons' ordnance specialists were also working out details for containing, controlling and directing the energy that resulted. The bomb assembly had become a jigsaw puzzle. Any one interlocking piece depended on the other. Those interlocking pieces were the checks and balances of its firing system, which was designed to prevent premature detonation.

Inside the barrel of the bomb, a five-pound "bullet" of U^{235}, triggered by gunpowder, would be fired rapidly into the hole of a seventeen-pound, donut-shaped uranium ring. Halfway into the ring, a radioactive metallic element would throw off an initial shower of neutrons. They would begin the chain reaction. If they scattered without bombarding other atoms, the reaction would "run down," and there would be no explosion. As long as a high-density substance corralled the neutrons, they would continue the chain reaction.

The uranium bomb, first named "Thin Man" after Roosevelt, now "Little Boy," was anything but little. With all of its firing mechanisms in place, it weighed nearly five tons. To accommodate the activity that would need to take place inside it required a housing ten feet long and twenty-eight inches in diameter.

Although the cigar-shaped superexplosive, painted an inconspicuous gun-metal gray, looked primitive, the "sweet simplicity of the thing" fascinated even Tibbets, the pilot entrusted to deliver it.

The potential for using atomic energy to create a weapon of war enthralled Caron. In high school, he had been awestruck by H. G. Welles' *War of the Worlds.* Now, unobtrusively, intricately, he had been woven not into fiction but into the fabric of twentieth-century reality, the imaginings and fabrications of Oppenheimer's geniuses its warp and woof.

In the dusty quiet of the library, Caron's own imagination ran loose. *If only an atom-splitter could be made small enough to fit in an airplane...and if it could pack enough wallop to force the enemy to its knees. But that's impossible. The magnets in Lawrence's cyclotron weigh tons. And yet.... Why are all those civilians dressed in khakis with no insignia trooping in and out of Wendover?*

He allowed the chain reaction of ideas to run down. Quickening his pace on the walk, he marched purposefully to Tibbets' house.

"Colonel, I'd like permission to work on an idea I have for putting a third machine gun in the tail."

"Sure, Bob. But do it on the QT. No requisitions. I don't know anything about it."

Before he could finish the gun's design and installation, the 509th began its long packing process. The extra machine gun would eventually be added to General Doolittle's 8th Air Force planes.

April 24, 1945

Dear Mr. Rickey,

I'm a deep-rooted Dodger fan...been one since I was old enough to tell a baseball from a football, having lived within walking distance of the Ebbets Field bleachers all my life....

It was one thing to be razzed by a cocky Giants' fan. It was quite another to see caps on some of the crews from big teams other than the Brooklyn Dodgers. Caron hoped to fix that. Ray Gallagher of the *Bock's Car* crew had written to the Chicago White Sox asking for baseball caps.

The Sox obliged, sending one for each crew member. The Brooklyn native figured a polite letter to Branch Rickey at the Dodgers' office might churn up a dozen for his crew.

Bob Finch, Rickey's assistant manager, cracked a smile in anticipation of his petitioner's next line:

> I've heard that major league clubs will send their hats to combat crews, and I wonder...

Finch poised for the pitch.

> ...if our crew could get some from the best club in any league, the Dodgers.

Even with all the soft-soap going to bat for the Dodger fan, Finch had no caps that weren't on his players' heads. He hated to write the tail gunner that, unfortunately, he couldn't send any.

Short in stature, but not on patience, Caron threw Finch an unexpected curve.

> May 8, 1945
>
> Dear Mr. Finch,
>
> I want to thank you for your very prompt and considerate reply to my request for a Dodger cap. I'm disappointed in not being able to get one, but I fully understand how difficult it is to meet all the similar requests you no doubt get. One of the boys suggested I make a similar request to another club, but I'll be damned if I will. Even if I haven't been home in three years to see a Dodgers' game, my kid sister is holding down my seat, rooting for me....

Not a home run, but good for a single. Finch buckled. "Anybody who can write that kind of letter in the midst of disappointment at not getting the right kind of answer to his first one deserves everything in the world," he flashed back, along with one lucky-charm cap. "I hope some day you wear it down the main street of Tokyo."

On warm summer days, young bespectacled Harry Truman practiced scales and sonatas. Over the cadences of his piano he could hear his schoolmates' cheers as one team or the other hit a triple or a home run. He longed to play ball with them, but his father had forbidden it. Harry could be injured, or break his glasses. The boy resigned himself to believe his father was probably right. He had never been particularly lucky. Over the years, his life had been guided less by good fortune than by sheer determination and the courage to forge past fear. Harry always seemed to muster that courage from some unknown depth, surprising himself and others. It would have been unlike him to bask in the glory of his gain. As commander of a battery under bloody siege in the French mountains, a more-seasoned Truman demanded of himself that which he didn't know he had and earned the respect of men who lived because he did.

Success. It had seemed always a chimera. Half a century of obstacles later, the man who had been denied baseball as a timid youth finally was going to bat in his (and, perhaps, history's) biggest game. Was it a choice morsel of fate, a delicious and succulent bit of luck that had rocketed him from obscurity to international prominence? Or was it a curse? Unknown to either of them, the President's destiny was about to become intertwined with another modest, ordinary young man, whose aspirations had been as simple and as honest as his own.

The twenty-five-year-old tail gunner from Brooklyn had not been the best first baseman on his junior team, or the biggest kid on the block, or even the smartest student in school, but he *was* going overseas and, perhaps, would *do* something for his country.

In Hiroshima, Caron's thoughts were mirrored by thousands of half-grown men. But their traditional views of service, life and death couldn't have differed more. Barely out of boyhood, scores of timid faces and bodies destined themselves to be dashed against the ships of their country's enemy in miniature torpedo submarines. Each *Kaiten* would ultimately make the "Turn Toward Heaven" alone. At Base P in Hiroshima Bay, the Navy would teach him how.

Kamikaze recruits, fresh from their university classrooms, their cheeks hot with purpose, wore as badges of their bravery simple white silk scarves tied around their foreheads. They were the Shimpu Special Attack Corps. Their wooden Yokosuka MXY-7 Ohka gliders, the fabled Cherry Blossom, dangled from the bellies of G4M2 bombers the United States Navy called "Bettys." At seven thousand feet, the gliders were set free. Within three miles of their targets, the pilots ignited the three tail rockets. At six hundred fifty miles per hour, their twenty-six hundred forty-five pound warhead unstoppable, the Cherry Blossom unfurled death. Instantly, *chu* and *ko* had been repaid.

His heart breaking, a Japanese admiral penned an elegy to the falling petals.

> In blossom today, then scattered,
> Life is so like a delicate flower.
> How can one expect fragrance to last forever?

Although worlds apart politically and culturally, United States Navy Vice-Admiral C. R. Brown would have understood the admiral's pain. The poetic deaths of the kamikazes roused in him a strange mixture of respect and pity. He watched their attacks with a "hypnotic fascination...and detached horror of a terrible spectacle rather than as an intended victim."

In Japan, destruction flowered everywhere. In its shattered cities, on the sea, in the air. Throughout Washington cherry trees exploded in a gentle pink profusion, bespeaking promises and rites that exist outside of man's capacity to alter them.

Admiral Brown's compassion was countered by Truman's contempt. Not for the young fallen Japanese, but for the demoniac warlords who pronounced them expendable. For them, he had neither respect nor pity. The President's mood was not one of munificence when he met briefly on April 22 in Washington with Vyacheslav Molotov. In fact, the Soviet foreign minister had been affronted by Truman's lack of diplomatic decorum. The President's unclothed threat to withhold reconstruction funds from Russia unless it honored the Yalta Agreement and reassessed its policies on Poland and eastern Europe only added insult to injury.

Roosevelt had carefully woven the Russians into the tapestry of his foreign policy. When Truman discovered a loose thread in the relic he inherited, he pulled it. At first, Admiral Leahy had misinterpreted the President's action as bungling, and it worried him. However, seeing Truman in the ring, sparring with Molotov, demonstrated he could get tough with bullies. Roosevelt had recognized the Soviet Union his first year in office and continued to mollycoddle her. Truman stood firm. The Admiral approved of that. Leahy knew one thing for certain. Like a pit bull, when the tenacious Truman bit, he wasn't letting go. The new atomic weapon would put even more power in his jaws.

In their September 1944 *aide-mémoire*, Roosevelt and Churchill had concurred that when the bomb was finally available, "it might perhaps, after mature consideration, be used against the Japanese." The ailing President's death had spared him the decision.

"This is a solemn, but glorious hour," Truman said on May 8 of the victory in Europe. Two days after Hitler's April 30 suicide in his bunker at the Reich Chancellery, Berlin fell. The Führer's death crashed like a tidal wave on Japan's shores. With V-E Day, Japan's 1941 solidarity agreement with Germany and Italy had became nothing more than so many handshakes and a worthless piece of paper. Now she stood alone against the Allies. They could concentrate their efforts entirely on her.

Slowly, the two subcritical halves of fissionable material were inching closer together. Oppenheimer's preliminary test of the new weapon had proven successful. At the same time, the small advance party of the 509th Composite Group arrived on Tinian to prepare for delivery of the bomb.

Thousands of miles east, a Midwest American town named for an Indian tribe was contributing its energies to winning the war. In Omaha, Nebraska, the C. A. Swanson & Sons Company was shipping nearly all its poultry to the armed forces overseas. Still another River City plant would play a significant role in the war. Overshadowed by the Boeing Company, an Omaha aircraft production facility had gone virtually unnoticed. That was about to change.

Two days after the end of the war in Europe, Colonel Paul W. Tibbets arrived in Omaha to shop for B-29s to replace his high flyers' well-used training planes.

Omaha had not long ago shaken off six months of Great Plains' winter. Frigid nights had released their crushing grip on the Missouri River. Creaking and groaning, striated ice floes heaved, broke free, jumbled and rushed jarringly Gulf-ward. Within weeks, a fragile, new green graced the cottonwoods. Tulips and narcissus dripped red and yellow onto lawns of proper Tudor residences. The inner city ambushed the longer days, imprisoning the radiant warmth in its brownstone and brick. Businessmen and women, who a month ago had measured every quickened step by the ferocity of head-bowing icy blasts, now protracted conversations on the corner and risked a last-minute cigarette on sunlit stairs. Birds trilled promise and renewal.

At Fort Crook, a few miles to the south, machines chirped and warbled at the aircraft assembly plant.

Like a goose whose goslings cluster about her, the bomb-proof main structure of the Glenn L. Martin Company hovered over its offspring with maternal watchfulness. Never mind that twenty-five full-size football fields could fit neatly into its one million two hundred thousand square feet of floor space. Or that ten miles of fluorescent tubing tracked back and forth across its ceilings. Martin's closely knit fourteen thousand five hundred twenty-seven-member family—nearly half women—punched time clocks day and night to meet the production schedule of its most demanding customer, Uncle Sam. The clan collectively reveled in its competitive edge: it was the nation's only aircraft assembly plant to achieve thirty-three consecutive months of on-schedule production.

On chilly December 7, 1941, dignitaries conducted a simple ceremony at Fort Crook to dedicate the main access road of the Martin plant in the memory of young native son, Marine Air Cadet Robert A. Nelson. Nebraska Governor Dwight Griswald and dignitaries spoke about honor, service, loyalty. Then, someone passed a folded note to the podium. Color drained from the speaker's face. He leaned into the microphone and stumbled over the words. "The Japanese have attacked Pearl Harbor."

If on April 26, two years later, the visiting President Roosevelt had arrived at Martin worn and weary, he left revitalized. Cheered by thousands of patriotic employees who championed the American way, he laid his doubts to rest. Here was proof that on the homefront the war was going well. Governor Griswald's Mid-American show-and-tell roused his spirits and quickened his resolve to achieve a swift Allied victory abroad. Martin would lay the golden eggs—or rather the silver superfortresses—of hope. It would be up to the Army Air Force to hatch a plan for their ultimate use.

By early 1944, Martin roofed in additional assembly area and retooled its B-26 Marauder production lines to accommodate the new four-engine, long-range bombers that were to deliver the final blow to America's enemy. On April 6, production of its first B-29 began. The first Superfortress was completed on May 24, one month ahead of schedule.

Its success was due in large part to the family spirit of its huge production staff. In lunch rooms, restrooms, near time clocks morale posters sprinkled God-and-Country messages. A hawkish, wide-eyed Uncle Sam, flamboyant in a stars-and-stripes coat, barked into a telephone receiver, "… But I need 'em NOW. I must have your B-29s on schedule. GET 'EM FLYING."

And they did. Nearly one Rosie the Riveter for every male kept the front-line-bound B-29s rolling off the assembly line. The Omaha Martin plant turned out fifty-five planes a month, nearly fourteen percent of the nation's total production of Superfortresses. Management pushed the production envelope to the limit by shuttling the planes' time-consuming modifications to a special hangar nearby. When the "mod" center couldn't keep up with the incoming stream, pilots picked up their partially completed planes as full of anticipation as suitors on their first dates and at their bases placed them in the hands of hot mechanics, engineers and armament men who rebuilt them by the seat of their pants, rewriting the manuals as they went.

Tibbets and an aeronautical engineer reviewed the Colonel's stringent specifications. The 509th's planes were to be the first equipped with fuel-injection engines and Curtis electric reversible-pitch propellers. Further, to lighten the planes and to save hundreds of man-hours modifying them back at base, Tibbets wanted four turrets eliminated during production.

"Trust me," said the Martin foreman, pointing to Number 82. "That's the one you want. It was built midweek, not on a Monday."

On his next visit to the plant, Tibbets brought a dummy bomb to try it out for size. But the forward bomb bay doors had to be enlarged. The same modification was then made on fourteen additional planes, enabling each to carry an identical, single, giant bomb suspended from a special mammoth hook.

Tibbets had faith that the plant foreman had selected for him the most mechanically sound plane on the line. Truman had become more incredulous. Brooding on the species' capacity for good and evil, he wrote in his May 22 memorandum to the Secretary of War: "The human animal cannot be trusted for anything good except en masse. The combined thought and action of the whole people of any race, creed or nationality, will always point in the right direction."

Perhaps the moon and stars had been in the right position, for May was a time to examine conscience and seek guidance. The Interim Committee convened in the Conference Room of the Pentagon to point itself in the right direction. It needed infinite wisdom to select cities as potential targets for the atomic bomb. Tibbets had no desire to usurp or involve himself in that ominous decision. Armed with Intelligence reports and recommendations, the committee could do its job. He had done his. Or nearly so. He announced that his fifteen flight crews were ready to deliver. Each bombardier had practiced at least fifty bomb releases. Some, like his best bombardier, Ferebee, had flown eighty to one hundred practice runs.

As Martin completed—to the degree it could—the 509th's special planes, one crew at a time arrived to pick them up. When the call came that Number 82 would soon be ready, Tibbets turned the crew over to Captain Lewis and sent them on without him.

When the C-54 transport touched down, the crew exploded onto the tarmac. Omaha suddenly looked as close to paradise as they were going to get. The countryside, greening with corn, undulated in surprising subtle rises and falls. That alone made it an agreeable diversion from the pastel landscape of northwestern Utah. To the New Jersey-born pilot, River City bore little resemblance to his East Coast haunts. But right now, Lewis couldn't think of any other cow town where he'd rather be.

Caron appreciated the chance to leave the cold .50 caliber turret guns and the smell of cutting oil behind. "No problem," the personable Captain Lewis assured him when the gunner asked to be dropped off in Dodge City to look in on Kay first. "See you in Omaha."

The disturbing call came while they were still at Wendover. On June 2, Kay had gone into a particularly difficult premature labor. Their baby was anxious to see the world more than two months early. The caller informed him that even if all went well, mother and baby would be hospitalized longer than usual.

Kay, happy to see her husband even for two days, felt strengthened, invigorated. Caron's suddenly expanded family was all he could think about on the bumpy bus ride from Dodge City to Wichita. Concern for their well-being remained with him throughout the flight to Omaha. Judy was so fragile, so unready to meet the world. He had never seen a baby so tiny. Still, the doctor assured him that she was perfect in every way. She's beautiful, he thought. Just like her mother.

"I'm very sorry, Sir." The clerk at the Fontenelle Hotel shook his head. "You might try next door at the YMCA." Caron took his suggestion, stowed his B-4 bag under the single bed that had just become his and returned to the elegant Fontenelle to spend time with the crew.

The Gothic Revival hotel, built four years before his birth, had been designed as a regional showpiece. Elaborate terra-cotta pinnacles, symbolizing the feathered headdress of the Indian Chief Logan Fontenelle, reached imposingly into the aquamarine Midwest sky. President Woodrow Wilson, a guest in 1916, complimented the Fontenelle's conspicuous grace. When Art Deco became the rage, it shed its heavy velour, mahogany and marble opulence for the new clean-line, sparingly elegant look that greeted the young New Yorker.

The proud new father discovered that his crew, ensconced comfortably in a suite of rooms on the eighth floor, had begun celebrating his good fortune without him. Lieutenant Stewart Williams was in his cups. Doddering to the window, he leaned out over Douglas Street.

"C'm 'ere," the lieutenant gestured to the crew. "See that Chevy down there? I bet I can hit it." He held the empty whiskey bottle like a chicken about to get its neck wrung, then made a ritual sweeping circle with it over his head. Bodies jammed the window casing next to him. Slowly, he stretched his unsteady arm far into the warm air and released the projectile. The hideous shattering sound seemed to take no time reverberating off the car's hood and into the ears of the shocked house manager.

Finding new quarters was no easy task. In less than a week, word of the crew's caprice and their churlishness had spread as quickly as chaff on the wind. Fortunately, while Caron was at Kay's side, Captain Lewis had befriended several pretty young women. Conveniently, one who was particularly sympathetic—and enamored—worked at the much smaller, but not inelegant Blackstone. As the crew settled in, Caron played it safe and retained his little bed at the "Y."

Throughout that ribald week, Lewis' people-savvy was on the line. When an irate husband discovered the naked truth about his wife's exercise program with one dashing crewman, he would have peeled both their hides and hung them on a fence post had it not been for Lewis. In a manner far different from Tibbets', Lewis was comfortable fraternizing with the enlisted men. He would go to unconventional lengths to be one of them, including slipping off his officer's jacket and donning Sergeant Joe Stiborik's. They were, after all, *his* crew. Rescuing them was part of his personality.

Early each morning the Martin bus picked up the crew and delivered them at the plant. Late each morning, the manager assured Lewis that his production staff was working as fast as it could, but Number 82 wasn't quite ready to go. Its many modifications, including a supercharged fuel-injection system and oversized bomb bay, were taking longer than anticipated. By noon, the bus redeposited the young and the restless downtown. For the rest of the day, they could play tourists or action-starved flyers.

Adrenaline surged in Lewis' veins. The feeling on June 14 of climbing into the pilot's seat of Number 82 was even better than the exhilaration he remembered when George W. Lewis handed his son the keys to his first car. The crew stroked Number 82's dazzling silver skin and caressed their way through a preflight check more intoxicated with her than they had been the previous night on women and whiskey.

The roar of her engines was sweet music to their ears. They circled the city once. Lewis gave Number 82 a little left aileron, then turned west. Teasing the Superfortress over poplar windbreaks separating grasslands, the Captain gleefully swooped over grazing cattle and laughed as they scattered in terror. Caught in the prop wash, a windmill reversed its direction.

Like a boy who had just taken the entire cookie jar, Lewis pressed his back against the padded seat cushion and was content. Subconsciously, he synchronized his breathing to the rhythmic murmur of the engines. His mood changed. The sun's warmth felt sensuously warm on his left shoulder. Gently, now, he guided *his* plane toward Utah.

At Wendover, the long working days now included readying the 509th's planes and equipment for the massive group transfer to the Pacific. To Lewis, Number 82 felt increasingly as though it had been custom-made for him. On a shakedown, he flew her due west over the Pacific to the Farallon Islands off San Francisco, then, at thirty-three thousand feet, south to Baja. Navigator Bud Rider calculated their ground speed on the return flight at an amazing four hundred ten miles an hour, until a front forced them down at the Port of Aerial Embarkation at Mather Field, near Sacramento, California. Negotiating the B-29 into position on the hardstand seemed to Lewis like a good time to try out its massive reversible pitch props. To the astonishment of the two men in the "Follow-me" jeep, he backed Number 82 into its parking spot with ease and grace. Caron and everyone else on the crew knew their plane had just performed flawlessly a maneuver the manuals didn't recommend. But what did the engineers who wrote the manuals know?

On May 6, eight hundred technicians attached to the 509th set sail out of Seattle bound for Tinian aboard the *Cape Victoria*. The B-29s, which shied from formations anyway, were assigned positions in the pipeline, flying overwater singly or in tandem. Number 82 was one of last planes to leave. On June 25 its wheels lifted off the Wendover runway for the last time. Caron was flying right blister for takeoff. "Let's drag the ramp and say good-bye," came Lewis' voice over the intercom. He taxied to the east end of the runway, put the right wing down and buzzed the ramp for the "So long, guys." Caron looked down and counted the cracks as they sped by.

"That's no damn stunt plane you're flying, Captain," a stern voice from the tower admonished. Within a minute Number 82 headed into the wind. Colonel Tibbets was waiting on Tinian.

Throughout the night-long layover in California, while Mather's Port of Aerial Embarkation crews checked to be sure that her life rafts, parachutes and other safety equipment were up to date and correctly stowed, Caron and the other enlisted men took turns standing guard over the plane. Tibbets had wanted assurance that absolutely no one looked into the bomb bay, where they would discover the conspicuous, special hook, modified from the Royal Air Force's Lancaster bombers to accommodate the secret weapon.

Again at Honolulu, they stood guard throughout the night. Caron loaded ammunition and prepared to ride the tail as the Japanese still held Wotje Island and their fighters could pose a threat. At Kwajalein, amid beached wrecks, landing LSTs and tanks, they slept fitfully in transient's shacks, while rats busily harvested anything edible and used the floor under their shaky cots for a racetrack. Before dawn, they were ready for the six-hour flight to Tinian, three miles south of Saipan and one hundred twenty-five miles north of Guam.

The Glory Boys

T
o the islanders and the Japanese troops who had been stationed there, Tinian seemed defensible. A tableland rising out of the waters, fringed with jagged, undercut walls of rusty brown lava, Tinian was not easily penetrable from the sea. For all the miles of coastal ramparts, only at two sites did the beaches break broad, tentative gateways to the interior. Asiga Bay on the eastern coast was one. Yet its four-hundred-yard entry was too narrow for a large-scale assault. On the island's southwestern coast, however, navigable channels stretched beyond the reefs and shoals of the mile-wide beachhead at Tinian Town.

The five-week-long struggle to wrench Tinian from Japanese control began on June 24, 1944. Protecting the island cost eight thousand Japanese lives. Taking it resulted in the deaths of one hundred ninety Americans. Strategically vital to Allied forces because it put Japanese cities within range of the B-29s, Tinian shortened Allied reach to Tokyo down to fifteen hundred miles. Only two and a half miles to Tinian's north across the channel lay Saipan, where twenty-three thousand Japanese troops died, and one thousand were taken prisoner.

One by one, the 509th's brand-spanking-new B-29s began to arrive at Tinian on May 8. From an altitude of three thousand feet, North Field's patchwork and grid pattern resembled a board game rather than a strategic offensive position from which to launch an attack on the enemy. The special planes entered North Field's sweeping flight pattern and touched down at the largest operational airfield in the world. From its four parallel eighty-five-hundred-foot macadam runways, as many as one thousand B-29s could take off at fifteen-second intervals. The Seabees had constructed broad hardstands of pale crushed coral. The 313th Bomb Wing, which was loosely attached to Tibbets' 393rd, had already been flying sorties from North Field. West Field, the island's secondary airstrip, had been adopted by the 58th Bomb Wing on its return from India.

To the American pilots who first flew over it, the shape of the island was reminiscent of Manhattan. Homesick engineers seized upon the similarity with joy, giving its latticed thoroughfares names like 42nd Street, Broadway and Lennox Avenue. The inner circle of Tibbets' Individual Air Force understood the ironies. Once the "Bronx Shipment" had arrived from Los Alamos, the Manhattan Project could be consummated.

When he first stepped off the plane, Caron was reminded more of Manhattan's sewers than its streets. He wondered if the terrible wind-borne smell was the earth belching up its cavernous stores of accumulated methane and other noxious gases, or if the natives who harvested sugar cane from fenced fields were brewing something more potent in their small processing plant.

Olive-drab, square canvas tents temporarily assigned to the crews checkered a well-worn area near low palms. The island's mosquito population sensed this assembly was mess, six men per serving. After two weeks, the ground crews moved to permanent tents in a tidier area. Although the crews left no forwarding address, the voracious insects found them. Flight crews took refuge indoors, assuming former Seabee Quonsets. Industrious Seabees had turned the section overtaken by the 509th Composite Group into a pleasant, walk-lined, livable place. **headquarters 509TH composite group** read a crescent-shaped sign, surrounded with flowers, then corralled in a grassy oval by a low rock wall. Queuing along a short dusty road were squat, rectangular buildings, their sameness broken only by the variety of their porch railings.

The compound's barbed-wire enclosure and carbine-carrying MPs, who stood guard day and night, were a strange incongruity to the attempted homey atmosphere.

Caron was among the twenty enlisted men assigned to the first Quonset in the row after the officer's club, nearest the gate. The mess hall was conveniently located across the road, graveled with crushed coral. The main road linked them to the airfield. Seabees had even left behind a backstop for playing softball, and Caron's group set up a horseshoe pit alongside their hut.

The first Quonset at Eighth Avenue and 125th Street was home not only to some of Lewis' Number 82 crew, but also to a handful of the enlisted men from Sweeney's *Bock's Car.* Some were familiar faces from the old XB-29 test crew. The other residents of the Quonset hadn't been assigned to it. When the bare bulbs that glared from tracks along the curved ceiling went out, the rats ran rampant. They scooted in and out of boots and duffels and devoured stashed Hershey bars. The second night that rodents robbed the high-paraffin chocolate—engineered to resist meltdown in the core of a volcano—several enterprising crewmen suspended a fine netting "hammock" from the ceiling. In the semi-darkness, the men watched their edibles and cigarettes swing overhead as silhouetted, hairless-tailed vermin tried unsuccessfully to negotiate the new obstacle course.

Sandwiched between two itchy wool blankets, flight crews slept on air mattresses issued exclusively to them to relieve discomfort of the narrow, slumped-center cots.

The first night rocks pelted the crews' corrugated-tin roofs, the men inside thought they had been shelled. By the time those in Caron's hut reached the door, squadrons of flight crews from other outfits, freshly returned from bombing raids, had already passed. But their jeers and heckling could still be heard.

"There's the Glory Boys.... Hey, Glory Boys, when're you guys ever gonna fly a mission?"

The 509th shared the island with others whom they couldn't see. Five hundred stranded Japanese bided their ascetic days in caves and trees and made stealthy supply and food forays to the compound by night.

For diversion, crewmen from various squadrons spontaneously raised night-time routing parties. On one occasion, Caron joined Shumard, Nelson and a handful of others to search the restricted southeast section of the island. Sometimes parties routed out a lone Japanese soldier, starved for a cigarette, and escorted him back to headquarters. Mostly, the sallies turned into scavenger hunts, gleaning souvenirs rather than prisoners. This time, they found nothing.

Thirteen of the 509th's fifteen flight crews (two crews remained at Wendover to transport components of the bomb) were assigned to attend ground school conducted by experienced combat crews from other outfits. Nearly all the rock-throwing night marauders resented the mollycoddled crews who continually tinkered with their heavily guarded, brand-new, stripped-down planes and occasionally flew sorties to drop a pumpkin on an enemy city.

Being the butt of frequent taunts was wearing thin. An anonymous headquarters clerk had written and widely circulated a poem that summed up prevailing contempt for the Glory Boys.

Into the air the secret rose
Where they're going, nobody knows.
Tomorrow they'll return again,
But we'll never know where they've been.
Don't ask us about results or such,
Unless you want to get in Dutch.
But take it from one who is sure of the score,
The 509th is winning the war.

When the other groups are ready to go,
We have a program on the whole damned show.
And when Halsey's Fifth shells Nippon's shore,
Why shucks, we hear about it the day before.
And MacArthur and Doolittle give out in advance,
But with this new bunch we haven't a chance.
We should have been home a month or more,
For the 509th is winning the war.

During orientation classes, other outfits continued to twist the knife and held their "pampered dandies" captive audience to blow-by-blow accounts of harrowing bombing missions and encounters with ground and air opposition. Sessions did offer vital information about enemy attack systems and anti-aircraft fire. But the 509th's armament men secretly felt there was little their counterparts could teach them about the B-29's firing systems. They had written the book.

Tibbets' crews cheered when the order finally came to resume flying. Long over-water practice flights to Japanese islands that offered no resistance would simulate the long haul to Honshu, the largest of Japan's home islands and where the capital and major cities were concentrated.

Though Caron flew Number 82 with "Cap" Lewis' as aircraft commander, he and the others sensed more intensely than before that when Tibbets was ready for the "big one," they would be the Colonel's crew.

As they waited for that moment to arrive, the men did what they loved most, flying. Short navigational runs to Guam evolved into bomb drops on the Japanese-held island of Rota. Missions didn't usually exceed the six- to eight-hour round trip to the northeast island of Marcus. Marcus, which had been an active Japanese airbase, was still occupied by troops.

From the air it looked to Caron like a grossly disfigured, pock-marked face.

Unlike the 313th, which sent out two-hundred to three-hundred planes at once, the 393rd flew sorties either singly or in tandem, seldom risking more than three of the special planes at a time.

Preflight briefings were conducted in a large, open-air theater with a stage and benches. Once the aircraft commanders, navigators and intelligence officers presented their instructions, gunners from experienced squadrons proffered their own. "Be sure to count the flak. Note its color and location." From that information, a gunner could determine much about the size and number of the batteries on the ground and relay that information to the aircraft commander. Experience had taught them that only the large 120 mm guns could approach them at thirty thousand feet. Once the nitty gritty of a briefing was out of the way, the tall, lean Chaplain William Downey offered a prayer for a successful mission.

In mid-July, flight crews were briefed that they would carry a single five-ton bomb on their first mission. It would be the familiar orange pumpkin like the dummies they had dropped over American deserts, the shape later dubbed "Fat Man."

General John Davies wanted to see for himself Tibbets' strange aberrations parked on the hardstand. The commander of the 313th Bomb Wing had been assigned only administrative responsibility for the 393rd. He could exercise no authority over it or the rest of the 509th. He stepped from his jeep and peered up at Number 82. An armed guard stopped him.

"General, sir, I have orders that only flight and ground crew and those with security passes are allowed to inspect the plane."

No matter how loudly the general roared his insistence, the MP maintained unflinching resistance.

"I'm sorry, Sir. The general does not have a pass. However, I have a gun, and I have orders to use it."

The vanquished general blinked astonishment, huffed, then climbed back into the jeep. The driver sped off to deposit the general at headquarters where he hoped someone recognized his authority.

The July 24th target was a plant in Kobe. To reach "God's Door" in the southern niche of Honshu, Number 82 would fly over the island of Shikoku. Captain Robert Lewis, aircraft commander, assembled his crewmen: Richard McNamara, co-pilot; Stewart Williams, bombardier; Harold "Bud" Rider, navigator; Wyatt Duzenbury, flight engineer; Robert Shumard, assistant flight engineer; Junior Nelson, radio operator; Joe Stiborik, radar operator; and Bob Caron, tail gunner.

From Tinian, the island of Iwo Jima was in direct line with most target cities. During flyovers, it served as a checkpoint for the navigator to set course for an identifying marker, the initial point. By the time they were over Iwo Jima, the B-29s had reached full or nearly full altitude and could slow their climb for greater fuel efficiency. At the IP, word spread through the intercom they were receiving flak. For the moment, Caron was watching its bursts behind the tail. Where the tail had been a second before, now were streams and clouds of sooty black smoke. Yet none of the fragments hit the plane. The enemy had locked onto Number 82's altitude and course, but couldn't keep up with its speed. Caron recalled scuttle-butt that the Japanese were using German guns. He counted the bursts. Five sets of four each, a set of three. One had been a dud. There must have been four batteries on the ground. For the first time Caron realized the really frightening thing about flak. There was nothing to shoot at.

At the sound of flak, the automatic pilot in Lewis' brain kicked in. In his usual insouciant manner, he handled the plane like it was a continuation of himself. They left the black bursts far behind them.

The airfield outside of Osaka was on the course home. Caron could see its airplanes, recognize the dummies.

"Cap, " he called to Lewis. "Can I release a little tension and fire a few bursts?"

"Let it out," came the response.

The tail gunner fired a few rounds of the .50 caliber, knowing the shells could reach the planes below. Then he settled back in his seat.

Because crawling forward out of the hatch into the waist involved depressurizing and temporarily going on oxygen, he remained isolated in the tail. On a few occasions, when they were on a long practice run and out of fighter territory, Caron would put on his mouton-collared flight jacket, raise his seat on its track and crawl into the frigid cat-sized space of floor to rest his buttocks and his eyes. When the amplidynes and dynamotors that supplied power to the turret system were on, they generated a little warmth within the cold steel.

"Select a target of opportunity," Lewis had been ordered. During the briefing, he told his crew that their July 26 mission to the west coast of Japan was unique in that a target had not been predetermined. Number 82 was headed into a front building over the mountains. Better not risk it, Lewis said over the intercom and turned east toward the heavily bombed Nagoya. The exhausted city yielded. It offered no opposition. No flak. Williams found a target from the little that remained unscathed and released an orange pumpkin.

The target for the July 29 bombing was an aluminum plant in Koriyama, north of Tokyo. At the last minute, Lewis was ordered to substitute another plane for Number 82. Caron found one of the .50 caliber guns in the tail of the borrowed plane was jammed. He crawled into the turret and discovered a ruptured case that couldn't be extracted before takeoff. He would have to leave it. The aircraft flirted with the coastline and finally coursed inland over a low ceiling. Tokyo was all but obscured. Rising like a proud sentinel above the strata, Mount Fujiama glowed in the sunlight. It caught the tail gunner by surprise and took his breath away. He had seen it in photographs, of course. But there was the god eternal in its heaven.

The aluminum plant and nearly everything else within miles of Koriyama lay beneath a dense vapor layer. Since their orders were for visual bombing only, no radar drop, Lewis planned to come in for a closer look.

"Fighters down low, Cap," Caron called forward. "They look like "Tonys". They must have spotted us because they just made a climbing turn."

"OK, boys. Let's get the hell out of here and find us an alternate target."

With an engine that had failed to generate full power since early in the mission, Lewis wasn't going to press their luck. The navigator plotted a new course, and the B-29 was a phantom before a single Tony reached its altitude.

Williams finally spotted a railroad yard with a long causeway over its tracks that would become their alternate target. Lewis lined up for the bomb run and gave Williams the controls. "Bomb away," he shouted. Caron watched the pumpkin hit the center of the causeway. Railroad tracks scattered like matchsticks. "Looks like you got yourself a causeway, Stew," he said.

Mission takeoffs at 2:45 A.M. gave the planes considerable air time under the cover of darkness and brought them at their targets in the early morning hours. Invariably, Caron crawled into the tail for takeoff. He had heard rumors that despite the horrible crash record of overloaded B-29s—"too many of those boys roll right off the end of the runway into the drink"—there was never a tail gunner lost in a ditching. The Superfortress simply snapped at the rear pressure section, near the put-put, and a bubble of air moved up into the tail.

A watery grave wasn't the only death to fear for the rest of the crew. No one could predict—and crews too often couldn't escape—the blazing torch that was an overloaded B-29 piled in a heap on the tarmac.

Tokyo Rose was not an enigmatic, evanescent entity. Rather, the creation called Tokyo Rose was a unique psychological emanation: multiple entities sharing a single personality. As many as a dozen voices articulated her message of demoralization. When it had the opposite effect, the Navy awarded the infamous voice a citation for *aiding* American morale. Tinian flight crews left their radio dial tuned to her sometimes coquettish, often sensuously breathy monologues. As was intended, the music she played reminded them of home. She made them laugh. And she made them angry. They called her lies "a lot of boloney," or something more profane. Still, it had unnerved them when she welcomed the Black Arrow Squadron—despite its carefully guarded B-29s being parked on restricted areas of North Field—and its orange pumpkins. Intelligence-gathering was a two-way street.

Lolly-pop sweet Shirley Temple had grown up. Even as a dimpled, vivacious teenager, she was less of a draw at the "Pumpkin Playhouse" than Rita Hayworth. Projectors rolled nightly at the outdoor theater, and rain or moon shine, its movies attracted more goers than the Navy's indoor theater. When Caron wasn't laughing or crying to a base movie, he and his barrack buddies were applying their carpentry skills to disassembling the least conspicuous parts of the officers' club and reassembling the salvage on the back of his crew's hut. The enlisted men appreciated the midnight requisitions that resulted in a porch more suitable to a Maine oceanfront than a Quonset on a recently occupied island in the war-torn Pacific. The retreat became a back-home place where they could prop their feet on the railing and spin a tale or two.

Between briefings and missions, Tinian skies invited romps on white coral beaches. Sometimes a lucky crewman brought a pretty nurse willing to prescribe a remedy for his homesickness. In the late afternoon, when towering thunderheads released their burden, the men grabbed a bar of soap and showered under the cool deluge.

The 509th's unofficial uniform became well-broken-in brown boondockers that barely cleared the ankle, "Tinian shorts," regulation Army Air Forces' fatigues cut off above the knee, and a white T-shirt.

W hile Tinian flight crews painted names on their planes, Columbia University professor Norman Ramsey rechecked the complex schedule before him. From the seventy-three-hundred-foot Los Alamos mesa, final components of the bomb were about to make their way to Tinian.

For two years Oppenheimer and the Los Alamos scientists coaxed a short Hungarian physicist's bathtub fantasy into being. They had solved the riddle: how much fissionable material was "enough" to explode. Ordnance specialists had taken potential and turned it into an eventual. Collectively, they had answered the question that Caron pondered on lonely afternoons in the Wendover library—how to make an idea practical.

Now, the responsibility for seeing to it that the various components of the bomb reached the man who would deliver it rested with Dr. Ramsey.

"Quantum physics," lectured Dr. Yoshio Nishina, his thin lips rippling like little pink ribbons, "can liberate us with the potential for boundless energy." His square face animated. He gave himself over to his students fully, enthusiastically. He, himself, had studied with the best. For six years in Copenhagen, he had learned everything that Niels Bohr could teach him, and that was considerable—Bohr, whose genius many of his colleagues ranked second only to Einstein's.

Nishina—*Oyabun,* the Old Man, to his assistants—had been commissioned to build an atomic bomb for Japan. The American embargo on exports of uranium strongly hinted to him that it, too, was undertaking the same task. If only the military could have left him alone to explore the vast potential of nuclear energy...harness it to rebuild his broken country and restore its prosperity, rather than to dash her headlong into cliffs of oblivion.

"What an insane war Japan has launched," he risked to a friend. "Any fool knows the power and might of the United States. The consequences to Japan can only be disastrous. We are all aboard a sinking ship."

How well he understood the Western mind. And how ironic that his own two-hundred-ton cyclotron was a sibling to Ernest Lawrence's, constructed with the help of Lawrence's own Berkeley whiz-kid assistant. But, then, pure science had always ignored political boundaries.

In April, the question of the military's sanity for entering a nuclear race with the United States became moot. Four months before Dr. Ramsey inched Little Boy closer to its destination, Nishina's Tokyo laboratory at the Institute for Physical and Chemical Research blazed a white-hot casualty of the "insane war."

THIRTEEN

Miracle of Deliverance

T he eight-square-mile volcanic island of Iwo Jima had been bought with blood. Thirty-five days of siege that began on February 19, 1945, claimed six thousand American lives and more than three times that many Japanese. It was a fragile victory that placed another stepping stone in America's path to Japan.

At home, Americans looked to the theater for diversion from the wounds of war. On March 31, Mississippi-born playwright Thomas Lanier, better known as Tennessee Williams, opened *The Glass Menagerie*, featuring Laurette Taylor and Eddie Dowling, at New York's Plymouth Theater.

Rogers and Hammerstein again dazzled audiences with their lavishly romantic production *Carousel*. Premiering on April 19 at New York's Majestic Theater with John Raitt and Jan Clayton, it would run eight hundred eighty-nine additional performances.

Time was in tune with the national pulse, and it throbbed with melodies such as "It's Been a Long, Long Time" and "Till the End of Time." Gospel singer Mahalia Jackson rhythmically infused hope with—and people, black and white, clapped to—"He's got the Whole World in His Hands." Before the year was over, Jackson's soulful song would sell more than a million copies.

Amid the rubble of charred wood, broken stones and crumbled concrete of Tokyo, delicate fan-shaped leaves opened triumphantly on blackened ginkgo branches. Oleander bushes burst forth defiantly, like miniature deep pink and white prayer flags, waving their brave blooms in the breeze.

Without Hitler to disfigure it, the face of Europe began to soften. Its diverse people, who for six years had tasted the bitterness of war, would be introduced to the effervescent sweetness of Coca-Cola, the red and white flag on its bottles as characteristically American as the Stars and Stripes.

Fatigue and sorrow lined the face of the forty-four-year-old reluctant deity-emperor of Japan. The nearly unbearable weight that pressed on him, reducing his five-foot, six-inch frame from one hundred forty-five pounds to one hundred twenty-three, was not his own mortality and vulnerability. The Emperor welcomed them. Most oppressive was the suffering of his people. All around the Imperial Palace, with its moat-rimmed walls, greenhouses and pavilions, the great city of Tokyo lay buried beneath ash. He had been aware that the Allies had deliberately spared the palace. On May 25, however, the Emperor and his residence were no longer inviolate. Incendiaries accidentally set some of its twenty-seven buildings afire. He and his wife, Nagako, took refuge in a concrete bunker beneath the rambling Imperial library where he passionately immersed himself in study. Now he knew something of the homelessness that surrounded him. Even one of the world's richest men could not buy peace.

He wondered what the Supreme Council for the Direction of the War thought when it gazed upon the destruction, heard the wails of the people. How had it come to pass that a handful of men held greater power than he and chose to prolong the agony of Japan?

Physicist Herbert F. York had been working with Lawrence on his Calutrons when he received a call from the Oak Ridge, Tennessee, scientists who said, "Come, we need you." One late spring day in the ancient Appalachians, York and his colleagues were given an unusual notice: be prepared to shut down all Calutrons in June. York analyzed his orders. Interrupting the Calutrons' month-long "run" was inefficient. Nevertheless, midstream, the machines were to be stopped, their uranium collected, processed and shipped to Site Y. York was certain the dramatic and costly move confirmed scientists as Los Alamos had eaten of the forbidden fruit.

Dr. Vannevar Bush, head of the Interim Committee, that motley crew over whom the tree of the knowledge of good and evil loomed auspiciously, explained to the assembled scientists, politicians and military experts that their function was to lay out "if" and "how" the new weapon was to be used.

At the committee's May 31 session, whispers subsided when Stimson spoke. Candidly, he told the small group that he regarded the bomb not as a new weapon, "but as a revolutionary change in relations of man to the universe." With that preface, he placed on their shoulders a weighty decision: Should the bomb be used on Japan?

When the committee reconvened the next day, they answered resoundingly, "Yes." Furthermore, the bomb should be dropped "without warning" and "as quickly as possible," before more lives were lost. The committee also recommended the bomb be used against a target that would sustain the greatest damage to show its devastating effect. Any other alternative "involved serious danger to the major objective of obtaining prompt surrender." Stamping their final seal on the operation, they concluded: "We can propose no technical demonstration likely to bring an end to the war; we can see no acceptable alternative to direct military use."

Leo Szilard was beside himself. His brainchild was now his tormentor. He had envisioned it a deterrent against German aggression. Not against Japan. With Germany's fanatic leader out of the picture, the Interim Committee faced new considerations. The Committee's decision to use the bomb countered Metlab's efforts to petition Truman for a demonstration only. They hoped that a display of the bomb's power would be sufficient to dissuade Japan from prolonging the war.

Metlab director Arthur Holly Compton, recipient of the 1927 Nobel Prize in physics, sat on the Committee's scientific advisory panel along with Oppenheimer, Teller and others. He read to the small group a poignant counterpetition that he had received:

> Are not the men of the fighting forces a part of the nation? Are not they, who are risking their lives for the nation entitled to the weapons which have been designed? In short, are we to go on shedding American blood when we have available a means of speedy victory? No! If we can save even a handful of American lives, then let us use this weapon—now! These sentiments, we feel, represent more truly those of the majority of Americans and particularly those who have sons...in the foxholes and warships in the Pacific.

His own convictions reinforced, Stimson took the Committee's recommendations to the President.

At Brookhaven, Long Island, the military was planning ahead for project "Olympic," General Marshall's November 1 invasion of the Japanese home islands. It began erecting temporary structures to treat the thousands of American soldiers who would suffer from a newly identified wartime trauma labeled "shell shock."

General George Marshall refined his three-prong plan for the invasion of Kyushu to avert a repeat of Okinawa. The high cost of securing the strategic island was fresh in his mind. When on April 1, 1945, Allied forces landed on Okinawa's west coast, they were outnumbered almost two to one. By June 22, the day Admiral Chester Nimitz, commander in chief of the Pacific Fleet, declared victory, one hundred three thousand Japanese troops lay dead, but so did forty-eight thousand Americans. Despite the toll and massive cleanup of the island, on July 2, General Douglas MacArthur established an air base there. Marshall knew all too well Japan had proven a formidable adversary. Although Japan's sun had shone briefly over much of Southeast Asia, uncounted Japanese souls gave silent testimony that the glorified bubble of an expanding Greater East Asia Co-Prosperity Sphere had burst.

That was not, however, the picture painted for the Japanese people. Printing the military's fabrications, the press promulgated the myth that Iwo Jima and Okinawa had been sacrificed as part of a grand strategy to lure American forces closer and closer to the homeland until they could be pounced upon and utterly annihilated.

As General Marshall planned his invasion, Imperial Army strategists formulated a counter-offensive: a "Basic Policy of the Future Conduct of the War." Its substance was as improbable as its title. Kamikazes would destroy one-quarter of the invaders while they were still at sea; another quarter while the vulnerable invading force attempted to land; remaining enemy troops would be crushed at beachheads. To Foreign Minister Shigenori Togo, the "strategy" was inconceivably naive.

The Imperial Army was grasping at straws. Early in the summer of 1945, militarists envisaged a massive guerrilla army of young and old, hurling the enemy back to the sea. In one desperate and fanatical move, the Army conscripted the entire nation, in essence mobilizing everyone under supreme command. There would be no personal choice.

July Fourth Americans celebrated freedom. Leo Szilard joined in, exercising his newly gained rights as a naturalized citizen. Mothers, children and grandparents picnicked and thought of loved ones far away. Old Glory unfurled in parades down America's main streets. Bands pranced to rousing marches. On that Independence Day, American, British and Canadian leaders met in the real and symbolic capital of world democracy to formulate the means to an end of the war.

The means had included major B-29 air-offenses against Honshu and Kyushu, launched from bases in the Marianas and Okinawa, to demoralize and cripple the enemy. The beleaguered Japanese nation, choked off from all sides, tightened its sash another few inches. An Imperial Army soldier subsisted on one bowl of scarce rice and one bean cake a day. Women prepared meager meals with a flour made from sweet-potato vines, mulberry leaves, pumpkins and horse chestnuts. Malnutrition and unsanitary conditions contributed to the prevalence of dysentery and stomach disorders. Most factories had been facing severe shortage of materials, including salt used in explosives, since early fall 1944.

"Japan was short on everything except courage," maintained Major General Seizo Arisue from General Army Headquarters in Tokyo.

With that mindset, Tokyo Rose brazened: "Come and get us."

Gripping the right handrail, Truman steadied himself as he crossed the gangplank and stepped down. Saluting sailors jammed the deck of the heavy cruiser U. S. S. *Augusta*, which would deliver the apprehensive President on July 15, 1945, to Antwerp, Belgium, for the journey to Berlin. In three fleeting months, he had made the passage from moon-faced obscurity to one-third of the Big Three. Why shouldn't he be nervous about the power-play to come when the stakes were so high? The crossing, with its upbeat band, first-rate movies and tranquil deck strolls, would ease his mind. But all the coaching from freshly appointed Secretary of State Byrnes couldn't help him play his hand any better than the card he was about to be dealt from home.

A Charleston, South Carolina, Democrat who served a decade in the Senate and sat briefly on the Supreme Court, James Francis Byrnes had plenty of advice for the President, especially regarding relations with Russia. And he would give it if only he could get Truman's undivided attention.

Days after Roosevelt's death, Byrnes had tried to expand the new president's horizons. Truman needed to think of the bomb as more than just a means to an end, explained the man next in line for the job. Quite simply, the bomb was clout. With such power in its grasp, the United States could unilaterally dictate the terms for peace and keep Russian hands off Manchuria and Japan.

W hile the physicist who had been so zealous to build a bomb just as zealously urged reconsideration of its use, the device was receiving copious attention in New Mexico. The U^{235} from Oak Ridge, which Oppenheimer's team had feverishly readied, was about to journey six thousand miles across the Pacific. Airlifting it seemed too risky. Major Robert R. Furman, Groves' quick-witted trouble-shooter, arranged the alternative—over-water passage.

On July 14, seven carloads of security agents flanked an inconspicuous black truck for its geared-down descent from the Jemez Mountains above Santa Fe enroute to Albuquerque. Cradled inside, Little Boy's cannon components rocked gently. From Albuquerque, an Army Air Forces' plane shuttled the special cargo to Hamilton Field near San Francisco. At Mare Island Naval Dock, crewmen loaded the mysterious fifteen-foot crate and bucket-shaped cylinder containing the uranium projectile aboard the cruiser U. S. S. *Indianapolis*. Another portion of the bomb, the projectile's "target," would be sent from Wendover later. The cloak-and-dagger operation, code named "Bronx Shipment," had begun.

M uch of Europe lay in shambles. Yet Villa Number 2, Kaiserstrasse, in the Potsdam suburb of Babelsberg outside of Berlin, rose from the bleakness like an oasis. Amid lush, well-groomed lawns and luxurious gardens, Truman settled into a three-story stucco to serve as the "Little White House." Not until the next day would he encounter for the first time the quintessential Englishman, Sir Winston Leonard Spenser Churchill.

Although they had never met the man they served, scientists half a world away at Los Alamos had been working around the clock to provide the President of the United States with clout for his forthcoming Potsdam negotiations.

For two years the assembly of brain power had meddled with fate, testing the criticality of various reacting masses. Oppenheimer aptly named it "tickling the dragon's tail." They played this Russian roulette with radiation at "Omega," a remote site in Alamos Canyon, where botched experiments were less apt to jeopardize the laboratories. Louis Slotin was the first fatality of the unseen force. He had been tickling the dragon's tail, pushing two subcritical hemispheres closer and closer, measuring the radioactivity levels as the two halves approached critical mass. Suddenly, the screwdriver—which he used to inch the masses slowly, cautiously nearer and nearer—slipped, sending one subcritical mass into deadly contact with its twin. With thought only for the safety of the other scientists in the room, Slotin instinctively ripped the two halves apart with bare hands. Then he sat down quietly, calmly to calculate the radiation exposure to everyone else. There was no need to consider the risk to himself. The dragon had turned on him, breathing the fire of death.

Oppie was jittery. Time was as critical as the limited supply of U^{235}. In fact, there was only enough for Little Boy. The uranium bomb would have to receive its test somewhere over Japan. By default, a demonstration would take place of its more complex plutonium sibling, the Fat Man, for which the pumpkin shape had been designed. Just as Klaus Fuchs conspired with the Russians to deliver the secrets of the uranium bomb on which he worked, David Greenglass would hand over blueprints for the plutonium bomb that detonated by implosion rather than explosion.

The megalithic facility at Oak Ridge was squeezing out enough of the more easily extractable U^{238} for an encore to the plutonium test, which had been scheduled for July 14. That was too soon, objected Oppenheimer. Groves relented. The test would be postponed until July 16.

As he often did to soothe his tattered soul, Oppie melted into the cadences of poetry.

> Batter my heart, three-personed God, for you
> As yet but knock, breathe, shine and seek to mend.
> That I may rise and stand, o'er throw me and bend
> Your force to break, blow, burn, and make me new.

John Donne's metaphysical verses struck a cord within him. Inspired by their potency, the scientist and literary scholar christened the plutonium test "Trinity." The name seemed as fitting as test director Kenneth Bainbridge's selection of the site. Oppenheimer approved Jornada del Muerto, two hundred ten miles south of Los Alamos. Bainbridge staked out an eighteen-by-twenty-four mile rectangle of flat scrub desert sixty miles northwest of Alamogordo.

Jornada del Muerto, the "journey of death." The desiccated strip between El Paso, Texas, and northern New Mexico easily overpowered body and soul. It had doubtless daunted Spanish explorers emboldened by their sacred quest and pioneers hardened to beauty by a harsh land. For the weak, cottony mouths, blistered faces and dry retching came as final warnings that there was no margin for error under these flawless skies. Purple basaltic mountains to the west offered no life-sustaining respite. In this hushed place where only the shimmering heat dared waver midday, long-eared jackrabbits paused in the illusory shade of four-wing saltbush. Under scorched rocks and whitened, supine yuccas, scorpions waited for nightfall. Sidewinders, fleeing the oppressive sun, left their obliquely looped signatures on tortured sand.

Groves arrived at the Trinity site the day before scheduled detonation with his usual bravado. Audaciously, as though Nature had pitted her strength against him, the incessant downpour shifted everyone's concerns to the potential for soggy circuits and indiscriminate lightning bolts.

Oppenheimer opened the door to Worry, and the harbinger of doubt became his constant companion. Sleepless nights etched his face. Little flesh padded his one-hundred-sixteen-pound skeleton. Groves kept his eyes on this wisp of humanity as he climbed the one-hundred-foot steel tower to check on his progeny. The grapefruit-sized plutonium sphere lay securely inside its special housing like a giant turtle egg about to be hatched. Seismographs, spectrographs, geophones, ionization chambers and assorted other testing devices thousands of yards away would measure the new force soon to make its debut.

Fizzle or fury? What were calculations on paper except blueprints to failure or success? Enrico Fermi feared the new force about to be loosed on the world would snowball into an uncontrollable reaction. One that would transform the land of enchantment into a greasy spot on the map. Or set the atmosphere on fire. "Nonsense!" said his colleagues.

The consequences of the gadget fizzling were unthinkable. Congressional inquiry into the Pentagon's biggest boondoggle would inevitably go down in history as Groves' Folly. It left a bad taste in his mouth. While the general splashed through puddles, senior physicists, chemists and metallurgists organized a betting pool that wagered the raw power of the blast in equivalent TNT tonnage would range from zero to forty-five thousand. "*If* it worked," added the pessimistic project director.

"Look Oppie," his trusted Russian friend George Kistiakowsky encouraged, "I'll bet you one month of my salary against your ten bucks that this bomb will work."

Oppie was about as lively as a glass of day-old seltzer water. He, too, was near implosion. If something went wrong, and a runaway chain reaction occurred, in his control bunker only ten-thousand yards south from ground zero, Oppie would be a crisp. That prospect mattered little now.

Storms raged over the Jornada and within the scientists. In the pre-dawn of July 16, Groves glared at the Heavens in defiance. At precisely 4 A.M., they dutifully called back their clouds. "Detonate," ordered Groves, "in an hour-and-a-half."

At the edge of the Jornada twenty miles northwest of the tower on Compania Hill, VIP observers readied themselves to lay prone in trenches, feet toward the blast. They had been instructed to stand and remove their protective goggles only after the flash. According to his calculations, Klaus Fuchs had found an observation point out of harm's way. This was his moment. He didn't want to miss a millisecond in the birth of his baby, his monster. Neither did Captain Parsons. The weapons specialist prepared to measure results of the blast from an instrument-packed B-29, as long as weather cooperated. Radio transmissions at the control center certainly hadn't. A California station, its wavelengths crossed with the frequency of the test site, beamed the "Voice of America" to a befuddled test site radio operator.

A loudspeaker boomed: "Zero minus ten minutes."

Sergeant Bob Caron fiddled with the dial. Tokyo Rose's silken voice draped the 509th's Quonsets. This time she glorified the brave kamikazes who, she said, inflicted heavy losses on American fleets and delayed the capture of Okinawa. Her words wound themselves around the men as they polished their boondockers, wrote letters to wives and lovers and passed boxes of cookies that took them back to an innocence lost.

"You just don't know what you're in for," Tokyo Rose taunted. "You won't be seeing Mom again."

The gambler held his aces close to his chest. He could call Stalin's hand, if he needed to. If the bomb worked, there would be no need, or desire, to hold Russia to the Yalta accord, anxious as she was for the return of territories and privileges lost to Japan forty years ago. Neither Stimson nor Byrnes doubted that as "reward" for her assistance with Japan, she expected Truman would forego the wrist slapping for having her hands already too deep into eastern European pockets.

"If [the bomb] explodes as I think it will," Truman confided, "I'll certainly have a hammer on those boys." Secretary of State Byrnes certainly hoped so.

If the bomb was a dud, Stimson advised Truman, then let Russia declare war on Japan. It probably would anyway. Hedging his bets, Stalin had already dissolved Russia's Neutrality Pact with the battered country. Stimson continued. Stalin's troops in Manchuria would distract and fragment Japanese forces, opening the door wider for an American invasion. The problem, of course, the two men agreed, was that the tactic also opened the door to Communism. Better to keep Russian hands home and encourage a friendly Japan's conversion to democracy.

Truman would put on his poker face and test how well he could bluff.

Klaus Fuchs' face gleamed with the pride of an expectant father. Hans Bethe, head of the Theoretical Division at Los Alamos, had praised Fuchs' theories for having made an "extremely great contribution" and speeding up bomb production. Stalin had praised Fuchs, too, for the speed with which he delivered to Russian intelligence highly classified information. Already, Fuchs had handed over blueprints and documents in hopes that Russia could lift itself from the age of oxcarts and rise with the dawn of technology as a contender in the world arena. As early as 1930, Russia had tried to do that for itself. The Supreme Council for National Economy funded physicist Abram Federovich Joffe's nuclear research, and centers sprang up in Leningrad and Kharkov.

Four months after America declared war on Japan, Stalin charged scientists at Volynskoye, near Moscow, with the auspicious responsibility of building a nuclear weapon. Director Igor Kurchatov filled his brain trust with hand-selected geniuses and captured German scientists.

While their cyclotron split atoms, Klaus Fuchs plugged their data pools with leaked American secrets.

"Zero minus ten seconds." Three...two...one.... Suddenly and without any sound, or so it appeared to physicist Otto Frisch when atoms split at Jornada del Muerto, "the hills were bathed in brilliant light, as if somebody had turned on the sun with a switch."

At that instant, Oppie's successes and failures melted like the steel tower at ground zero. All humankind's previous acts seemed timorous and small. The flash pierced Oppie's consciousness and imprinted a prophetic passage from the sacred book of the Hindus, the *Bhagavad-Gita*:

> If the radiance of a thousand suns
> Were to burst at once into the sky,
> That would be like the splendor of the Mighty One...
> I am become Death,
> The shatterer of worlds.

That Monday morning, July 16, 1945, *Times* science writer Laurence wrote furiously:

> Up it went, a great ball of fire about a mile in diameter, changing colors as it kept shooting upward, from deep purple to orange, expanding, growing bigger, rising as it expanded, an elemental force freed from its bonds after being chained for billions of years.

For a long moment, the beginning and ending of time mingled in silence. Then nothingness collapsed in a heaven-splitting roar. The earth trembled. Dishes and windows rattled two hundred thirty-five miles to the northwest in a town called Gallup. Sky watchers in Amarillo witnessed a strange new sun. An old blind woman experienced a miracle called light. Trinity lived up to its name.

Stimson waited in the dilapidated summer house assigned to him for word of Trinity. At 7:30 P.M., it came. The old gentleman's heart-rate increased. Without haste, the Secretary of War carried George

Harrison's message from Washington to the President, just returning to Potsdam from Berlin.

> Operated on this morning. Diagnosis not yet complete but results seem satisfactory and already exceed expectations. Local press release necessary as interest extends great distance. Dr. Groves pleased. He returns tomorrow. I will keep you posted.

On July 17, Groves went home to Washington. At headquarters in Germany, Supreme Allied Commander Dwight Eisenhower had just finished a "nice dinner" with Stimson and "everything was fine," when a second message from Harrison broke the spirit of the evening.

> Doctor has just returned most enthusiastic and confident that the little boy is as husky as his big brother. The light in his eyes is discernible from here to Highhold....

The metaphor was in poor taste, Eisenhower said. Stimson was more pragmatic. The new information helped clear the fog. Harrison's reference to Highhold, the elderly host's own Long Island estate, conveyed Trinity's now-unquestionable power. Not until shortly before noon on Saturday did Stimson receive the eyewitness narrative Groves and his deputy, General Thomas Farrell, had painstakingly drafted.

> The effects could well be called unprecedented, magnificent, beautiful, stupendous and terrifying. No man-made phenomenon of such tremendous power had ever occurred before. The whole country was lighted by a searing light with the intensity many times that of the midday sun. It was golden, purple, violet, gray and blue. It lighted every peak, crevice and ridge of the nearby mountain range with a clarity and beauty that cannot be described but must be seen to be imagined. ...Thirty seconds after the explosion came, first the air blast pressing hard against the people and things, to be followed almost immediately by the strong, sustained, awesome roar which warned of doomsday and made us feel that we puny things were blasphemous to dare tamper with the forces heretofore reserved to The Almighty.

Trinity had not marked the first time that humankind had been tempted by forbidden fruit. The Almighty had imbued the human mind with vision and the capacity to fulfill it. Next to the "stupendous" power of atomic energy, everything paled in Stimson's eyes. "What is gunpowder? Trivial. What is electricity? Meaningless." The test had turned the war inside out.

Farrell's poetic superlatives "tremendously pepped" Truman. Stimson called his attention to other new reports. If the war were to continue, one had predicted, by March 1946, an estimated seven-million Japanese will have died of starvation alone. In addition, Washington had released figures that put the cost of the war at seven billion dollars per month. According to Groves' calculations, the bomb could pay for itself in nine days.

From the first news of Trinity's success, Truman was certain that he had measured twice and cut once. His self-doubt slipped into Potsdam's moist night air and was carried away on silver wings. He was a new man.

Churchill also felt restored by the promise of the new bomb. Later, he reflected: "To avert a vast, indefinite butchery, to bring the war to an end, to give peace to the world, to lay healing hands upon its tortured peoples by manifestation of overwhelming power at a cost of a few explosions, seemed after all the toils and perils, a miracle of deliverance."

While Dr. Groves was completing his delicate New Mexico operation, Stalin's physicians were laying their hands, however healing, on their recovering leader. His diagnosis would remain their secret. Although Stalin's mild heart attack had delayed departure for Potsdam, he was certain it would not interfere with his ability to strong-arm the Big Two.

As far as Truman was concerned, Stalin's delayed arrival at the conference on July 17 had been made to order. When the two leaders scrutinized each other for the first time at the Little White House, the President invited the general to lunch. Although Stalin politely declined, the cocky Truman challenged, "You could if you wanted to."

A game of one-upmanship had clearly begun. The two roosters postured and strutted and kept a keen eye on the other. Invigorated by the bomb's success, Truman symbolically positioned himself as the center of control in an official photograph. A pale Stalin in a crisp, white military jacket stood to the President's left, the rotund Briton to his right. Truman crossed his arms in front of him for the three-way handshake. As the shutter clicked, he flashed the Russian a vainglorious smile.

It was not a handshake gesture of peace Truman would soon extend to Japan in the Potsdam Declaration, but a gripping ultimatum as plain-spoken as he: Surrender immediately or face "prompt and utter destruction." Later that day he appended the long, apocalyptic entry in his diary: "...we will issue a warning statement asking the Japs to surrender and save lives. I'm sure they will not do that, but we will have given them the chance." Power was exhilarating, and addictive. Deftly, he arranged for Stalin's signature to be absent from the document.

At the conference round table, each player knew the cards held by the other. Truman had read the cable intercepts between Japan and Russia. He was well aware that it served Generalissimo Stalin's purpose to stall the Japanese ambassador to Moscow, who would request that Russia act as intermediary in peace negotiations with the West.

By the same token, Stalin had eliminated one of Truman's bargaining chips. A Russian agent had already informed him of the Trinity test. But Truman did not know that the well-kept secret he had hoped to trade for concessions in Europe was already in the back pocket of a tyrant.

He still tasted Trinity's sweet success. At first, said Churchill, "I couldn't understand it. When he got to the meeting after having read this report, he was a changed man. He told the Russians just where they got on and off and generally bossed the whole meeting."

As scientists at Alamogordo analyzed test data, Bill Laurence took Harvard chemistry professor George Kistiakowsky aside. "Tell me," he said, "how to put what's happened here in perspective." Kistiakowsky was only to happy to oblige. "I am sure that at the end of the world, in the last millisecond of the earth's existence, the last human will see what we saw."

To me, said the reporter, thoughtfully filtering the experience through rosier glasses, it was "like being witness to the Second Coming of Christ." At Potsdam, Churchill imagined a different scenario. As was his wont, he adroitly cut to the quick, equating the new dawn he had witnessed only through the eyes of others to the "Second Coming in Wrath."

After Laurence walked away satisfied, Kistiakowsky slapped Oppie on the back. "Old buddy, you owe me ten."

In the Soviet Union, Sato, the Japanese ambassador to Moscow, frantically vied for an ear willing to receive Prince Funimaro Konoye's peace initiative from the Emperor. Frustrated by Russia's stalling, on July 20 he cabled Foreign Minister Togo:

Just as we can assume that the enemy will one day attempt a landing, it is also clear what Russia will do after our fighting strength has been destroyed. By placing our government on a more democratic basis and by destroying the despotic bureaucracy, we must try to raise up again the real unity between the Emperor and his people.

Togo read into Sato's cable the urgency intended. Japan had "plunged into a great world war which was beyond our strength," Sato admitted. "...but I have taken such a stand because I believe that this is the only way to save our country."

Churchill broached a relaxed Truman at the July 22 luncheon. The President knew what was on the eminent statesman's mind. To both men, dropping the bomb blotted out the specter of Marshall's massive land invasion.

"Now," wrote Truman in his diary, "all this nightmare picture had vanished. In its place was the vision—fair and bright indeed it seemed—of the end of the whole war in one or two violent shocks. Moreover, we should not need the Russians. The end of the Japanese war was no longer dependent upon the pouring in of their armies for the final and perhaps protracted slaughter. We had no need to ask favors of them."

The one or two violent shocks were being readied. On Tinian, Tibbets' crew was practicing for the event they all hoped would bring about the vision fair and bright.

Pictures Worth a Thousand Words

July 22, 1945

My Dearest Kay,

Hi Honey, how're you feeling today? I feel swell because when we landed yesterday afternoon there were three letters from you. One was an old one forwarded from Wendover, but the other two were written July 8th and 11th. In one of your letters you said you were sending some pictures, but I didn't receive them yet. I'll let you know when I do. I'm glad Judy's christening came along nice. Now I'll be sweating out those pictures. I'd give anything to have been there. I envy Judy's party with the ice-cream. Boy, I'd love to have a dish of it and about a gallon of fresh milk. We had our two bottles of beer last night and tonight we get some kind of juice.

I'm sure glad harvest is coming along now. It's good Dad was able to get some help. You said you were going to take Judy in to see the Dr., but in the next letter you didn't say what the results were. I hope he was able to help your pains. Are they still bothering you? I'm getting your letters O.K., but they come in bunches and yesterday's were the first in a week. That's probably the way they will come in. We all would like it if you could send me Reader's Digest, too, because we can't buy any reading material over here. When you do, would you send me the shaving mirror and pillowcase? You sure are right, Honey. I do wish I was there to help you take care of Judy. I'd even do her three-cornered pants without a squawk and it must be quite a task if she has such a goofy "plumbing system." It's a good thing that she does keep you busy, though, because it will take your mind off me being so doggone far away. Even so, it's sure nice to know you miss me so much, cause I miss you and Judy a powerful lot. I'll bet she sure is cute. She'll be wearing your high heels before you know it.

Yesterday's mission was O.K. except for that getting up at 2 A.M. I was sure busy after we took off. One of my guns acted up, and I had to fix it in flight. It's good I'm skinny, or I'd never have gotten in the turret to fix it. I got it working O.K., but nothing came up to shoot at so I just fired down on the target.

Honey, Tinian is only three miles from Saipan and in the Marianas chain islands. It's about 130 miles north of Guam, so maybe now you can find it on the map. I guess in the letter where I told you the stops coming over the censor cut them out. First they said we could tell them, then after the letters *were mailed, they said not to. Anyhow, it's not very important cause they weren't much to write about anyhow.*

Well, honey, I better close for now as I have to scoot out and clean my guns this morning.

Take good care of yourself and give my best to the folks. Tell Aggie to take care of herself, too, and not galavant around on the tractor. Give 'lil Judy a big kiss from her Daddy and heap a million or so on yourself. Keep writing to me, Sweetie, 'cause I live for your letters. Bye now,

All my love,
Bob

Letters from home did sustain Americans abroad. They gave reason to living and dying. The nation flung itself into a flurry of words. Letters of pride, passion, regret and discouragement flowed back and forth across continents and oceans. Filtered through censors, addressed to APOs half a world away, letters served as tattered surrogates for shining eyes and warming smiles. Love, fury and compassion found expression eloquently, simply or profanely in every conceivable hand. Arranged by date, bundled with string, letters ritually made their way to hat boxes, shoe boxes, dresser drawers, steamer trunks, under pillows, beside photographs. Back and forth went snippets of hair, bits of ribbon and lace, headlines, pressed flowers, scented handkies, silk panties, snapshots of children never seen.

Military leaders have long known the power of words to move. On June 2, 1945, from the front cover of the *Saturday Evening Post*, the military addressed the citizens of Everytown, U.S.A, in an open letter. With Independence Hall in the background, the patriots appealed for moral and financial support.

TO THE AMERICAN PEOPLE
Your sons, husbands and brothers who are standing today upon the battlefronts are fighting for more than victory in war. They are fighting for a new world of freedom and peace. We, upon whom has been placed the responsibility of leading the American forces, appeal to you with all possible earnestness to invest in War Bonds to the fullest extent of your capacity. Give us not only the needed implements of war, but the assurance and backing of a united people so necessary to hasten the victory and speed the return of your fighting men.

G. C. Marshall   William D. Leahy
Douglas MacArthur   E. J. King
Dwight D. Eisenhower   C. W. Nimitz
H. H. Arnold

Newspapers, magazines, billboards and radio played a prominent role in disseminating propaganda. Their colorful images and slogans galvanized the nation. They challenged and persuaded with fact and fiction. Public relations campaigns were often clever and sometimes obnoxious. Some were both. But they were seldom bland.

> Are you worth dying for? They land on the rocky islands of the Setting Sun. And they fight. And they win. And some die. For you. Are you worth dying for? Don't try to answer. Your conscience will do that for you when it sees what you do in the 7th War Loan. Stay in the fight to the finish. Buy more bonds."

Americans received two messages that appeared contradictory. One encouraged them to spend, investing in their country "to keep the factories moving and people in jobs." The other urged them to "make it do," "reuse it" and "wear it out." At every turn consumers were reminded:

> Meeting the nation's used fats needs is one of the war-time jobs of individual homemakers. One pound of fat is one step toward final victory.

> We are at war. Remember, every Wednesday is waste-paper collection day.

Paper, like scrap iron and steel, became particularly crucial to the war-time effort. It wrapped supplies and ammunition and was in short supply as was photographic paper for reconnaissance prints.

For all its belt-tightening, the nation experienced a vigor unknown in peacetime. The War Man-Power Commission found jobs for the unemployed, linking people with paychecks. Although they didn't know it, ten thousand male and female physicists, chemists, chemical engineers, electricians, carpenters and even bricklayers in New York state put their own energy into the atomic bomb. Seven thousand of those recruited by the W. L. Maxson Corporation of Manhattan for "work of a highly confidential nature and one which would contribute to the war effort" were transferred to the Manhattan Project in Pasco, Washington, and Oak Ridge, Tennessee.

Thoroughly red, white and blue, the work force regretted war, but hated draft dodgers. At the University of Texas in Austin, for example, young scientists were recruited for secret research on the atomic bomb. They were among the thousands of Americans who had a job to do, but couldn't talk about it. Anyone not visibly involved in the war effort was labeled a "slacker," "dodger," or "feather merchant."

Industry was mass producing more than the implements of war. The rosy-cheeked girl next door in prim dress and high heels promoted Kelvinators, Buicks and even Texaco's coast-to-coast "Registered Rest Rooms." Phillip Morris appealed to those who wanted to be among the "Intelligent, enlightened men and women who *demand* a cigarette" that permitted the "full enjoyment of rich tobacco unhampered by throat irritation." Ads admonished: "Don't be a fat man. Check that growing waistline with 'The Bracer,' the new, amazing supporter belt that makes you look better and feel better." Stepping out on the town helped some step into a smaller clothing size. Arthur Murray promised that they would help even those with two left feet "cut a fine figure on any dance floor," trim their midriffs and "feel light and supple, gloriously self-confident."

In a whirl of patent leather and dapper hats, Gene Kelly and Fred Astaire set the example, singing and dancing their way through travel bans and gas rationing.

For forty-eight dollars, smart Fifth Avenue businessmen were well-suited, crisp and seasonal in their double-breasted tropical wool worsteds. In Des Moines, the middle class wore sturdy gabardine and put the change in groceries. Republic Steel launched a "Can you pick the woman from Dubuque?" campaign. Thanks to its trucks and trains, Miss Dubuque's high-style wardrobe sped along America's super highways from the fashion centers of New York to department stores in the Heartland. Soup to nuts moved by road and rail. To keep up with the momentum, rapid-transport carriers added lines to haul raw materials to factories and finished defense products to shipping centers.

Insurance promotions targeted the family breadwinner and urged him to "consider his own back yard as part of the nation's front line." Strength means more than armament production, claimed ads that evoked conscience. "Nationally strong is individually strong." Those who purchased insurance not only protected their families, but also their country. Companies promised that portions of every premium dollar directly supported national defense.

Nostalgia for a gentler time made popular reminders of how life used to be, or how one imagined it was. Children redeemed box tops for small treasures that were sometimes worth the wait. Young homemakers sent Del Maiz ten cents in stamps and received a steadying depiction of rural stability—a poster of the ideal grandmother putting the glow in a growing boy's cheeks with corn on the cob.

There was nothing nostalgic, however, about the daily reminders of separated families, or fatherless sons. Newspapers reported that every week the war claimed another thousand American lives. That was the most painful of all messages the media and mail brought home.

The message Truman had been waiting for arrived on July 24 from George L. Harrison, secretary of the Interim Committee, whose task was to study the use of the bomb. Relayed through Stimson, the message informed Truman the date that the bomb would be ready. The capstone had been laid in place. In his diary he wrote: "I had made the decision."

Final decision for selection of a target city from four possibilities had been dropped in Groves' lap. When he phoned General George C. Marshall about it over the scrambler, Marshall put the onus back on Groves.

The next day, Groves wired his bombing order to the President at Potsdam. "The 509th Composite Group, Twentieth Air Force, will deliver its first special bomb as soon as weather will permit visual bombing after 3 August 1945 on one of the targets: Hiroshima, Kokura, Niigata and Nagasaki."

Throughout the twelve-square miles of Japan's seventh largest city, the inflooding of soldiers made residents feel uneasy. Rightly so. The troop-buildup had been a contributing factor in Hiroshima's selection as a primary target.

Kyoto had teetered on the brink of being targeted for annihilation until Stimson interposed his personal veto. When he served as Governor General of the Philippines, he and his wife had been captivated by Kyoto's transcendent beauty and religious and cultural richness. In her defense, Stimson argued that her ruination would be a loss to all humanity. Not to mention that indiscriminate destruction of a non-industrial, non-military site was immoral and would blemish American credibility. The clergyman in him could see it no other way. Thus, Kyoto owed its reprieve to the man whose business was war.

The Hiroshima Prefecture belonged to one of forty-odd administrative divisions comparable to states. Built on a delta, it was inundated by water. Lush hills and mountains on three sides gave it a bowl shape that scientists believed would intensify and spread the bomb's force.

Only a twenty-one-gun battery on Mt. Futaba defended it.

Anxiety-peaked Hiroshima feared most of all for its children. Over time, it shuttled twenty-five thousand of them to the safekeeping of aunts, uncles and friends in the countryside. The older school children who remained worked eight hours each day making weapons or clearing debris from the fire breaks.

Intuition had nothing to do with it. The flagship's admiral, Raymond A. Spruance, needed only his common sense to see that the *Indianapolis* was a candidate for disaster. She was fast and big—the reason she had been chosen to transport much of Little Boy across thousands of miles of open water. But her towering rigging set the cruiser's center of gravity far too high. One direct torpedo hit, and it would all be over. Already the *Indianapolis* had used up more than one of her lives. At Okinawa, a kamikaze killed nine of her crew and turned her hull to hash. A new port quarter, new radar and fresh crew later, the *Indianapolis* pushed its prow westward through pacific waters toward Tinian.

Her captain, Charles Butler McVay III, had an uncomfortable suspicion that the coffin-like, pine crate strapped to his deck and guarded by marines and the three-hundred-pound lead bucket bolted to a cabin floor were some kind of bacteriological weapons.

As McVay dropped anchor on July 26 a thousand yards off Tinian's reefed shore, the Oak Ridge plant extracted the final forty-percent of the bomb's U^{235} and flew it to Los Alamos. Overnight, Oppie and his assistants processed the substance and divided it for transport on three ATC C-54 twin-engine Dakotas bound for Tinian.

At 7 P.M., Truman's staff released his Potsdam Declaration to the press for dispatch two hours twenty minutes later. Stimson had argued the phrase "unconditional surrender" would pose a potential stumbling block to peace. Truman remained intractable. The ultimatum's full text flowed over San Francisco airwaves. At 7 A.M., July 27, shocked Japanese monitors picked it up.

That day, Togo delivered the English version of the American, British and Chinese "opportunity to end this war" to his Emperor. It was a most curious and mysterious document. While it called for the unconditional surrender of all Japanese armed forces, it made no mention of the Imperial House. As Stimson had predicted, the Emperor's status had become a sticking point. A Japan bereft of her territorial possessions could be tolerated. But dissolution of the throne? Furthermore, he found the declaration's reference to "occupying forces," albeit forces that "shall be withdrawn...as soon as these objectives have been accomplished," excessive.

Now what? Clearly, Japan should not act hastily. He must think. Wait, he implored, at least until Ambassador Sato has enlisted Russian cooperation. Prime Minister Suzuki was dubious, but agreed. Militarists, as hot as ever to brandish swords, called for the declaration's immediate rejection.

The next day, Japanese newspapers printed a censored version of the declaration. Omitted were assurances that the Japanese people would not be enslaved, and their country would not be destroyed. Surrender would disband the armed forces and send them home.

Suzuki did not look forward to the afternoon press conference. "As for the government," he announced to eager reporters, "it does not find any important value in it, and there is no other recourse but to *mokusatsu* it and resolutely fight for the successful conclusion of the war."

The press was ready to take Japan across the chasm between peace and a fight to the death on the rickety bridge of semantics. As diplomat Toshikazu Kase later explained, the unfortunate and ambiguous word was to connote "refrain from comment." *Mokusatsu* also could be interpreted as "treat with silent contempt." It was a fatal miscalculation.

The jingoistic Japanese press heard with both ears closed. Banner headlines labeled the proclamation "Absurd!" and claimed the government found it ludicrous and, therefore, chose to "ignore" it.

"In the face of this rejection," Stimson reflected nearly two years later, "we could only proceed to demonstrate that the ultimatum had meant exactly what it said...."

"The incident was thus a deplorable one in its embarrassment of our move for peace, and was most disadvantageous for Japan," Togo wrote shortly thereafter. Disadvantageous was an understatement. And so it happened that Japan and the United States had also tickled the dragon's tail. The two subcritical masses called pride and cultural misunderstanding had been shoved together into one critical mass.

By this time, each side was engaged in second-guessing the other. American Intelligence, certain that the Japanese press would censor the declaration, rained tens of thousands of leaflets with the complete text onto Japan's twelve largest cities. In their debris-littered streets, on remaining operable streetcars, the Japanese people confronted the startling revelation that their country was not on the verge of victory, but at the brink of defeat. Furthermore, the United States government was assuring the Japanese people that surrender would free them from tyrannical leadership and bring their sons and fathers home to rebuild the nation. "The time has come for Japan to decide whether she will continue to be controlled by those self-willed militaristic advisers whose unintelligent calculations have brought the Empire of Japan to the threshold of annihilation, or whether she will follow the path of reason." Nothing short of surrender would save her from "utter devastation of the Japanese homeland." It was strong language.

As neighbor whispered to neighbor in Japan, Britons made their voice heard with political aplomb. Clement R. Attlee's Labour Party busied itself replacing the portly prime minister and his Conservatives. Attlee was Potsdam-bound.

July 27, 1945

My Dearest Kay,

Hi Sweetie, how you be tonight? How's Judy doing too? I received another letter from you written July 18th. I sure love to receive your letters because you tell me so much about you and Judy. Honey, in one of your letters a few days ago, you said you were sending me some pictures of Judy. I haven't received them yet. How did you send them? From what you tell me, she sure must be a cute baby. Cutest in the whole wide world I'll bet....

July 28, 1945

I got too sleepy to write last night so I put it off till this morning. I had the best GI sleep last night I've ever had. Yesterday they issued the combat crews new air mattresses. After the hard canvas cots, they were like floating on a cloud.

I thought sure we were going on a mission last night because they were coming along every other day. The second one was better than the first 'cause they didn't throw any flak at us. Didn't even see a fighter. We can't understand what keeps those people fighting after seeing the destruction we are handing out. I've seen quite a few of their airfields and they really are beat-up. Let's hope and pray this ultimatum the United Nations sent Japan will make them realize they don't have a chance.

Boy, we saw a swell show last night. Eddie Bracken, who played in the Miracle of Morgan's Creek, and Peggy Ryan, who plays with Donald O'Conner in lots of pictures. They had some gals who weren't very talented but boy they sure were sexy individuals and really threw it all over the stage.

One gal paraded around in slacks and a sweater. WOW! What a show for rock-happy guys. Peggy Ryan is really a dynamic fire-ball and Bracken is very funny.

My mother surely will go to Kansas to see Judy just as soon as the traveling eases up and the weather gets a bit cooler. She said my Dad would probably go too if he could get away from the business for a couple of weeks. They sure love to get your letters and hear all about 'lil Judy.

The Dr. bill was much lower than I expected. How much was the total cost for Judy including hospital, medicines, etc.?

Honey, if the radio doesn't work, maybe you haven't put the new tubes in the right place. The bum ones were in place and if you followed the nos. on the new ones and removed the corresponding nos. from the radio, the new tubes should be in their correct sockets. If that doesn't work then I guess you will have to take the radio to the shop.

Honey, I haven't received the copy of Reader's Digest as yet, but I'll look forward to reading it.

I had a nice dream about you last night. We went to Salt Lake City on a three day pass and had a swell time, just like when we went in from Wendover.

I like the poems you put in your letters. I just know they're your sentiments exactly. I may not express my sentiments too fancy but you can read between the lines and realize how much I love you and Judy, also how much I miss you both.

They sure play nice music all day and evening. There is a station on Saipan which replays all the big programs and also plays a lot of recorded music. One of the boys in the hut got a nice radio and it really does work overtime.

I received a nice long letter from Chris. They will stay at his home during the week and go to Lynbrook for weekends. They are looking for an apartment, but I guess it's quite a job to find one anyplace, these days.

Here's a million kisses and all my love to you and Judy. Keep writing often and I will do likewise. Bye now Sweetheart,

All my love,
Bob

Early Sunday morning, July 28, the voices of ten church-bound pedestrians were forever silenced as a United States Air Force B-25 bomber gashed the Empire State Building between the seventy-eighth and seventy-ninth floors and it plummeted to the street. All three men aboard were killed.

July 29, 1945

My Dearest Kay,

Hi Sweetie, how're you and our cute little daughter doing tonight? There wasn't any letter from you when we got back this evening but I received one from you yesterday afternoon.

Boy, I sure am tired tonight. Our mission was over thirteen and one-half hours and I flew the tail for eight and one-half hours. I don't mind it back there because I really get a good view of where we've been. It's just so crowded with all the junk that there's hardly any room to breathe, much less stretch my legs. Only thirty-two more missions to go. If we keep going at this rate, it won't be too long. One night's rest in between isn't bad, but two nights' rest is better. I just want to get those thirty-five missions in so I can get back to see you and Judy. I want so much to see Judy while she is still just a little baby. They're so doggone cute then. I feel sorry for the fellows who don't see their kids until they are two or three years old.

I can't kick on the way I'm receiving your letters. I may miss a day or two, but they come along pretty regular. It was just that once that I waited for seven days to hear from you. I think all the letters forwarded from Wendover are here. I just live for your letters, Honey, so keep them coming as regular as you have been.

I know my folks would like to have you with them in Lynbrook for the winter, but I know it would be too much of a trip for you to make alone. Even if my mother did come out to help you with Judy, I wouldn't want you ever to go by coach. It would be too hard for you being Judy is so young. If my mother did come she would travel by Pullman and make the arrangements so you could have a berth or compartment going back with her. That could only be if the ban on traveling eased up. So, Honey, don't try to decide on going to N.Y. for this coming winter until you find out if my Mom is going to Kansas. When I write to her, I'll explain the situation, but I'm sure she already understands it. I know she wouldn't expect you to make the trip alone.

Well, Sweetheart, I guess that's about all for tonight. Take good care of yourself and stay as sweet as you always are. Give my best regards to your folks. Give Judy a big hug and kiss from her Daddy and take a few million for yourself. Bye now, Honey,

All my love to you and Judy,
Bob

Captain McVay had been relieved when the suspicious cargo had been removed from the *Indianapolis*. But it was a false sense of security he felt. Less than four days after the critical components of Little Boy left his deck, Admiral Spruance's worst fears were realized. In the Sunday midnight stillness of the Indian Ocean, the *Indianapolis* was not alone. Lacking sonar, it was unaware that Japanese submarine I-58 listened attentively, silently, plotting bearings of what it mistook for a battleship. From fifteen hundred yards, I-58 fired six torpedoes. Its power center destroyed, the *Indianapolis* could issue no SOS. Within twelve minutes, her stern rose a hundred feet into the choking, smoke-fouled air, and the *Indianapolis* was sucked to her death. Only three hundred fifteen of her one thousand one hundred ninety six crew members survived. The *New York Times* lamented: "Her loss just before the dawn of peace marks one of the darkest pages of naval history."

JAPAN OFFICIALLY TURNS DOWN
ALLIED SURRENDER ULTIMATUM

Anne Caron read the Monday, July 30, 1945, headline to her husband. Like seven swords, the words carved out her heart. They took so little space. Yet they were potent beyond imagining. Hadn't she and mothers of fighting sons around the world prayed for their safe return? How many times had her fingers marched across the beads of her rosary... "Hail Mary, full of grace, the Lord is with Thee...." Where was this elusive peace for which mothers petitioned saints and angels? She would count down the missions until her son returned.

In the meantime, she would save all his letters with their peculiar, rectangular censor stamp on the front. In precise, handsome cursive that trailed squarely across unruled pages (the engineer in him, she thought), he would write what he could. The where, what and why of missions he self-censored so efficiently that only a few letters arrived with a sentence sliced out. All George and Anne knew was that their son had been involved in something top secret ever since Colonel Tibbets selected him to join the 509th at Wendover.

This evening, when Anne had settled into her favorite chair with the paper, her spirits had been light. The President had issued an ultimatum to Japan she was certain it would accept. In anticipation, George had been in a celebratory mood, suggesting that they plan something special for the weekend, just the two of them. She had wanted to see Frank Sinatra, Gene Kelly and Katherine Grayson in *Anchors Aweigh* at the Capitol. But the bold, black headlines announcing Japan's rejection of a peace initiative drained that desire away.

Words—written, spoken, coded and uncoded—communicated to both sides the activities of the other. The Japanese gleaned nearly as much about America, its war efforts, troop movements and battle casualties from the *New York Times, Colliers, Life, The Saturday Evening Post* and *Time* as it did from its own intelligence-gathering.

At a Hiroshima nerve center, English-speaking Japanese monitored the American airwaves. Day and night they listened to the enemy's news broadcasts, comedy, drama and musical programs for a loose word, a clue to the enemy's Achilles' heel that would turn the tide of war in their favor. The penalty for a Japanese citizen caught listening to American shortwave radio was death. Many felt the risk worth taking.

Only a few hours remained before dawn on August 2 as the Potsdam Conference came to an official close. Six years to the day had passed since Einstein's letter urgently advised Truman's predecessor of an "extremely powerful bomb of a new type." Now, the man who had authorized its production was dead, but the issue of its use was still very much alive. Its demonstration of American potency would be tested on a different aggressor than the one for whom it had first been intended. A new president, freshly bolstered, would cut a potential threat—Russia—no slack. The bomb had been and would be the doughty Truman's Sword of Damocles.

Long before the concessions of the Yalta entree had been served, Stalin's friends had been eyeing the dessert tray that was eastern Germany. If one world leader intended to carve away at a solemn agreement, then so be it. Truman had a dainty of his own. His chefs had prepared a precious morsel to be savored at the last. And it would, indeed, be carried out on a silver plate.

Truman's power swelled within him. The Russian would soon know he had met his match. The President had come a long way from a shilly-shally youth. At the conference *finis*, he shouldered up to the general. Conscious to temper his inflection with a "by-the-way" tone, he uttered his aside through Stalin's interpreter. "We have a new weapon of unusual destructive force."

"Uncle Joe" Stalin had been engrossed in a discussion of

Russian transportation problems and double-track railroads. Yet he readily picked up on the game and responded duly matter-of-fact. He hoped the new weapon would be put to "good use" against Japan, he said. The President felt robbed. Stalin hadn't chomped at the bit. Though Truman could not know it, Fuchs had stolen his thunder. He had supplied Soviet nuclear cooks with Truman's secret recipe.

Although its effect had fallen flat, the presidential bombshell did receive Stalin's left-handed endorsement, and that vexed Truman not at all. He shed his initial disappointment and swaggered away, more confident than a week earlier that he was about to put the Japanese in the soup. Stalin, too, was confident as he prepared to let the broth mellow.

Only seven days remained before his target date to enter Manchuria.

A Thousand Years of Regret

O n August 2, the day Truman left Potsdam, Tibbets returned to Tinian, and eleventh-hour communiqués crisscrossed the globe. Sato and Togo feverishly exchanged cables. Togo was a man of carefully chosen words. At Tokyo Imperial University, he had majored in German literature. He married a brilliant German woman, even at the risk of his career. From extensive European and American contact, he gained insight into Western thought. "Do not risk a war with the West," he had warned his government, a warning it did not heed. Yet, for all his military and political savvy, he remained naive about Russia's hungry eyes.

"We have only a few days in which to arrange the end of the war," he wired to Sato in Moscow. "At present, in accordance with the Imperial will, there is unanimous determination to ask the good offices of the Russians in ending the war. Under the circumstances there is a disposition to make the Potsdam...Declaration the basis of our study concerning terms.... If we should let one day slip by, the present situation may result in a thousand years of regret."

Too many days had already slipped by. Precious minutes lost triggered the complex firing system of military momentum. Fifteen minutes after noon, Tinian time, the final components of the bomb landed at North Field, and they were hustled to a well-guarded security hut in the 509th area.

In the Banda Sea, the United States Navy Seventh Fleet destroyers *Charrette* and *Conner* captured a Japanese hospital ship and escorted her to an Allied port. In every nook and cranny she had stowed ammunition.

T ruman, who had scattered circulars over pastoral Missouri villages nearly a quarter century earlier to win votes for a county judgeship, now ordered leaflets of a quite different nature. On August 4, the propaganda fluttering down on Hiroshima warned its citizens: "If the war goes on, Japan will be destroyed. It is not difficult for a man to give up life for his country, but true loyalty now means the termination of the war and the concentration of the national effort on the rehabilitation of the country."

Time had not stood still. With every second, the chain reaction escalated.

By mid-morning August 4, the air on Tinian was already sticky and oppressive. As he walked to the 3 P.M. briefing, a dark, sweaty "V" spread from the collar of Captain Lewis' suntans to his belt. Flight crewmen flashed their I.D.s at the carbine-carrying MPs posted at the entry to the narrow 509th briefing hut, next to Intelligence Headquarters. Just returned from a test run to Rota, Caron and the other enlisted men filed in, still wearing their flight suits. Tacked to the wall a sign warned: "Careless talk costs lives." Lewis sat down and read in Tibbets' and Parsons' faces that graduation day was close at hand. The briefing was about to confirm his suspicions.

Seven of the 509th's fifteen flight crews were present in the briefing room. Aircraft commanders and their officers casually lounged on the front benches. Enlisted men took up seats toward the rear. Caron shoved his Brooklyn Dodgers' cap a little higher on his forehead for a better view of the blackboards and the enlarged reconnaissance photographs that two Intelligence officers just uncovered. He didn't have to strain to see one Japanese city was divided by rivers and spread like the fingers of an outstretched hand. *"Natural Features of Rivers"*...fleetingly, the association to a book he had rescued from extinction long years ago washed into and out of awareness.

He concentrated on Colonel Tibbets' words. They had all been waiting for the big one, and now, from the dais, Tibbets was telling them it had arrived. With luck and skill, the special mission for which they had trained eleven months and fine-tuned their planes could end the war. "That makes you the hottest crews in the Air Force," he warned, a grin crept into his serious expression.

Parsons picked up the introduction where Tibbets left off. "The bomb you are going to drop is something new in the history of warfare. It is the most destructive weapon ever produced. We think it will knock out almost everything within a three-mile area." Then he added, "No one knows what will happen when the bomb is dropped from the air. It has never been tested before." A murmur vibrated through the heavy air.

He explained that the recent Trinity test in New Mexico detonated a less-powerful bomb of a similar nature from one hundred feet off the ground. The crews could see for themselves its effects. Someone tripped the lights. A movie projector threw its piercing white beam onto the screen. Suddenly, it sputtered and whirred. Then its gate chewed the film's sprockets. The shredded cellulose strip snaked viciously until the projectionist shut the machine off. Unruffled, Parsons improvised with black and white slides showing a smoky column topped by a funny, dirty-looking cloud. Everyone seemed to be having trouble getting any kind of perspective of the mushroom shape, much less visualizing it as any more threatening or impressive than a smoke bomb on the Fourth of July. Yet Parsons was now describing a weapon as potent as twenty thousand tons of TNT. That was something to fathom—the equivalent of two hundred thousand of the two-hundred-pound bombs conventionally dropped on Europe! What such a thing would look like going off a third of a mile above the earth remained beyond imagination.

Parsons passed out to each crewman protective, tinted goggles. Quinine crystals within the lenses filtered out all but purple light. The Captain pulled a pair over his eyes and adjusted the nose bridge knob to demonstrate their maximum darkening capacity. Finally, he warned the pilots to stay clear of the cloud. It would be radioactive.

To no one's surprise, Number 82 would drop the single bomb. Because the effects of the blast and shock wave were still unknown, she could risk no fighter escorts to protect her. Furthermore, the Japanese had been carefully conditioned to tolerating solitary planes over their island. Only two observation planes would follow a short distance behind. Major Chuck Sweeney's *The Great Artiste* would carry monitoring instruments. Mounted in the belly of Number 91, commanded by Major George Marquardt, a K-17 aerial camera would document the event.

Weather planes would proceed ahead of the *Enola Gay* and radio conditions over each of three targets. Captain Claude Eatherly would fly his *Straight Flush* to the primary target, Hiroshima. Major John Wilson, commanding *Jabbit III*, would radio conditions at the secondary target, Kokura. From Major Ralph Taylor's *Full House*, Tibbets would receive cloud-cover information over the tertiary target, Nagasaki. The seventh plane, *Top Secret*, would be commanded by Captain Charles McKnight. It would stand by at a bomb-transfer pit on Iwo Jima, prepared to replace Number 82 at their rendezvous if she should get into trouble.

For a moment, the men in the hut could have heard a pin drop. All eyes were on Tibbets. When he broke the ripple of tension, they were grateful. He told them that whatever any of them had done before was "small potatoes" compared to what they were about to do. He said he was proud to have commanded their group. And he was proud to be involved in a raid that would shorten the war by at least six months. Then he warned his crews: "No talking, even among yourselves. No writing home until the mission is over."

The people of Japan understood that the typhoon battering its islands had given them a temporary reprieve from the battering of *B-sans*. Sunday, August 5, the steady rain and wind subsided, and a storm of activity arose on Tinian. Early that morning, General Farrell had a visitor.

"General, if we crack up at the end of the runway on takeoff for tomorrow's mission, there's a strong probability that the bomb will go off and blow up all this end of the island," Captain Parsons said.

"Yes, I know," the general responded thoughtfully. "What can we do about it?"

"Just this. If I could make the final assembly of the bomb in the plane, after we are well clear of Tinian, there wouldn't be a nuclear explosion if something goes wrong."

"Isn't that nice? In case of a crackup, then, we'll lose the plane, crew, bomb *and* you. But we won't blow up the island. What makes you think you'll know how to connect all the right stuff once you're airborne?"

"I've got all day to learn."

As if he were pushing a baby carriage across a busy intersection, Captain Lewis gently taxied Number 82 onto the strip for a brief, early morning test flight before the big day. He noticed his palms were damp.

Like a birth in reverse, at 3:30 P.M., tarpaulin-covered Little Boy, escorted by eight MPs and assorted vehicles, rolled out of the highly guarded Tech Area into the brilliant sunshine and was lowered into a six-foot by thirteen-foot pit. Tibbets stood by and puffed on his pipe. Ground crews towed Number 82, freshly painted with its new name, *Enola Gay*, beside the pit. They pivoted the plane one hundred eighty degrees until she squatted squarely over it. To one of the crewmen, Little Boy looked like an elongated trash can with fins. Scrawled on its dull finish were graffiti jabs at Emperor Hirohito "From the boys of the *Indianapolis*." The B-29's single bomb shackle swung overhead. With a little jockeying, the bomb and hook aligned, and a hydraulic winch drew Little Boy deeply into *Enola Gay's* womblike bay.

The bomb wasn't the only last-minute preparation for the next day's mission. Electronics controlled navigation, radar, countermeasures, communications and bombing equipment on B-29s. Anything that had to do with electronics, on the *Enola Gay* as well as the group's other bombers, was the responsibility of Lieutenant Jacob Beser. During the last two days, he had added to his already considerable duties installing the radar system within the uranium bomb. Elaborate countermeasures had been taken to prevent enemy radar interference with the bomb's frequencies, reducing the risk of premature detonation. Allied planes with missions over southern Japan had been ordered to release no chaff, the small, fine strips of foil that act as a reflective decoy to confuse enemy radar. From now until the bomb was dropped, every circuit and fuse had to be checked and rechecked.

At 4:15 P.M., Stiborik, Shumard, Nelson, Duzenbury and Caron had been playing softball with a handful of crewmen when they were called to operations. Tibbets, Lewis, Van Kirk and Ferebee were waiting. The group photographer juggled his Speed Graphic and directed the sweaty men in their Tinian shorts to kneel in front of the standing officers.

By dinner, the planes had been fueled and inspected. The squadron insignia, a black arrow within a circle painted prominently on the special plane's vertical stabilizer, had been removed and replaced with an adopted Circle R. When Tibbets' Individual Air Force had arrived on Tinian, Tokyo Rose had broadcast a spine-chilling welcome to the "Black Arrow Squadron" and its "pumpkins." Recognizing his B-29 was branded, for mission Number 13, the Colonel ordered painters to confuse spotters by switching the *Enola Gay's* insignia to Circle R.

Tibbets reviewed his mental checklist, then tried to nap. It was futile. Visitors kept bringing him back from the verge of unconsciousness.

Writing feverishly on a clipboard, Captain Parsons made a checklist of his own, spurred by the alert and perceptive Lieutenant Jeppson. Their goal was to ensure every connector, switch and monitoring system would get the attention it needed once the *Enola Gay* was airborne. Over the long, unbearably hot day in the bomb bay, Parsons had successfully wired and unwired the delicate detonating system, slicing his hands on the sharp interior of the bomb's cylinder jacket. He had been up to his elbows in graphite and much of it was still with him. The Captain knew Groves would have quashed his plan to arm the bomb in flight. He, Tibbets and General Farrell agreed to keep it the 509th's little secret.

Writer Bill Laurence, though disappointed he wasn't going to be aboard for the story of a lifetime, came up with an alternative that pumped a little wind into Captain Lewis' deflated sails. "Keep a journal for me," Laurence said, handing a notebook to the man who was not happy about being bumped from pilot to co-pilot for the "big one."

Behind the small confessional screen that separated him from the priest, Stiborik whispered, "Bless me, father, for I have sinned...." He would be sure nothing separated him from whatever lay ahead. In the Quonset, Caron stretched out on the scratchy wool blanket and stared past the bare bulbs at the curved white ceiling. Perhaps it was the brightness, perhaps his mind would have taken him there anyway, but his thoughts skipped to the sight of Kay in the snow at Monarch Pass. Their time together passed so quickly, and now he was a father. Nelson propped himself on one elbow and escaped within the pages of *Reader's Digest*. Shumard rolled away from the lights, pulled his knees close to his chest and tried to lose consciousness, however briefly, in the cradle of his bunk.

At the "Dog Patch Inn," officers—segregated from enlisted men—piled ceramic plates high with real eggs and sausages, blueberry pancakes and samples of mess officer Perry's other preflight smorgasbord delights. He had not forgotten Tibbets' favorite, pineapple fritters. The EMs chowed down from their metal mess kits. As he had learned to do before early morning flights, Caron put away pancakes until he had no room left. When the flight crews picked up the sack lunches Perry prepared, he and his staff plunged into plans for a blowout return celebration.

Lewis looked at his watch. It was 11:26 P.M., and nearly every man from all fifteen crews was at the chapel. As they did before other missions, the men sat quietly. Some looked straight ahead at the pulpit but into another world. Others, eyes closed, savored the silence and peace. This evening, the hush seemed somehow different.

"May they, as well as we, know Thy strength and power, and armed with Thy might may they bring this war to a rapid end," prayed Chaplain Thomas Downey. From the benches rose, "Amen."

Caron, Shumard and Nelson, loosely abreast on the narrow walkway leading to the briefing hut, didn't speak. The rest of the crews quietly filed through the tropical darkness in front of and behind them. Crushed coral crunched underfoot and blotted out the drone of racing minds.

Like a splash of after-shave, the brightness of the briefing hut stimulated their senses. Tibbets reviewed the schedule with the airmen who would be part of Mission Number 13. Weather officers projected that cloud cover over the targets should break up shortly after dawn. Caron and the other gunners were to be sure that they had a thousand rounds of ammo. For the twenty-eight-hundred-mile trip, each of the planes would carry seventy-four hundred gallons. To make takeoff easier, the *Enola Gay* would carry only seven thousand. Even with the reduction, she would still be overloaded. Finally, her radio designation had been changed from "Victor" to "Dimples," to "confuse the enemy." Tibbets closed by telling the men, "Do your jobs. Obey your orders. Don't cut corners or take chances."

Crewmen grabbed their flight bags and bulky survival vests. In the vests' many pockets they stashed a fishhook and line encased in paraffin, emergency rations and water purification tablets. A parachute harness with clips for a small life raft crisscrossed their flight suits. Because Caron's tail compartment space was limited, he relied on the single, compact, reserve chest chute. Each man also tucked into one of his suit's many pockets a talisman unique to him. This night, Tibbets carried a very small box. Rolling around inside were twelve cyanide capsules. One for each member of the crew.

At 1:12 A.M., the crews of *The Great Artiste* and Number 91 piled into a truck. When a six-by-six arrived three minutes later to pick up the men flying the *Enola Gay*, they looked more the motley crew than ever. Adhering to regulation dress codes, Tibbets believed, had nothing to do with the stuff a man was made of. Each of his men—private on up—was a peerless individual whose signature was the roll of cuffs, flip of a collar, cock of a hat. Even his choice of hats marked the man. For this mission,

Van Kirk had replaced the usual peaked flight cap with the pointed "fore-and-aft" hat. Stiborik chose his charmed knit ski cap, which had been showing signs of his affection for it since Wendover. Caron's icon, the familiar Brooklyn Dodgers' cap that Bob Finch pitched in to the war effort, was right where it always was. But appearances were deceiving. Though they consciously asserted their individuality, they were one of mind and purpose.

Straight Flush, Jabbit III and *Full House* taxied into position and took off at 1:37 A.M. from the mile-and-a-half-long North Field runway. As orders were for visual bombing only, their reports of cloud cover over each of the potential targets was critical. At 1:51 A.M., *Top Secret* left Tinian for Iwo Jima.

In the last year, Tibbets had come to expect General Groves capable of almost anything, but he did not anticipate the theatrics the blustery general staged for Mission Number 13. The flight line resembled an MGM set. Bright spotlights raised the *Enola Gay* to stardom and abruptly isolated her from the surrounding darkness. Nearly one hundred scientists, military personnel, maintenance and ground crewmen tried to look and act like directors, producers, grips and technicians. Groves had gone all out "for posterity."

Caron dodged the cameramen and brass and walked under the *Enola Gay's* belly. In the dark cavern of her bomb bay, the "gimmick" snuggled securely. It was only a little different from the bombs they had dropped on practice runs. Suddenly, he caught himself and glanced about. Security had been so strict over the past eleven months that everyone had been conditioned not to see what they shouldn't. It was odd, even now he was reluctant to take a good, hard look. He gave the awkward device another quick glance and hoped that it would do what it was supposed to do. So did several thousand men from Washington to Los Alamos.

A shadowy figure pressed toward Caron. Jerome J. Ossip, photographic officer of the 509th, had counted on documenting this historic event himself, whatever it turned out to be. He had loaded the cumbersome K-20 camera, preset the controls, then covered them with strips of medical adhesive tape. At the last minute, however, Ossip's request to ride along had been denied.

"Here," he said, thrusting the camera in the tail-gunner's hands. "Pull the trigger on the pistol-grip shutter like this...don't change the aperture...and shoot anything you see."

Caron now had plenty in his arms and on his mind. He still had to retrieve components of the guns that he kept in a can of kerosene and cutting oil in a maintenance tent at the hardstand.

Since he hadn't boarded the *Enola Gay* from the nose wheel hatch, he missed Parsons' complex console that monitored every second of activity within the baby in the bay. Instead, he entered through the aft hatch and, wearing the parachute harness with the chest chute clipped on, pushed the camera, flak jacket and guns ahead of him, crawling a little, pushing gear, crawling again, past the put-put and oxygen tanks into the tiny hole that would be home. As he was putting his guns in their mount, he heard someone shout for him to climb back out.

"Give us two rows...EMs squat in the front," a silhouette ordered from behind glaring floods. Caron gave his cap a light tug and looked at Stiborik. He was obviously enjoying this.

"Closer...squeeze in closer," another faceless voice shouted. Caron could feel Van Kirk's boot against his backside. The symbolism made him smile. He figured there were plenty of officers who would like to boot a few EMs in the rear. From their short exchange moments after the briefing, Caron knew Dutch wasn't one of them. He liked the good-looking Captain's easy laugh, his warm, relaxed, yet confident manner. His temperament mattered to Tibbets, too. Dutch had been the Colonel's navigator in Europe, and Tibbets wouldn't have asked him to join the 509th if he wasn't the best.

At 2:20 A.M., Tibbets called a halt to the public relations session. He had a mission to keep on schedule. As crewmen attempted to climb the ladder into the hatch, they were intercepted by cameramen, military reporters and others who tugged on their flight suits and pulled them aside. "Wear this for me," implored one after another, pressing bracelets, watches or rings into the crews' hands, trinkets they hoped would become keepsakes from historic Mission Number 13.

For luck Caron tapped the photograph of Kay and Judy stuck in his oxygen flow chart. He put on his headphones and turned the jackbox switch to "inter." "Roger," he answered to Tibbets' interphone check. The valve that controlled pressurization through the four-inch pipe that ran through the unpressurized compartment to his was OK. His oxygen pressure gauge showed four hundred twelve pounds. He pulled a test breath from his oxygen mask and found it was working smoothly. Gasoline and oil supply for the put-put were fine. He located the two emergency gallons, turned on the put-put, then strapped himself in behind his twin rear guns.

"Crew prepare for takeoff," Tibbets' voice squeezed through his microphone. Slowly and methodically, he ran down the checklist. The 509th regularly flew its B-29s ten thousand to twenty thousand pounds over maximum take-off weight. Between the weight of the bomb and its extra fuel, the sixty-five-ton *Enola Gay* was overloaded by sixteen thousand pounds. Tibbets was going to treat her with a great deal of respect.

Duzenbury had been running through his own preflight check.

At 2:27 A.M., Tibbets called for startup of engine Number Three. Throughout the engine run-up, blue-eyed Duzenbury remained keyed to his maze of dials and gauges. The nose and rear oil pressure gauge at the left of his instrument panel indicated normal. As he ran the engine up to one thousand revolutions per minute, he was satisfied that the mags and cylinder head temperatures were below one hundred fifty degrees Centigrade. Cruising, their temperature would not exceed two hundred thirty-two degrees. Directly below the tachometer, in the center of the panel, were the manifold pressure, and below it, the fuel pressure dials.

"Number Three operating properly," he reported. "Ready to start engine Number Four."

"Clear on Number Four," Tibbets responded.

When engines Two and One had also been turned over and Duze was assured vacuum and hydraulic pressures were within limits, he made his final takeoff power check at twenty-seven hundred rpm with full brakes. Pulling the four throttle levers gently down together, he prepared for taxiing at seven hundred rpm. The throttles now belonged to Tibbets.

The pilot and co-pilot checked their gyro instruments to be sure they were uncaged. Ferebee closed the bomb-bay doors. Having double-checked that chocks had been pulled and parking brakes released, Tibbets radioed the tower for taxi and take-off instructions.

"Dimples Eight Two." "Dimples Eight Two from North Tinian Tower. Take off to the east on Runway A for 'Able.' "

The runway would more appropriately have been labeled "D" for "Disabled." Charred carcasses of four B-29s, lumped at the end of the runway like broken sarcophagi in a vandalized tomb, had not been cleared from last night's crash. Fire trucks poised at intervals created dashes between the white pin-dots of runway lights.

Earlier, Tibbets had ordered his deputy commander, Tom Classen, to remove the scientists and key military personnel to a "safe" area far from North Field. Several of the scientists refused to budge from the tower, arguing that—considering the *Enola Gay's* cargo—there was no such place on the island.

It was 2:45 A.M. Lewis listened carefully for even the slightest engine sputter that indicated—as he put it—the crew had "bought the farm." The B-29s' powerful torque made them want to veer left during takeoff. At Wendover, Tibbets had trained the 509th's pilots to forget what they learned about canceling torque by braking right wheels, which could dangerously slow takeoff. Instead, his pilots led with the left engines, advancing those throttles first. Now, at eighty miles an hour, Tibbets had full rudder control. He advanced the right throttles full power. The *Enola Gay* raced toward the obsidian ocean below the edge of the cliff. Caron watched the pin-dots sprout under him, only to fall into darkness seconds after they appeared. Lewis' hand was itchy to lift her off, but Tibbets wasn't ready. The *Enola Gay* wasn't ready. She sliced through the thick air at two hundred five miles per hour. Lewis could have sworn the runway had ended yards before her hot wheels were free of Tinian and her nose pierced the space over moonless water.

Mission Number 13 was underway, on its north-by-northwest course. A twelve-man sigh of relief spread through the intercom system. Abdominal muscles relaxed. Not so long ago Admiral Leahy labeled the fantasy of a bomb to end the war a "professor's dream." But this was no dream. The *Enola Gay* was on its way to Japan with reality tethered in its bay.

Lewis hauled up the wheels and milked the flaps. Once Caron heard and felt the familiar thump, he called to Duzenbury that he was turning off the put-put.

Consecutively at two-minute intervals after *Enola Gay's* takeoff, *The Great Artiste* and Number 91 took to the air.

Six hundred twenty-two miles away, Iwo Jima's eyes were open. Black velvet stretched seamlessly before the *Enola Gay* and engulfed her crew. Only a thimbleful of people had whispered her dark secret. Though Americans were lunching at this very moment in the brightness of the sun, their eyes had been closed to the mission now taking place.

Darkness lay about the people of Japan. Those with the candle were too irresolute to light it. Russia was moody. She mourned her losses. The world was sullen.

Caron flipped on the main power switch to his radar sighting control box. It would take fifteen minutes to warm up. Once he had adjusted the intensity knob on the side of the sight, the familiar dot-and-wing presentation brightened and the reticle illumination lights automatically turned on. Manually, he increased and decreased the size of the dots in the circle. Once the gunner had set the wing span of a target in his sight, its computer automatically determined its range. The equipment seemed to be working as it should. Caron hoped he wouldn't need to use it.

When they were far enough from the island, he called Tibbets for permission to test fire the guns. The turret operated smoothly and he fired a few rounds through the .50 caliber guns. Their metallic rattle echoed through the fuselage. Caron had wiped his guns so clean (excess oil at high altitude would freeze them up) that only the faintest smell of cordite, an explosive sulfur, and burned oil, lingered in the tail. Satisfied with the guns' performance, he shut the power switches off until the *Enola Gay* broached Japan. He placed his armored vest, which was too clumsy to wear, on the floor beneath his feet, just in case the plane took flak from below. Flak jackets on the floor were a standing joke among the crew. That's where they would do the most good, protecting the "family jewels."

To save fuel, Tibbets flew under five thousand feet. By the time they were ready to climb, the plane would have less fuel weight to lift. At low altitude, the cabins remained unpressurized, enabling Parsons and Jeppson to work in the bomb bay.

In the waist, Shumard, Stiborik and Beser felt the telltale boot of the elevators as "George," the automatic pilot, kicked in. The tail shimmied so much that such subtle vibrations were undetectable to the gunner.

Near the waist scanners hung a second photograph of Kay that Caron had slipped inside another checklist plastic pocket. By the hatch, he had taped a picture of a nude. "Wendover Mary," her assorted male acquaintances had named her. Just over the state line into Nevada, Wendover Mary merrily distracted GIs from their loneliness. Rosy and glowing and lean in sexy high-heel shoes, she posed for their snapshots amid the natural splendor of nearby mountains. Caron thought the crew chief's copy would brighten things up for the guys.

Mary's image had created a stir at the Port of Aerial Embarkation at Mather Field, California. The two females assigned to inspect Number 82's life rafts, parachutes and other safety equipment were making their rounds under the strict supervision of the tail gunner. As Tibbets had ordered no one be allowed in the bomb bay, Caron led the two women from the nose though the tunnel to the waist. "Who's that?" asked one inspector, pointing to Wendover Mary. "That's my wife," Caron fibbed. "You have a picture of her, like *that?*" "Why not? It's good luck. I'm going overseas."

Because a man never knew how much luck he might need, Caron also kept on board the rosary that his mother had given him. But he refrained from bringing the two Mary reminders together.

As the plane droned toward Iwo Jima, Shumard vaguely recalled that there were two or three pairs of lace and silk panties stashed in one corner of the bombardier's compartment. He pictured them tucked underneath a book on venereal disease. Moments earlier, he let himself think about getting to the target, about flak and fighter opposition. That wouldn't do. He told himself to keep repeating, "I'm coming back...I'm coming back...all in one piece." The panties, wherever they were, would bring good luck. Stiborik's ski cap, purchased in Salt Lake City, was like Caron's baseball cap, only a lot dowdier. A photograph had been stuck up of the lobby of the Hotel Utah. It documented the lobby's swift, but brief, occupation by the dashing Ferebee. The Major had commandeered the space for his personal office of public relations. Nelson had attached his good-conduct ribbon to the radio set. He figured it might just as well assure safe conduct. Someone shellacked over a lipstick kiss print on Number 82's glistening nose. It was signed, "Dottie. Omaha, one time." Whenever they paid homage to it, the crew raised their right arms high and rallied, "Omaha, one *more* time."

J ust before 3:00 A.M., Tinian safely out of range if the bomb accidentally detonated, Parsons slipped his lean frame into the cool, restrictive chamber of the bomb bay and inched along the catwalk. Jeppson followed. Had it not been for a coin toss with another electronics officer a few days earlier, Second Lieutenant Morris Jeppson, assistant weaponeer, would not have been in this place at this time. Now, he was Parsons' surgical nurse. In less than thirty minutes, the team activated half of the "double plug" safety system that kept the two pieces of U^{235} apart and connected Little Boy to the electronic monitoring panel in the forward cabin. Only one critical electrical circuit remained to be completed. Jeppson would take care of that task after the rendezvous at Iwo Jima. Then, he could safely replace three green safety plugs with three red arming ones. The useless green plugs would end up souvenirs in his pocket.

Parsons and Tibbets had momentously and bilaterally decided that as long as the *Enola Gay* could fly, they would release the bomb rather than risk returning to Tinian with it. If not on one of the designated targets, then way the hell out in open water.

A Physicist's Nightmare

S ince the *Enola Gay* would not climb to altitude and pressurize for some time, Caron—as he had gotten into the habit of doing on long flights—came forward to stretch his legs and shoot the breeze with the men in the waist.

The midnight breakfast pancakes had burned out fast and Bob was getting hungry. So were Shumard and Stiborik. As the officers were hoarding Perry's lunches in the nose, Caron crawled through the long tunnel to raid the brown bag before none were left. The mess officer apparently kept the crew's waistlines in mind when he prepared their allotment of half a diagonally cut turkey C-ration sandwich each and an apple or an orange. Caron pushed what remained of the sandwiches and rolly-polly fruit in front of him as he wormed his way back through the tube.

For the past three and a half hours, the exhausted Jake Beser had been napping on the floor at the entrance to the tunnel. Caron, figuring the best way to expedite the movement of food, rolled the apples toward Stiborik. One bounced out of the tunnel and landed on Jake's head.

Jake needed to get up, anyway. Black coffee fought back his numbness and cleared the haze. Shortly, he would monitor Japanese radio for wavelengths that too closely approximated those selected to activate Little Boy's complex proximity fuse. Every time one of the proximity fuse signals bounced back from the earth's surface, it closed another circuit, until a sequence had been completed and the bomb detonated. Just before takeoff, Beser had been given a small piece of rice paper listing the newly designated top secret wavelengths. In the event of capture, the rice paper would end up in his digestive track.

Even in the midst of war, miles above the earth, the physical body still required attention. Caron had hooked his green canvas-covered canteen onto his web belt and brought it forward from the tail with him. He double-checked that he had the right one. The guys were always switching his good water canteen with the old one that he used to take a leak in. Before takeoff, he'd make sure that the right canteen was in the right place.

At 4:25 A.M., Shumard, Stiborik and Beser were teasing him about taking a slug from the wrong canteen when Tibbets' dark, wavy hair broke through the light at their end of the tunnel. He spoke to each of them, then squatted beside his tail gunner.

"Bob, have you figured out what we're doing this morning?"

"Colonel, with all the security you've had us under, I'm afraid to guess."

"It's OK now. We're on our way. You can guess anything you want."

"Is it a chemist's nightmare, Colonel?" he asked, thinking of the superexplosive they were carrying.

"No, not exactly."

The light lit. Lawrence's cyclotron and splitting atoms and a process called fission came off the pages of books and into his imagination.

"Is it a physicist's nightmare?"

"You might call it that."

The five exchanged a few more words, then Tibbets began to wriggle forward through the narrow, padded tunnel. When nothing but his foot stuck out, Caron yanked on it. The gesture was inappropriate between an enlisted man and his commanding officer. But it was too late. Long ago Caron realized Tibbets was no ordinary commander. The Colonel put himself in reverse.

"What's the problem?"

"Colonel, are we splitting atoms this morning?"

Tibbets knew his tail gunner's fascination with physics. The question didn't come as a surprise. "Yep. We sure are." Without explanation, he re-entered the tunnel. A short while later, the pilot who had been given the awesome task of preparing for this historic morning announced that the *Enola Gay* was carrying the world's first atomic bomb.

Of the men in the waist, only Beser had been in on the nuclear secret since Wendover. Now, Stiborik, Caron and Shumard scrutinized each others' faces with as much care as they scanned their engines. Throughout their preparation, the term "atomic" had never been used. The crewmen were not physicists, but neither were they fools. They talked about the slides at the briefing. Without some sense of scale, the test explosion's residual cloud could have come from a firecracker. Tibbets' announcement helped put the new weapon in better perspective. "The world's first atomic bomb...." It even sounded big. Tibbets and Parsons said they thought it might end the war. The three enlisted men and one officer huddled in the small, dull lime green space sure hoped so.

Tibbets was beginning his climb. Pressurization of the compartments meant Caron would be locked in the tail. He crawled through the small hatch and reached behind him for the little fold-down seat. Attached to a rail on the back of the bulkhead, the wooden seat slid down and locked into position. Its small, fabric-covered cushion offered minimal padding, especially to a man whose weight had dropped to less than one hundred twenty pounds. Because the seat's safety belt restricted movement, he normally buckled up only during rough weather. This time, however, he snapped the quick release buckle together, leaving just enough slack to lean into the gun sight.

An hour out of Iwo Jima, the moon arced over the horizon on the *Enola Gay's* right. From his lonely compartment, Caron watched mesmerized as the silver slivers below connected like the giant sterling links of Neptune's necklace. Finally, the deep blackness between the swells gave way to shimmering pools of liquid dawn. In the narrow cleft near the horizon, the sky blushed, rendering distant stars invisible. As the veil of darkness lifted from the *Enola Gay,* morning light transformed her argentine fuselage to gold.

Stiborik spotted Iwo Jima in his scope. At 5:20 A.M., the three planes were rendezvousing only three minutes past Dutch's calculations. The *Enola Gay* was performing flawlessly. Captain Charles McKnight's *Top Secret* would not be needed. From nine thousand three hundred feet, the *Enola Gay* circled left. *The Great Artiste* and Number 91 slipped smoothly into a loose formation with her, and the three soaring eagles glided back over open ocean.

Parsons and Jeppson steadfastly watched the thirty-inch-high and twenty-inch-wide console panel that monitored Little Boy's vital signs. Umbilical cords linked the bomb's batteries and electrical circuits to the monitor where gauges blinked and dials oscillated. Once the bomb-bay doors opened at thirty-one thousand feet and Little Boy began its fall, the umbilical arming wires would be severed, activating the timing devices within the bomb.

"What in hell do all these green lights mean?" asked Lewis, glad to be standing and feeling circulation return to his buttocks.

"Captain," said Parsons dryly, "if all those lights remain green, we're in good shape. If some of them go off, and red ones come on, that's not so good."

His fellow crewmembers' calm unnerved Jeppson. Nelson was reading...*reading!* Even if Jeppson had felt like burying his nose in a book, it wouldn't have been *Watch Out for Willy Carter.* Other crewmen struggled to banish the tension with affected lightness. Their abrupt and overly boisterous laughter punctuated bouts of crushing silence.

Caron chain smoked. Overseas, smokers lit up whatever brand base exchanges could stock. He flipped the metal lid of his Zippo lighter with his thumb. A steady flame from one-hundred-octane flight fuel shriveled the tobacco and it glowed red. Slowly and deliberately, he exhaled a thin, continuous stream of smoke through pursed lips, then watched it rise and curl away from the top of the tiny compartment. As casually as the Lucky Strikes and lighter would lay on the dash of his convertible, they rested on the narrow ledge alongside the gun sight. Lighter fluid scarcity led to occasional pirating of aircraft fuel. During preflight inspection, the ground crew checked for accumulated water in the fuel by draining a petcock on the underside of the wing. With a few tools and a few minutes, Caron could remove the safety-wired inspection plate covering the petcock, squirt a few drops of fuel into his lighter and batten it all down again.

As the Plexiglas windows magnified the sun's warmth, the tail got hotter than a greenhouse. Caron unzipped his flight suit to its web belt and stripped down to his T-shirt. As usual, the Miraculous Medal of the Virgin Mary that hung from his neck was tangled with his dog tags. The I.D. bracelet on his right wrist, a gift from his mother that first Christmas in the service, gleamed in the slanting sun. Crewmember wings, his name and serial number were engraved on the back. On his left wrist he wore the fine Swiss watch with the leather band that Maxson's presented him when he enlisted. It felt like lifetimes ago that he had worked among the rows of drafting tables in the big brick building. If Wendover had seemed worlds away from the familiar landscape of New York City, to what could he compare Tinian? Or the yet-to-be-known and experienced city that was simply their "target"? Caron shifted his buttocks on the small seat. The .45-caliber revolver holstered on his right hip poked its reminder. If the plane was downed in enemy territory, capture was a possibility.

The black and white photograph of Kay, which he had meticulously hand-tinted, bobbed and darted about in the shimmying space.

Much to his pleasure, he had found his steady, precise draftsman's hand a natural for applying the tricky, delicate oil tints. Coloring prints for the men in the squad as well as for his dates was a satisfying diversion.

From his starboard scanning position, Shumard peered through the small porthole, which replaced the wide blister of most B-29s, and kept a watchful eye on the engines. He would have bet his next paycheck some puff-chested brass would have bumped him to ride along. Yet, here he was, on his way to dropping the world's first atomic bomb.

Captain Lewis was making observations about anything he thought Laurence might find pertinent to the flight. "Outside of a high, thin cirrus and the low stuff, it's a beautiful day," he entered into the journal.

When Jeppson exchanged Little Boy's plugs, and Captain Parsons announced the bomb was now "final," Lewis waxed philosophical. "The bomb was now independent of the plane. It was a peculiar sensation. I had a feeling the bomb had a life of its own now that had nothing to do with us."

Claude Eatherly's *Straight Flush* had everything to do with Hiroshima's 7:09 A.M. air-raid alert. To the ground operator who spotted it, the B-29 looked no more threatening than the other lone reconnaissance planes that frequented the island's airspace. Yet, better to be safe. He triggered the minute-long "mild" siren. It signaled that danger was only "slight." The main Hiroshima radio network interrupted its programming with the alert. People came and went from their shelters.

At 7:25 A.M., as the *Enola Gay* was at twenty-six thousand feet and climbing, Caron heard Eatherly's voice on the intercom. Nelson had picked him up at the designated 7310 kilocycles.

"Cloud cover less than three-tenths at all altitudes," Eatherly radioed. "Advice: bomb primary."

A visual drop at Hiroshima now seemed a foregone conclusion. Actually, Tibbets had not anticipated otherwise. Lewis switched off the IFF—Identification, Friend or Foe—and watched for landmarks. The island of Shikoku rose to meet them. Beyond it opened the Inland Sea.

From wind and drift calculations, Dutch Van Kirk reset their compass heading to three hundred forty-four degrees. At landfall, they swung east, their altitude thirty thousand seven hundred feet.

At 8:05 A.M., the navigator announced ten minutes to AP.

Caron tried to wriggle into his flak jacket. It was useless. He put it back on the floor where it might do more good. Unrestrained, he rubbernecked for fighters and black puffs of smoke that signaled flak from antiaircraft batteries on the ground. Nothing. Thank God! In rapid-fire succession, his mind conjured images of Zero shells and flak, connecting with the device harpooned like a mighty whale beneath them.

Antiaircraft fire wasn't what concerned Lewis most. The star center of his high-school football team tackled run-ins head on. They were something he could control. Turbulence was another matter. He had logged enough hours to know that as a land mass heated up—especially one surrounded by water—thermals could become an unpredictable problem. The challenges of the next ten minutes and anticipation of their dangerous dive-turn maneuver brought Lindbergh's counsel clearly to mind. "Watch trim and attitude. Be sure to pick up enough speed in the dive...."

Eatherly's cryptic message had been correct. "Some vagrant winds had cleared a ten-mile hole in the cloud cover," Lewis scratched into his journal. The ill-fated city was bathed in sunlight.

Automatically, Ferebee positioned his damp forehead against the specially designed brace on his M-9B Norden bombsight. He knew the gyroscopically stabilized aiming device that determined correct flight course and bomb release point perhaps better than any bombardier. While bombardiers in other squadrons checked out on the Norden after twenty visual and five radar drops, Ferebee and his fellow 509th bombardiers had honed their eye-hand coordination on thirty bombs a week for eight months, dropping sixty on radar. During test runs over Japan, he had plunked every one of his practice bombs right into the "pickle barrel."

Dutch changed their heading to two hundred sixty-four degrees. At 8:12 A.M., from thirty-one thousand sixty feet, he spotted their initial point sixteen miles from the Aioi Bridge. "IP," he called to Tibbets.

Although Ferebee and Lewis teamed effectively, the bombardier and Tibbets worked as one. They synchronized their instruments.

At 8:13:30 A.M., Tibbets watched an intent Ferebee press his forehead against the sight. "It's all yours," the pilot said. Ferebee made the final adjustments on the Norden, touched the ailerons to maintain his alignment.

"On goggles," Tibbets' voice crackled over the intercom. When he could see nothing with his goggles on, the pilot snapped them back onto his forehead. Lewis quickly wrote in his journal, "There will be a short intermission while we bomb our target." Then he pulled down his protective goggles.

Ferebee had already ruled them out. Colorful frames of Hiroshima began to appear in his viewfinder, like a tinted newsreel in slow motion. The exceedingly handsome officer had nearly made it into big-league baseball. The war had a way of waking people from their dreams. Now, he was aiming for a different sort of goal. He turned on the low-pitched tone signal that alerted the crew they were in the final fifteen seconds of the bomb run. One and two miles behind, respectively, *The Great Artiste* and Number 91 heard the tone. So did the weather planes and the radio operator of *Top Secret* at Iwo Jima.

The bombardier concentrated on his aiming point, the T-shaped Aioi Bridge, that was moving from east to west into the sight's cross hairs. He took a shallow breath and held it. At 8:15:17 A.M., the bomb-bay doors burst open. Released from its menacing hook, Little Boy ripped away from its monitoring cables. The tone stopped.

"Bomb away," Ferebee said loudly, compressing his lungs with release of the words.

Nearly five tons lighter, the *Enola Gay* bolted upward.

"It's clear," Ferebee said into the intercom. But it was by no means free. In Harry Truman's mind, plummeting six miles to earth was the world's biggest gamble—a two billion dollar crap shoot—and nobody had dared name the odds.

Tibbets nosed the *Enola Gay* into a sixty-degree bank to gain speed throughout the sharp right turn. The "g" forces pinned Caron against the window hatch. He struggled to point the camera in the direction of the horizon, but he couldn't find it.

Tibbets asked if he could see anything yet. Nothing. He knew that *The Great Artiste* mirrored their turn, releasing instrument-filled cylinders on parachutes to measure effects of the blast, but he couldn't see those either.

Hiro (wide) and *shima* (island) was one hour behind Tinian. Yet, culturally, ideologically, it was light years away. Now it was about to become the "place eternalized." As the island city wiped sleep from its eyes, a weary mother pushed aside the *shoji* to the room where her two young children lay on their *tatami,* dreaming the dreams of angels. It was past time for them to waken. She, like many hundreds of thousands of Hiroshima citizens, believed what she read in the *Chugoku Shimbum.* The army's stratagem had been to lure the enemy closer, closer. Get him on Japanese soil and unleash on him all the fury of bamboo spears and ancient muskets, rocks, stones and even bodies. Victory belonged to the Emperor.

It had been a long time since Hiroshima's schoolchildren could linger on their mats. Instead, each day they rose hurriedly to work in the fire breaks. Thousands gathered more than a million metric tons of acorns that was ground into flour. Families ate roasted worms and beetles, river weeds and pumpkin stalks. Someone respectfully tended every patch of earth. Longing gnawed at their bellies and encircled their eyes. Each day Hiroshimans filled the city's twenty-three hospitals and clinics and its thirty-two first-aid centers to be treated for stomach disorders and acute diarrhea.

The four-hundred-foot main span of the Aioi Bridge linked the Honkawa and Motoyasu rivers. Fifty yards from the Aioi Bridge stood the Town Hall. Mayor Senikichi Awaya, a dedicated pacifist and antimilitarist, had just received a report from his statisticians. As of August 3, more than seventy thousand wooden dwellings had been demolished. After evacuations, two hundred eighty thousand civilians were thought to be left in city. Many of these were needed at the Mitsubishi factory. Ten thousand were employed at the Toyo factory that produced six thousand rifles each week. Japan Steel and small manufacturing plants for kamikaze aircraft parts employed still others.

Downstream along the Motoyasu River, one hundred yards from the bridge, the "Fuel Hall" controlled and distributed the prefecture's fuel. Nippon Motor Oil Company, as well as aircraft parts plants, aluminum and chemical factories dotted Hiroshima's many riverbanks.

Built on a mound less than a half a mile from the Aioi Bridge and surrounded by a moat, four-hundred-year-old Hiroshima Castle headquartered the Second Army's forty thousand troops. Located in and under the Castle were ammunition and supply depots, civilian defense headquarters and the control center for the city's antiaircraft batteries. A score of small factories that circled the castle produced artillery.

At 8:16 A.M., the last of the complex series of detonation circuits closed within the bomb. Missing its target by eight hundred feet, it released its fury more than a third of a mile above the Shima Clinic.

Forty-three seconds after Little Boy's umbilical ripped away from the *Enola Gay*, the blast's blinding flash reached Caron's eyes. When his vision had been partially restored, he saw nothing outside his right side window but blue sky. Suddenly, an unholy globe of compressed air rose to eye level. Like some protoplasmic substance from a science fiction movie, it threatened to engulf them. Caron was flabbergasted. Before his unintelligible warning reached the crew, it struck with violent force.

What the jolt did to his engines, flight engineer Duzenbury wasn't sure. But it gave him a moment of pause. He was relieved that all instruments indicated normal function.

Almost instantaneously, the ricochet wave rushed toward them. Caron shouted a warning. Four seconds after the first, it bounced the plane.

The bomb did what it had been designed to do: destroy by heat and blast. The subtle secondary consequences of uranium fission, visible only in the coming days and months as changed cell structures, were vastly underestimated and little understood.

Survivors nearest the hypocenter saw only the *pika* (flash). "The light of many suns in one," Laurence had written of Trinity, yet his description was appropriate for Hiroshima as well. Farther away, others heard the *don* (boom) that they described as "a hundred thunders sounding at once, shaking the earth on its axis." Trinity's awesome roar was the equivalent of only half the Hiroshima *pika-don*. The only thing relevant was an object's distance from the point directly beneath the burst. Like a wheel whose crushing weight converges at the hub, the epicenter collapsed. At the rim, life was meted out by long, fragile spokes. What heat hadn't turned instantly to vapor, the blast and shock wave—potent as a dozen typhoons—smashed to bits.

In his cubicle, Caron pointed the cumbersome K-20 camera toward the spectacle outside, but the gun sight and window frames blocked the view. The escape hatch window on his right offered the least obstruction. Quickly, he asked Tibbets to turn the plane just five or ten degrees. Now he could see Hiroshima—or what was left of it (Captain Lewis noted he had just seen a city disappear in front of his eyes). *Airplanes...there was an airport and part of a harbor, out beyond the lavalike flow. No...it was more like bubbling molasses the way it spread over the city and crept up into the foothills.* Melted earth and steel roiled in the mass of energy that consumed all matter in its path.

"Holy Moses, here it comes," Caron said to no one and everyone. Rapidly, he collected his thoughts and directed his words toward Tibbets. "Colonel, it's coming toward us...the head of the cloud is coming toward us." The pilot instantly changed course.

This *had* to mean the end of the war, nineteen-year-old Nelson said aloud when he could finally see for himself. Such raw power could only horrify the enemy into submission.

"A caldron." Shumard associated the boiling action of the cloud, full of all kinds of colors, with an unearthly brew. It sent shivers up his spine. And terrified him. "There's nothing but death in that cloud," he said. Then he thought he heard a voice say, "All the Japanese souls are rising to heaven."

The great whirl of soot, vaporized matter and earth fanned upward, then crowned like a giant umbrella, casting the disconsolate city into shadow. Hiroshima, like Jornada del Muerto, had become a scorched desert.

Caron snapped the shutter until there was no more film to shoot. As Tibbets requested, all the way back to base, Caron kept his eyes on the cloud. When he finally lost sight of it, the *Enola Gay* was an hour and a half south of Hiroshima. The leviathan still hadn't disappeared below the horizon. It had been merely obstructed by high stratus clouds. He informed Dutch. The navigator indicated that the city was three hundred and sixty-three miles behind them. Caron calculated the curvature of earth at that distance was roughly twenty thousand feet. Since the cloud had risen above them when Tibbets leveled off at thirty-one thousand, then, it had apparently attained a height of fifty thousand feet.

Tibbets was surprised that the mission had been so easy, one of the most routine he had ever flown. Everything had gone according to his meticulous plans. "You go ahead and fly. You'll be all right." Enola Gay Tibbets was always right. During his many missions in Europe and Africa, testing aircraft, and the long preparation for Mission Number 13, he had seldom indulged in the luxury of concern for himself. By the same token, if he was "all right," so was his crew. He had picked the right name for plane Number 82.

Crewmen blotted out the engines' monotonous drone. Stillness was an eerie counterpoint to the shock and horror of the fearsome sight they had just witnessed. The flurry of activity since Tibbets' September 1 meeting in Colorado Springs had been directed to that historical moment. The scientists had delivered. So had Tibbets. But would the punch Japan had just taken score a knockout? Or would the bloody opponent get up, stagger dazed and senseless across the ring to fight on? Surely the power display behind the *Enola Gay* made such a prospect unthinkable. Made all war unthinkable. Tibbets' hope was mirrored by every man on board. In fact, each of them wrestled with his ideal of peace and the price paid for it. Caron's question fractured their introspection.

"Colonel, how many people did it take to pull this thing off?"

He had opened the floodgate. A tide of questions poured into Tibbets' headset. How had it all begun? How much did it cost? Who were the key players? Wasn't it ironic that most of the scientists were immigrants? Patiently, fully, Tibbets answered them all.

Oddly, everyone had been so preoccupied with two seemingly disparate paradigms—the intellectual exercise of understanding the most basic concepts of nuclear physics and the emotional exercise of hoping for peace—to acknowledge that they had survived the blast *and* the shock wave. Enola Gay's spirit was with them all.

"Fighter at two o'clock."

Caron didn't know to whom the strained voice belonged. He hit the black box on the wall and threw all his control switches on at once.

"What the hell's going on? Who's taking all my power?" flight engineer Duze yelled into the intercom. Because Caron's two amplidynes and dynamometer drew four hundred amps each, ideally, they were to be switched on at ten second intervals to avoid a sudden drain on the generators. But ten seconds times three was a long time to wait for guns to respond.

Fortunately, the threat was over before it began. Again Caron rubbernecked, searching for danger. Whatever had been at two o'clock was no more. The only speck now in the sky had the cigar shape of a B-29. The tail gunner was sure that the *Enola Gay* was now enjoying the pleasure of *The Great Artiste's* company for the long flight home.

Thirty-eight minutes out of Tinian, Tibbets took General Farrell's congratulatory call from the North Field tower. Caron cut power to his guns, stowed the tail mount and started the put-put. Anticipating the *Enola Gay* would be greeted by a welcoming committee, *The Great Artiste* and Number 91 courteously dropped back to let her touch down well ahead of them.

Twelve hours and thirteen minutes after the *Enola Gay's* breath-holding takeoff, she received a rousing homecoming from several hundred officers and enlisted men, cheering from the flight line. A ring of tan uniforms closed in behind them on the taxiway.

Caron had no sooner squeezed out of the hatch when photo officer Ossip pulled alongside in an MP-chauffered jeep. With few words, he relieved Caron of the bulky K-20. Once he had removed the K-17 film magazines from *The Great Artiste* and Number 91, he rushed the world's only documentation of the historical event to his lab technicians for processing.

Wing Commander General Davies waited for the pilot of the *Enola Gay* to step forward ceremoniously. He was honored, he said, to award Colonel Paul Warfield Tibbets the Distinguished Service Cross. Tibbets was still fumbling with his pipe, palming it up his left sleeve, when four gleaming stars approached him. General Carl "Tooey" Spaatz, commander of the Strategic Air Force, shook Tibbets' hand and pinned the medal on his coveralls. The two men who had known each other for many years stepped back several paces and saluted. At a later ceremony, the remaining crewmembers would be awarded the Silver Star.

In the years to come, the nail-driving Groves would commend the pilot: "Your performance and that of the 509th was perfect." The operation had been like the movement of a complex organism in which its many systems executed their individual tasks flawlessly for the benefit of the whole.

Often after missions, flight crews marched to the Group dispensary. The 509th's medics, although interested in the physical effects of prolonged, high-altitude sorties on the flyers, had other motives than physical examinations for seeing the men. They dispensed psychological anesthesia—a single, medicinal shot of high-grade bourbon.

This afternoon, however, the medics and the medicine came to the men. After a quick once-over of the crew by the medics, the informal debriefing began. At the table were thirst-slaking glasses of lemonade and something a little stronger to mix in them, for those who were so inclined.

Caron was not so inclined. He sat near the foot of the table opposite General Spaatz and to the right of Intelligence Officer Hazen Payette. Under his Brooklyn Dodgers' cap, the tail gunner still brandished the reminder of Duze's spirited attempt at barbering. The regrettable episode had been Shumard's idea. Duze, his state of awareness heightened by an unknown quantity of Navy torpedo juice tempered with pineapple, was going to save Bob the price of a haircut. Instead, he saved Bob only a few islands of burr isolated by great seas scalp. A crewmember remarked that the tail gunner's pate resembled a "cross between a Blackfoot Indian and a patch of sprouting prairie."

"Psst, Bob...." Tibbets, several chairs away, pointed to the navy-blue cap.

Bob sucked air between his teeth. Reluctantly he raised the cap and tipped his crown in the commander's direction.

"Do you still want me to take it off, Colonel?"

General Spaatz scanned the pink and brown geography. He and the interviewers filled the debriefing room with uproarious laughter. Still not fully composed, he addressed Caron.

"Sergeant, leave it on."

Like stories about the fish that got away, the crew's recounting of the bomb's spectacular power display seemed to interviewers exaggerated almost beyond belief. Even the precision timing of the drop was extraordinary. The *Enola Gay* had just flown nearly six hours, yet the bomb was released only seventeen seconds later than scheduled.

By the time the interrogation was over, so was the elaborate barbecue celebration mess officer Perry had prepared for the 509th. Numb and famished, the crew scavenged the few leftovers and partied with the rest of the group until midnight.

In the photo lab, Captain Ossip pressed his right eye against the enlarging loupe and examined the big 70 mm negatives from the K-17 aerial cameras. What he saw surprised him. The fixed-position cameras had clicked away, all right, but not at the bomb strike. The film captured whatever was in the lenses' angle of view as the planes executed their evasive dive turn. There was nothing but uninformative sections of off-kilter horizon and obliterated ground. That left the K-20! He whistled. There on the light table, the awesome atomic cloud appeared for the first time. Frame by frame, it rose higher and higher. Hurriedly, Ossip selected the sharpest negative and ordered prints. Wait till the world sees this.

The Irish septuagenarian who waited with the President aboard the U. S. S. *Augusta* for word about the Hiroshima bombing had more than half hoped the "damned fool thing" would fizzle.

During a luncheon in honor of Truman aboard a British cruiser off Plymouth, England, Admiral Leahy had voiced these feelings to King George VI. "I don't think the thing will go off," he said with conviction. "It sounds like a professor's dream to me."

"Admiral, would you like to lay a little bet on that?" the King asked.

Groves didn't like waiting for anything. He made things happen. Waiting was a waste of time. For something constructive to do, he threw his weight into a serve on the Army-Navy Country Club tennis court. The longer he played, and the longer he remained in the dark about the strike, the more he convinced himself that the "one-two punch" to end the war made the most sense. He reasoned the first bomb (why was it taking so long to get news of its success?) merely demonstrated to Japan what it was. The second bomb would prove there was more than one. Japan would have no choice but to capitulate.

Truman sat down at his diary: "The fourth day of the journey home from Potsdam came the historic news that shook the world. I was eating lunch with members of the *Augusta*'s crew when Captain Frank Graham, White House Map Room watch officer, handed me the following message:

> To the President:
> From the Secretary of War
> Big Bomb dropped on Hiroshima 5 August at 7:15 P.M.
> Washington time. First reports indicate complete success
> which was even more conspicuous than earlier test.

"This is the greatest thing in history," he exclaimed to the sailors who peered at him quizzically. "It's time for us to get home."

Shikata ga nai,
"It Could Not Be Helped"

T here was to be no homecoming yet for Caron, his fellow enlisted men or superiors. The instantaneous surrender Captain Lewis naively hoped to hear over the *Enola Gay's* radio as the crew returned to Tinian on the Hirohito Highway was not forthcoming.

"The atomic bomb," broadcast Truman to millions of Americans who had also been praying for surrender, had been used "against those who attacked us without warning at Pearl Harbor, against those who have starved and beaten and executed American prisoners of war, against those who have abandoned any pretense of obeying international laws of warfare. We shall continue to use it until we completely destroy Japan's power to make war. Only a Japanese surrender will stop us."

Anne and George had been in their pajamas and striped robes for several hours when they heard Truman announce a B-29 had dropped a lone atomic bomb on Japan. There were hundreds, perhaps thousands of B-29s in the Pacific, George said. What made her think it had anything to do with their son's outfit? A short time later, news services broadcast the name of the pilot who had dropped the bomb. It was Colonel Paul W. Tibbets.

When the Army Air Forces released the names of the crew, New York stations wasted no time in finding the local angle. "Captain Robert Lewis of New Jersey, co-pilot, and Sergeant George Caron of Lynbrook, tail gunner, were aboard the plane that dropped the atomic bomb on Hiroshima. At this time, the Army Air Forces has neither confirmed nor denied that the crew are alive."

Anne knew. The telephone began to ring as quickly as reporters looked up "Caron" in the directory. All night, she and George, still in their pajamas, answered the same questions. Reporters hastily scratched notes and dashed back to their newspapers to pound out copy.

At the same time, the Office of War Information printed millions of propaganda leaflets and tabloids in Japanese, urging citizens to support a military surrender. As quickly as they came off the presses, they were shipped for air-drops over Japan.

The Japanese picked up Truman's broadcast from San Francisco radio. In Tokyo, diplomat Kase and his Cabinet were stunned. An atomic bomb had leveled Hiroshima! Staggered, they tried to fathom a single bomb with the destructive force of twenty thousand tons of TNT. Around them was evidence of the destruction wrought by hundreds of conventional bombs dropped by B-29s. But a single bomb....?

Field Marshal Hata had reported from his headquarters a mile outside of Hiroshima that the early morning B-29 strike had "little effect. Only those caught without protection suffered injury."

The illusion had continued. An almost inconsequential bulletin on Tokyo's 6 P.M. news promulgated the myth of invulnerability. "A few B-29s hit Hiroshima city at 8:20 A.M., August 6, and fled after dropping incendiaries and bombs. The extent of damage is now under survey."

Armed Forces Radio beamed the harsh reality. Sixty percent of the city had been obliterated. However, broadcasts from Manila and Okinawa intended to assure the Japanese people that the bloodshed would stop if their leaders surrendered were never heard. The Imperial Japanese Army ordered transmissions jammed.

"To continue the war is mass suicide," Kase told the Cabinet. Common sense says surrender. He risked yet another heretical statement. "The Army is a stranger to common sense. As ever, it is riding a hot steed headlong to self destruction."

The Japanese press condemned the attack on Hiroshima as "barbaric." Confusion reigned as fifteen million American propaganda leaflets and news sheets fluttered onto Japan's cities and towns. On their front pages, the news sheets carried one of Caron's photographs of the atomic blast. Three Japanese officers captured at Okinawa had translated surrender appeals written by former reporter Major John Moynahan and the poetic General Farrell. The leaflets said to the Japanese people:

> Before we use this bomb again and again to destroy every resource of the military by which they are prolonging this useless war, petition the Emperor now to end the war. Our President has outlined for you the thirteen consequences of an honorable surrender. We urge you accept these consequences and begin the work of building a new, better and peace-loving Japan.

Still, Japan's leaders remained silent. At 11:01 A.M., August 9, 1945, *Bock's Car* dropped "Fat Man" on Nagasaki.

Word of Japan's unofficial surrender filtered into Washington on August 10, picked up from Japanese radio broadcasts before the official notification had arrived by way of Switzerland. Even as arrangements were being made for the formal surrender, Japanese military extremists plotted to overthrow the government and continue fighting. A peace treaty was signed on September 2 aboard the battleship *Missouri* in Tokyo harbor. World War II, which had involved fifty-seven nations, was over. It claimed an estimated fifty-four million eight hundred thousand lives, mostly civilians. Seven and a half million belonged to the Union of Soviet Socialist Republics. The United States claimed losses of two hundred ninety thousand.

With the exception of Tibbets, Van Kirk and Ferebee, who had already returned to the States, throughout the summer and fall, Caron and the *Enola Gay* crew remained on Tinian. In early November, Lewis received orders to bring the plane and its crew to the new 509th home at Roswell, New Mexico. By the time the flight and ground crews boarded with their gear, the plane was bulging at its seams. Caron returned to his niche in the tail and flew the Pacific in the little compartment he had come to know so well.

The pipeline allowed for five B-29s to fly at night, while B-24s and B-17s flew by day. Twilight hadn't descended on the island when Lewis lifted the *Enola Gay* off the North Field runway for the journey home. Its first stopover would be Kwajalein, then Hawaii and, finally, Mather Field, California.

By takeoff time the next evening, the B-29 was boxed in from the front on the Kwajalein runway. Anxious to be airborne, Lewis threw the props in reverse, backed out of the slot, then taxied the Superfortress around and through the maze of planes. The tower buzzed him. "What's your hurry?" "We want to get the hell out of here," he radioed back.

At Honolulu, the press was waiting. With interviews and photographs finally over, the men satisfied their craving for thick, juicy steaks. Full, content and tipsy, they stopped briefly at a tattoo parlor, determined to bring home yet another souvenir. The line was long, the day longer. They shrugged off the opportunity and headed for a bunk.

Lewis flew by day from Mather to Roswell. The Colonel, whom Caron had served two and a half years, greeted them.

Discharge processing, which included turning in equipment, filled the next two weeks. Crewmen's pay was docked for missing gear, although men were allowed to purchase keepsakes. Caron laid claim to his A-2 and B-4 jackets. Then he signed up for the Reserves.

Kay drove down from Dodge City, Kansas, and hardly recognized her one-hundred-sixteen-pound husband. They remained on her parents' farm until February to give baby Judy time to recover from her high fevers and her father to restore flesh to his boney frame.

Caron approached the price board to set the resale value of the 1940 Chevy convertible. Scarcely had he advertised the car at the six hundred forty dollars fixed by the board that buyers clambered to pay it. Later he learned that under-the-table deals usually doubled a selling price. He would have been uncomfortable with such an arrangement, and the cash was enough to purchase plane tickets to the East Coast, where he hoped to find work.

Engineering positions were at a premium in New York City. Maxson's, which had boomed during the war, had let all but its most senior engineers go. Apartments were as scarce as jobs. George and Anne insisted that Bob, Kay and Judy move in with them. George made room in his display shop for another hand.

In April 1946, Tibbets flew the *Enola Gay* into LaGuardia Field for the Armed Forces Day Parade. Caron served as grand marshal. In addition, he and Lewis were the welcoming committee. Crowds lined Fifth Avenue. As the parade passed, onlookers yanked at servicemen's ribbons and uniform buttons, tearing off mementos.

By late fall 1946, Bob and Kay had a new son, Bobby, and a Cape Cod cottage in a sparsely populated area on Long Island heavy with oak trees.

Ed Sullivan wrote in his *New York Daily News'* column that Bobby was the first of many babies born to *Enola Gay* crew members, proving unfounded the prediction of one scientist that the bomb's radiation would make them sterile.

Resilient, the Japanese people began the long process of patching their tattered lives. Pragmatically, they summed the means to the end of the war as *shikata ga nai*, it could not be helped.

To Truman, the means had been "no great decision. ...It was merely another powerful weapon in the arsenal of righteousness." His philosophy remained simple. Behind his desk in the Oval Office, Truman displayed a small frame in which was lettered Mark Twain's axiom: "Always do right—this will gratify some and astonish the rest."

The one morality of the war had been victory. Truman had chosen one path to achieve it. The bomb dropped on Hiroshima had the explosive force of twenty thousand tons of TNT, nearly twice the power of Trinity. In 1948, Operation Sandstone's test explosion yielded the equivalent force of forty nine thousand tons. Only seven years after the first atomic test, Operation Ivy's thermonuclear device released the force of ten million four hundred thousand tons of TNT. Ever more powerful nuclear weapons were maintained throughout the Cold War as deterrents.

"More than an end to war, we want an end to the beginnings of all wars," Roosevelt intended to say during his Jefferson Day broadcast to Americans on April 13, 1945, the day after his sudden death. An excerpt from that speech reveals his thoughts.

> Today, we are faced with the preeminent fact that, if civilization is to survive, we must cultivate the science of human relationships—the ability of all people, of all kinds, to live together in the same world in peace.

The eye-stabbing flash that temporarily blinded Sergeant Caron on August 6, 1945, six miles above Hiroshima, led to a greater clarity of sight. After witnessing the unimaginable, surveying the unthinkable, peace becomes paramount. Caron is plain-spoken, yet emphatic in his sentiment.

"I hope no one else will ever have to see the sight I saw that morning from the tail of the *Enola Gay*."

A s *Fire of a Thousand Suns* goes to press, five of the six surviving members of the *Enola Gay* crew remain in contact with each other. However, they have lost touch with the sixth.

For nearly five years following the war, George Robert Caron worked in his father's display shop on Long Island. In 1950, W. L. Maxson's executive vice president and chief engineer, Jack Vaughn, offered his former employee a job designing a machine gun pod to be hung under an airplane wing and a bombing computer.

But visions of Denver remained in Bob's memory. An engineering position with Boeing in Wichita brought him one step closer to the Rocky Mountains he learned to love. In 1954, the dream to relocate in Colorado became reality when Stanley Aviation of Aurora hired him.

Nearly two years later, he joined Denver's new Sundstrand Corporation to design the first constant-speed drive for a Swedish jet fighter. Throughout his twenty-seven years with the company, he worked on various aerospace projects and was one of a three-man nucleus chosen to begin the commercial division plant in Arvada. He retired from Sundstrand in December 1983.

Daughters Janey and Kathy were born in 1950 and 1961. Bob and Kay are great grandparents. In 1957, George Jay and Anne Westrick Caron left the cold of New York for Arizona.

P rior to his involvement in the Pacific, Paul Tibbets had flown General Mark Clark to North Africa and General Eisenhower to Gibraltar. After the war, he became a test pilot for the Boeing B-47 jet bomber and later was assigned to the NATO staff with Allied Air Forces in central Europe. He was promoted to brigadier general and, in 1959, was given command of a B-47 Air Division, followed by a posting to the Military Assistance Group in India. In 1966 he returned to the United States and assumed a position at the Pentagon. After thirty years of distinguished military service, he retired and began a second career with Executive Jet Aviation, becoming its president in 1976. Currently, he is enjoying a second retirement, skeet and trap shooting.

Thomas Ferebee, who had been Tibbets' bombardier in England and Europe, had flown an extraordinary sixty-four combat missions. When World War II ended, he became involved with Tibbets in the atomic bomb tests on Bikini. When that duty was completed, he attended Command and Staff School. Thereafter, he was attached to NATO, followed by an assignment as A and E commander of a B-47 squadron, where in 1959 he was promoted to colonel. Ferebee accompanied the first B-52 wing sent to Guam during the Viet Nam war. After an illustrious Air Force career, he retired in 1970 and earned his real estate license. His favorite pastime is golf.

Theodore "Dutch" Van Kirk enlisted in the Army Air Corps in October 1941 and graduated from navigation school in April 1942. He was assigned to the 97th Bomber Group, the first operational B-17 group in England, and served as navigator for Tibbets. By the end of the war, he had flown fifty-eight combat missions and eight transport missions. He also participated in the Bikini atomic bomb tests. After he left the military in August 1946 with the rank of major, he returned to college and earned bachelor and master's degrees in chemical engineering from Bucknell University. His civilian career in research, marketing and management with a major domestic chemical corporation spanned thirty-five years. He retired in 1985.

Richard "Junior" Nelson, youngest of the *Enola Gay* crew, entered the Army Air Forces in August 1943. He completed a College Training Detachment Program and, after radio school, was assigned to B-29 replacement training, becoming the only member of his group to be attached to the 509th at Wendover, Utah. Following discharge, he returned to college to earn his degree. He accepted a position with a major United States firm and eventually was promoted to Western Regional Sales Manager. Retired but remaining quite busy, he operates his own orange grove in California.

Morris Jeppson, who served as assistant weaponeer for the Hiroshima mission, became a physicist and businessman following the war. He is believed to be residing on the West Coast.

Deceased members of the *Enola Gay* crew are: William Parsons, weaponeer (1953); Robert Shumard, assistant flight engineer (1967); Jacob Beser, electronic countermeasures (1983); Wyatt Duzenbury, flight engineer (1983); Robert Lewis, co-pilot (1983); and Joseph Stiborik, radar operator (1984).

Alperovitz, Gar. *Atomic Diplomacy: Hiroshima and Potsdam, The Use of the Atomic Bomb and the American Confrontation with Soviet Power.* New York: Elisabeth Sifton Books, Penguin Books, 1965.

Anders, Gunther. *Burning Conscience: The Case of the Hiroshima Pilot, Claude Eatherly.* New York: Monthly Review Press, 1961.

Associated Press. "Atom Bomb Destroyed 60% of Hiroshima. Pictures Show 4 Square Miles of City Gone. B-29 Dropped New Explosive by Parachute." *New York Herald Tribune,* (August 8, 1945).

Associated Press. "Atom Bombing is Sensational News in Russia." *New York Herald Tribune,* (August 9, 1945).

Associated Press. "Atomic Bomb Personnel Commended for Work." *New York Herald Tribune,* (August 9, 1945).

Associated Press. "Austrian Woman Won't Discuss Her Role in Developing Bomb." *New York Herald Tribune,* (August 8, 1945).

Associated Press. "Bomb Workers Taken for Slackers." *New York Herald Tribune,* (August 9, 1945).

Associated Press. "Col. Tibbets, Pilot of B-29, Tells of Raid." *New York Herald Tribune,* (August 8, 1945).

Associated Press. "Domei Hits at American 'Sadism' in Using New 'Diabolic' Weapon." *New York Herald Tribune,* (August 8, 1945).

Associated Press. "FBI Says Nazi Agents Tried to Get Atom Data." *New York Herald Tribune,* (August 9, 1945).

Associated Press. "Japan Calls Cabinet, Fears More Raids." *New York Herald Tribune,* (August 8, 1945).

Associated Press. "To Destroy a City...We Were Getting Into God's Territory." [*New York Herald Tribune?*] (n.d.).

Associated Press. "Tokyo Rose Gets Navy Citation for Aiding U.S. Morale." *New York Herald Tribune*, (August 8, 1945).

Associated Press. "2 Local Flyers on Superfort That Dropped Atomic Bomb." *New York Herald Tribune*, (August 9, 1945).

Associated Press. "Yawata Blasted in Daylight by 225 Superforts." *New York Herald Tribune*, (August 8, 1945).

Associated Press Wirephoto. "Pilot's Wife Busy Receiving Congratulations." *New York Herald Tribune*, (August 9, 1945).

"Atomic Bomb, Hiroshima, The." *Caron scrapbook clipping*, U.S. Air Forces, (n.d.).

Bigart, Homer and Mac R. Johnson. "Hiroshima Ruin is Scrutinized in Photograph." *New York Herald Tribune*, (August 9, 1945).

Bruckner, Karl. *The Day of the Bomb*. New York: Van Nostrand Reinhold Co., 1962.

Caron, Anne Westrick. *Personal Correspondence to Bob Caron*, (August 8, 1945).

Caron, George R. *Personal Correspondence to Katherine Younger Caron*, (July 22, 1945); (July 27, 1945); (July 29, 1945).

Clark, Ian. *Nuclear Past, Nuclear Present: Hiroshima, Nagasaki, and Contemporary Strategy*. Boulder and London: Westview Press, 1985.

Columbia Dictionary of Quotation, 1992, s.v. "Nuclear Armageddon: Douglas MacArthur."

Columbia Encyclopedia, Concise ed., 1991, s.v. "Atomic Bomb;" "Great Depression;" "Hiroshima;" "Japan;" "Roosevelt, Franklin Delano;" "Truman, Harry S.;" "World War II."

Crosby, Joan. "Dodger Baseball Cap Charm to Hiroshima Atom Raider." [*New York Herald Tribune?*] (n.d.)

Cross, Robin. *The Bombers*. New York: Macmillan, 1987.

Cummins, H. J. "Fontenelle Hotel...Future Is Uncertain." *Omaha World Herald*, (September 4, 1985).

Department of the Air Force. "B-29 'Crew Duty Check List,' RCT 6·2·1" *Historical Data and Properties*. Offutt AFB, (July, 1944).

Department of the Air Force. "B-29 'In Air Check List,' RCT 6·2·1" *Historical Data and Properties*. Offutt AFB, (July, 1944).

Department of the Air Force. "B-29 Operation" *Historical Data and Properties Manual #AN 01-20EJA-1, Section I, II, IV, V*. Offutt AFB, (August, 1944).

Department of the Air Force. "B-29 'Post Flight Check List,' RCT 6·2·1" *Historical Data and Properties*. Offutt AFB, (July, 1944).

Department of the Air Force. "B-29 'Pre-Flight Check List,' RCT 6·2·1" *Historical Data and Properties*. Offutt AFB, (July, 1944).

Department of the Air Force. "History of Building 'D' 1941-1981." *Historical Data and Properties Pamphlet # 210-1*. Offutt AFB, (April 17, 1981).

Department of the Air Force. "Supplement to Gunner's Information File, 'Harmonization in the B-29.' " *Historical Data and Properties, Air Forces Manual #20*. Offutt AFB, (August, 1944).

Dumas, Alan. "Photo an unnecessary memento of what he saw from the Enola Gay." *Sunday Magazine, Rocky Mountain News*, (n.d.)

Duncan, Val. "The Day—Aug. 6, 1945; The Place—Hiroshima." *Newsday*, (August 5, 1960).

Durant, Will. "No Hymns of Hatred." *Saturday Evening Post*, (June 4, 1938).

"Dying and the Buying, The." *Saturday Evening Post*, (October 18, 1941).

Farrell, Maj. Gen. Thomas F. "A-Bomb Assembled En Route to Target."
   Daily Mirror, (February 9, 1946)

"15 Years Later: The Men Who Bombed Hiroshima." *Coronet*, (August
   1960).

Fogelman, Edwin. *Hiroshima: The Decision to Use the A-Bomb*. New York:
   Charles Scribner's Sons, 1964.

Harper, Stephen. *Miracle of Deliverance: The Case for the Bombing of
   Hiroshima and Nagasaki*. Briarcliff Manor: Scarborough House, 1986.

Herald Tribune Bureau. "Invasion Plan Holds Despite Atomic Bomb." *New
   York Herald Tribune*, (August 8, 1945).

Herald Tribune Bureau. "Oppenheimer's 11th Hour Doubt Cost Him $10
   Bet at Bomb Test." *New York Herald Tribune*, (August 8, 1945).

Hersey, John. "A Reporter at Large—Hiroshima." *The New Yorker*,
   (August 31, 1946).

"History of War In Pacific From Pearl Harbor to Peace." [*New York
   Herald Tribune?*], (August 18, 1945.)

Huie, William Bradford. *The Hiroshima Pilot*. New York: G.P. Putnam's
   Sons, 1964.

Kilbourn, Cpl. Jonathan. "The Mighty Atom." *Yank*, (n.d.).

Kosakai, Yoshiteru. *A-Bomb: A City Tells Its Story*. Hiroshima: Hiroshima
   Peace Culture Foundation, 1972.

Kurzman, Dan. *Day of the Bomb: Countdown to Hiroshima*. New York:
   McGraw-Hill, 1986.

Lawrence, W. H. " 'Incredible Sights' in Hiroshima." *New York Times*,
   (September 8, 1945).

Lewis, Maj. Robert A., as told to Eliot Tozer. "How We Dropped the A-
   Bomb." *Popular Science*, (August, 1957).

Malcomson, Ralph W. *Nuclear Fallacies: How We Have Been Misguided Since Hiroshima.* Kingston: McGill-Queen's University Press, 1985.

Marshall, George C., et al. "To the American People." *Saturday Evening Post*, (June 2, 1945)

Marxs, Joseph L. *Seven Hours to Zero.* New York: G.P. Putnam's Sons, 1967.

O'Hara, Tom. "75 Atom Bombs Could Destroy New York City." *New York Herald Tribune*, (August 9, 1945).

"1,000 in New York State Helped Produce the Bomb." *New York Herald Tribune*, (August 9, 1945).

Pacific War Research Society, The. *The Day Man Lost: Hiroshima, 6 August 1945.* Tokyo; Palo Alto, California: Kodansha International Ltd., 1972.

Pair, George. "I Saw it First." Transcription of recorded interview with George Robert "Bob" Caron." *Caron scrapbook*, (n.d.).

People's Chronology. Henry Holt, 1992. "Communications and Media: 1938, 1939, 1940, 1941, 1942, 1944, 1945;" "Political Events 1941: Pearl Harbor;" "Political Events:1945."

Perlman, Michael. *Imaginal Memory and the Place of Hiroshima.* Albany: State University of New York Press, 1988.

Reid, Jay. "Truman Back, Atom Bomb Use Is Big Question." *New York Herald Tribune*, (August 8, 1945).

Rhodes, Richard. *The Making of the Atomic Bomb.* New York: Simon and Schuster, 1986.

Schwartz, Robert. "Atomic Bomb Away." *Yank* , (n.d.).

Snow, Edgar. "Who is Winning the China-Japan War?" *Saturday Evening Post*, (June 4, 1938).

Stevenson, David. "High Flyer." *Wings West*, (May/June, 1994).

Thomas, Gordon and Max Morgan Witts. *Enola Gay*. New York: Pocket Books, 1978.

Thomas, Gordon and Max Morgan Witts. *Ruin from The Air: The Atomic Mission to Hiroshima*. London: Hamish Hamilton Ltd., 1977.

Tibbets, Paul W., with Clair Stebbins and Harry Franken. *The Tibbets Story*. New York: Stein and Day, 1978.

U.S. Army Air Forces. "Trick That Won a Stepping Stone to Japan, The." *Caron scrapbook clipping*, (n.d.).

United Press. "Atomic Bomb Worker Still 'Scared' to Talk." *New York Herald Tribune*, (August 9, 1945).

United Press. "Secret Once Imperiled." *New York Herald Tribune*, (August 9, 1945).

United Press. "Two Captor Ships Identified." *New York Herald Tribune*, (August 9, 1945).

Wyden, Peter. *Day One: Before Hiroshima and After*. New York: Simon and Schuster, 1984.

World Almanac and Book of Facts, 1994. s.v. "United States History, 1945."

Yearbook. Brooklyn: Brooklyn Technical High School, June, 1938.

York, Herbert F. *Making Weapons, Talking Peace: A Physicist's Odyssey from Hiroshima to Geneva*. New York: Basic Books, Alfred P. Sloan Foundation Series, 1987.